THE FREEDOM FRAMEWORK

BUILD A LIFE ON YOUR TERMS BY
MASTERING YOUR MIND, BODY, AND MONEY

PETER CHEMELLO

COPYRIGHT

Cover design and interior illustrations by the author, created with the assistance of AI image-generation tools. Final image selection, editing, layout, and publishing decisions are the author's own.

DISCLAIMER

This book is intended to help you pause, reflect, and make more deliberate choices about your life, health, money, and future. It is not here to tell you exactly what to do, and it cannot take into account the full context of your personal circumstances. It is not intended to constitute medical, psychological, financial, investment, tax, or other professional advice.

Use what is helpful, adapt what fits, and seek qualified advice where your circumstances require it.

Nothing in this book should be taken as a recommendation to buy, sell, or hold any particular investment, financial product or asset class. Investing involves risk, including the risk of loss. The health and fitness information in this book is not a substitute for professional medical advice, diagnosis, or treatment.

The reader remains responsible for their own decisions, actions, and outcomes.

CONTENTS

INTRODUCTION

PART ONE — YOUR MAP

PART TWO — YOUR VEHICLE

PART THREE — YOUR FUEL

EPILOGUE

CLOSING PAGES

INTRODUCTION

THE FANTASTIC JOURNEY

When was the last time you questioned why you do what you do? Why you work where you work? Eat what you eat? Buy what you buy? Act how you act?

If you're like most people, the answer is probably never. On the odd occasion we do, it tends to be at a surface level. We rarely, if ever, explore our true underlying drivers.

Whether we realise it or not, we've all been conditioned by the sum of our life experiences. Friends, family, culture, and upbringing all heavily influence our thoughts, behaviours, and actions. We like to think we're making conscious choices, yet most of the time we're following scripts written by others long before we even knew we were in the story. If your first thought is "*maybe others, but not me*", that reaction is simply part of the conditioning.

The truth is that most of us aren't consciously living; we're simply existing. We're reacting rather than choosing, drifting through life on autopilot, mistaking motion for direction. Drifting may not sound like a big deal, but it's far from harmless. When you don't choose a direction, one is chosen for you. As the years pass, your options begin to narrow. What feels comfortable in the moment extracts a heavy cost over time, often too late to realise the price you paid.

Think of your life as a road trip you only get to take once. Your mind is the map, your body the car, and your money the fuel. You think you're driving, yet you're half-asleep at the wheel, while a force you barely understand is steering in the background. But we're getting ahead of ourselves...

Run out of fuel? You'll never reach your destination. Trash the car? You'll end up broken down on the side of the road. But the biggest thing that can derail your journey is your map. Navigate it poorly and you'll waste every drop of fuel driving in circles, only to end up somewhere you never wanted to be. Oh, and you'll burn out the car while you're at it too.

You might not start with a full tank, but you need the means to top it up. Your car may not be perfect, but you still need to look after it. Your map may be incomplete, but you must take the time to understand it. Ignore any of these for long enough and the journey begins to unravel.

Most people neglect something. Some spend half their lives stockpiling fuel but never decide where they're going. Others thrash their vehicle without ever popping the hood. Many hit the road aimlessly, never pausing to understand their map. Meanwhile, the odometer continues to climb, and the vehicle wears down. There is no escaping the fact that each of our journeys will end, and at a time we cannot predict. What remains undecided is whether we reach our destination having ever truly lived.

Dreams of freedom

I was once a stockpiler myself – building towards freedom, yet often depriving myself of it in the process. I saved aggressively, avoided spending, and treated money as protection against some vague future threat. In trying to make myself safe, I had become a doomsday prepper hoarding for a crisis that never came. This realisation did not come to me overnight. It was only on looking back over my journey that I came to understand the reasons why.

As a kid, I loved puzzles, brain teasers, and problem-solving books. Everything in life felt like a puzzle just waiting to be solved... if only you knew where to look. As the youngest of four kids in a single-income household, money quickly became the biggest puzzle of all. I witnessed the stress and arguments it could create. I saw how it dictated decisions around what we could and couldn't do. I noticed how it seemed to set invisible boundaries on how we lived our lives. It made a deep impression.

I decided then and there that I didn't want such limitations on my life. I didn't want to be restricted by something as arbitrary as my bank balance. Money was just another puzzle; there had to be a solution. After all, there wasn't anything inherently special about it. It was just another human invention. If I could understand how it worked, I'd never be limited by it. Freedom was the goal, and money, I believed, was the path. So began my journey to master it.

I followed the usual path at first, getting a full-time job and saving as much as I could. It became clear over time, however, that I wasn't really getting any closer to freedom. I figured that I simply wasn't earning or saving enough, and that a higher income was needed to solve the issue. So, after some research, I decided to pursue a career as an actuary, a field built on understanding risk and forecasting outcomes. It seemed like the ultimate solution. It promised higher pay, but more importantly, knowledge of how money really worked. I'd learn how to invest, how to plan and manage risk, and how to be in control of my future.

With renewed motivation, I set out on my new path and immediately hit my first speed bump. None of the local universities offered the course, leaving me no choice but to buy the materials, teach myself the content, and sit the twice-annual exams. So that's exactly what I did.

Eight units and eight massive binders of content. The guidelines recommended four years of study, but I set my sights on two. Time is money, and I had no time to waste. For those two years, I lived and breathed actuarial science. When I wasn't working, I was studying. Nights, weekends, and even annual leave were all consumed in pursuit of the riches that would surely follow.

Two years of sacrifice later, I had done it. The failure rate on these exams was staggering, yet I'd passed each one on the first attempt. It was one of my proudest achievements at the time. I was elated, and at the same time, relieved that it was over. I was ready to move into the industry and change the trajectory of my life.

Only, *nothing changed.*

Sure, I got a new job, but the pay was no better. That higher salary the career promised was still years off in the future. This might have been acceptable if the work had been anything like I had imagined. Instead of complex risk assessments and interesting financial problems, I was writing computer code for hours on end. While I loved the theory and the maths I had studied, I found the day-to-day work to be soul-destroying. Realising what my next few years at work looked like, my motivation fell off a cliff.

At least I knew how to invest money now, right? In theory, yes, but in practice, nothing changed. The education had given me all the technical knowledge I needed, yet for some reason, I failed to act on it. It was like having all the skills and tools to build a house yet never laying a single brick. Instead, all my hard-earned savings remained where they always had – in the bank. Safe and untouched but going nowhere. Bricks, just waiting to become a house.

I'd poured two years of my life into chasing a promise that never arrived, and all I had to show for it was my exhaustion. Six weeks later, I quit and, with my tail between my legs, returned to my old job. My ticket out had led me right back to where I'd started. Sitting back at my old desk, disillusioned, I asked myself, "*What went wrong?*"

The salary I could chalk up to my lack of research on the industry. But why wasn't I investing my savings? The course *had* delivered on that promise. In fact, the tools I'd learned were far more sophisticated than those I'd actually need to become financially free. That was the moment I realised the flaw in my plan. I'd assumed that having the knowledge would be enough to get me moving. Instead, I discovered that without a clear understanding of my map, that knowledge served only to weigh me down with the guilt of inaction.

So, I began to ask a different question. Instead of asking how to make money, I began to reflect on why I wanted it in the first place. What was I really searching for, and why?

"Why?"

It's such a simple yet powerful question. As kids, it's one of our favourites. "*Why is the sky blue?*" "*Why can't I eat dessert first?*" "*Why do I have to go to bed?*" Of course, the answers would rarely satisfy us, so we'd follow up with our second favourite question – "*But why?*" – much to the frustration of our parents. It was rarely the truth that would end the chain, but rather a weary "*Because I said so!*"

What parents brush off as an annoying enquiry is wisdom that we've lost as adults. Kids ask why. Adults forget how. Kids want the truth while adults settle for stories. That's why most people drift through life unwittingly answering to someone else's *why* and never their own.

Whether you realise it or not, it's this very lack of questioning that defines your life. It determines what you do, and more importantly, what you don't do. That pet project that's still a note on your phone, never quite making the cut on your to-do list? Or the dream trip you never seem to book because you tell yourself you can't find the time? We all have our backlog of things we'd like to do, the things that would bring real joy and meaning to our lives, and yet they somehow seem to fall behind the things that we actually do. It's like having two boxes, one with $10 and one with $10,000, and picking the $10 box every time. Madness. Nobody would consciously do so, yet it's exactly what we do every day. Why?

Because we don't stop to question it.

When I finally started questioning my actions, and more importantly, my inactions, everything changed. I realised that knowledge alone isn't power; it's only potential. Power comes from applied knowledge, from taking action. I changed my question from *what* to *why*. Knowing what to do is less important than knowing *what's stopping you from doing it*. All the knowledge in the world wouldn't have helped because it wasn't what was holding me back in the first place. The real issue was that I'd never stopped to study my map.

It was at that moment that I decided to take accountability for my mindset. I got clear on what I truly wanted and why. I examined my relationship with money, my habits, my thought patterns, and the reasons behind my behaviours. For the first time, things began to make sense. With clarity, direction replaced drift, and I began to make real progress.

Over the years that followed, that clarity changed the way I approached every area of my life. I became more intentional with my decisions, developed better habits, increased my income, and steadily invested towards the future I wanted to create. The changes were rarely dramatic, but their cumulative effect was profound.

Fast forward eight years, and a meeting with my boss changed everything. My role had just been made redundant. Under different circumstances, the news would have triggered concern: "*What now? Where do I go next? How long can I afford to be without work?*" Instead, I simply smiled. As my boss spoke, I realised I didn't need another job. I wouldn't have to update my resume, trawl through job ads, or worry about my next paycheque. I had already crossed my finish line. My childhood dream of financial freedom had been achieved, all while I was still in my thirties.

Despite its significance, the moment itself was unremarkable. There was no big milestone, no sense of arrival. It hadn't happened all at once. It had crept up gradually, then suddenly it was just... done.

The plan had worked. I had achieved exactly what I'd set out to accomplish; I'd solved the money puzzle. What I hadn't done was give serious thought to what I would actually do when I got there. I had spent years building fuel for the journey, but now that I had enough, I had to pause and decide how I actually wanted to use it. Freedom wasn't the end of the road, but rather the ability to choose which roads I wanted to travel.

It was time to take the wheel and create a journey on my own terms.

The journey ahead

You might be wondering by now what this book is all about. Initially, I set out to write a guide to achieving financial freedom, but in reflecting on my journey, I realised there was more to it. Money alone doesn't create freedom. Many people find themselves wealthy yet living a life that is anything but free.

More important than money itself is the order in which freedom is built. I had assumed that more money would buy more freedom, when in reality it's the other way around. It's your mindset, patterns, and behaviours that ultimately drive your financial outcomes. Personal freedom isn't the result of financial freedom; it's what makes it possible in the first place.

Focus only on fuel while neglecting your map, and you're unlikely to get where you want to go. The map must come first. It determines the direction you take, the decisions you make, where you end up, and whether you make it there at all. That's why this book is about something far broader than just money. It's about understanding yourself, learning to live by your own *why*, and creating true freedom from the ground up.

This isn't just a checklist of tips and tricks. It's a framework for doing the deeper work that makes those tactics effective. It's the map before the route. Without clarity on who you are, what drives you, and why you act the way you do, even the best strategies will eventually break down.

The goal is to build your awareness first. We'll begin by learning how to navigate your map, avoiding needless detours that waste years and derail your progress. Next, we'll look at how to maintain and care for your vehicle, so it doesn't break down along the way. Finally, we'll cover how you manage and replenish your fuel, so you never run out halfway there.

Think of this book as a course in self-mastery, complete with practical exercises and habits that you'll apply along the way. It is a practical guide to transforming how you think, act, and live. Doing so will require you to examine your patterns, habits, and excuses. At times, this will be confronting, but the aim here isn't to comfort, nor is it to judge. It's accountability.

This book can show you the path, but it can't walk it for you. You have to be willing to do the work. It comes down to facing your excuses, owning your direction, and acting on it. Ultimately, the quality of your journey is determined by the choices you make, and those choices are yours alone.

The road is waiting. The only question now is whether you're ready to take the wheel.

◇

EXERCISE 1

First steps

Before moving forward, it's important to understand how this book is designed to work.

Reading builds awareness, but it's only through action that you create change. To help you get the most from this book, most chapters include a short exercise. These exercises are where you apply the ideas to your own circumstances and begin turning knowledge into results. If you skip them, you may understand the concepts yet still fail to create meaningful change.

We'll start simple. Take a few minutes to reflect on the questions below. Don't rush through them and make sure to write your answers down.

- What led me to pick up this book?
- What am I hoping will be different after reading it?
- How willing am I to approach these ideas with an open mind, even when they challenge my current thinking or feel uncomfortable?
- How much time, energy, and attention am I prepared to invest in working through this book properly?

PART ONE

Your Map

Before you set out on any journey, the very first thing you need is a map. It guides your path, ensuring that every step you take is in the right direction. But a map is only useful if you know how to navigate it. Skip that step, and you risk winding up exhausted at a destination you never consciously chose.

That's why we start here, with the most important map you'll ever use: your mind. It is the lens through which you interpret the world. Every decision and every behaviour is influenced by your mind. This is where the real work begins.

To do this, you'll need to harness your awareness. You'll begin to recognise the influence of your ego, witness your thought patterns, and notice when you're running on autopilot. You'll discover where your control truly lies, and where your efforts are best placed. As you peel back these layers, you'll discover a compass that points towards what truly matters to you.

This is the work that many people skip. They look for tactics, shortcuts, and step-by-step guides, while overlooking the very foundation those tools depend on. It's one reason why so many self-improvement systems fail to stick. It's not your knowledge alone that counts, but your level of awareness.

This part of the book asks that you slow down and look at yourself honestly. It won't always be comfortable, but it's the groundwork that makes everything else possible. Understand your map and you can start to make sense of the road ahead.

So, before we climb into the vehicle or worry about fuel, let's take a moment to lay the map out on the table in front of you. It's time to look at where you are, what's been guiding your journey, and how to chart the course forward.

◇

CHAPTER 1

THE FIRST STEP IS ADMITTING YOU HAVE A PROBLEM

Most of us are addicted to lying. Like most addictions, we'll outright deny it. But as they say, the first step is admitting you have a problem.

We lie to ourselves every day, in ways so subtle that it often slips beneath our awareness. We deny our true power and potential, place limits on what we can achieve, and then look for evidence to support our claims. For the most part, this isn't something we've consciously chosen to do. To break the pattern, we must first become aware of it.

The world's greatest jigsaw

Imagine your entire life as a gigantic jigsaw puzzle. Work, health, relationships, emotions, habits, fears, desires... everything you can think of is just another piece of the puzzle. At first glance, trying to piece it all together feels overwhelming. Where do you start? How do you even begin to make sense of the almost endless number of pieces?

Much like an actual puzzle, you start by looking for patterns. You pick up pieces that look related, group similar colours, and gradually small sections start to form. With each connection, the bigger picture becomes clearer.

What if you can't find some of the pieces? You may end up frustrated, convinced you're missing pieces and that the full image isn't possible. At this point, many people choose to give up. They decide the puzzle is too hard. Yet by accepting defeat, they never get to see what their life could be.

Awareness is the light that helps you find those pieces. It reveals what you've ignored, denied, or overlooked. It allows you to arrange your life in ways that make sense. Simply put, it is the key to seeing the bigger picture clearly.

Working on our own puzzle is important, yet it's easy to forget that we're not solving it in isolation. There are roughly eight billion others out there, each forming their own unique picture. No one can complete it alone. Those missing pieces others are searching for may be in your pile, just as some of yours may be hidden among theirs.

Awareness not only helps you build your own puzzle, but it also helps others build theirs too. In doing so, your understanding of both yourself and others deepens, making every interaction more meaningful. As we help each other complete our puzzles, a larger mosaic begins to appear, one far richer than any image by itself.

Developing deep personal awareness is a skill which must be cultivated over time. For some, it comes relatively easily. These people are naturally more present and tend to have a questioning nature. For most people, it's far more challenging. We settle into habits, stop asking questions, and narrow our identity to whatever we've decided our world deems it to be. In doing so, we become trapped in a prison of our own design, built from the lies we've accepted as truth. To break free, we must first build awareness of the bars that are confining us. So, what's stopping us?

If awareness is so powerful, why don't we all apply it? The simple answer is that part of us doesn't want us to. Its very existence is threatened the moment we notice it, so it goes to great lengths to stay hidden. It acts as a saboteur, undermining our attempts to wake up and realise what's really in control.

Wait... so who's really driving?

If our mind is the map, our body the vehicle, and our money the fuel, who do you think the driver is? Pause for a moment and genuinely reflect before continuing.

What did you come up with? Let's start with what it's *not*. Most people believe they're in full control when in reality there's a backseat driver calling the shots. You know the one, that noisy voice that has an opinion on everything, second-guesses every decision, and refuses to stay quiet. It's persistent, impossible to ignore, and it isn't going anywhere. It's time to meet your ego.

To be clear, we're not talking about being *egotistical*. When people say, "drop the ego" or "they've got a big ego", they're talking about someone who's boasting or arrogant with an inflated sense of self-importance. Here, we're referring to the psychological construct known as the ego. It is your sense of self: the collection of thoughts, labels, roles, and beliefs about who you think you are. If you're unfamiliar with the concept, you might be thinking to yourself, "*Wait, but isn't that me?*" That's the voice of the ego, trying to trick you into identifying with it.

It can be a hard concept to grasp initially. One of the best ways to see it for yourself is through *mindfulness*, the simple act of paying attention to the present moment, deliberately and without judgement. Think of mindfulness as the exercise that builds your awareness muscle. Every time you practise, you strengthen your capacity for awareness. It is the foundation for everything that follows for the simple reason that you cannot change what you cannot see. Mindfulness is how we open our eyes.

One of the best tools to cultivate it is mindfulness meditation.[1] Many people confuse the goal of the practice and attempt to completely silence the mind, yet that misses the point entirely. The mind isn't meant to go quiet on command. Rather, the practice is to simply observe. Thoughts will arise, pull at your attention, and invite judgement. Instead of engaging with them, you learn to watch your thoughts without attachment. Over time, this creates space between you and your thoughts, allowing you to see them for what they are, instead of being carried away by them.

Your awareness is like the sky, expansive and calm, while your thoughts are merely clouds passing through. Clouds come and go, often out of nowhere. The sky, however, is ever-present. Even in the deepest of storms, the sky remains, waiting to re-emerge once the clouds begin to clear. Your ego is the part of you that attaches your sense of self to those thoughts. "*I think, therefore I am.*" This is one of our psyche's greatest traps. You are not the clouds. You are the sky, the space in which thoughts arise.[2] A more accurate expression is simply "*I am.*"

Through mindfulness, you notice the voice of the ego. You start to observe the constant commentary playing in your mind, telling stories about who you are, what you deserve, and who's to blame.

---

[1] There are plenty of fantastic guided meditations available for free on websites such as YouTube. If you've never practised mindfulness meditation before, I highly recommend you do a few guided ones first to get the feel for it. Once you get the hang of it, you can practise just about anywhere and anytime.

[2] Eckhart Tolle expresses a similar idea in *A New Earth*: "What a liberation to realize that the 'voice in my head' is not who I am. Who am I then? The one who sees that."

By witnessing it in action, you recognise its patterns, seeing how it feeds on fear, comparison, and control.

Even those who are strongly attached to their ego still glimpse this truth from time to time. The concept of intrusive thoughts offers one such example. We all experience them: thoughts so strange that you know you couldn't possibly be the one responsible for thinking them. They must have come from somewhere else. Why would you think about suddenly veering off the road? Or randomly pushing someone over? Or any of the other weird and wild thought bubbles that suddenly pop up in your head?

It's interesting that we label certain thoughts intrusive when none are more so than others. The label simply allows us to distance ourselves from the ones that don't fit the person we believe ourselves to be, while holding onto those that do. This is just another way the ego protects itself. That moment of distance, where you recognise a thought as separate from who you are, is your awareness breaking through.

Recognise your backseat driver

Pay close attention and you'll start to see the ego lurking in the shadows of your mind. You begin to recognise how it manifests, through patterns such as:

- Playing the victim;
- Comparing yourself to others (whether feeling superior or inferior);
- Feeling offended;
- Complaining or fault-finding;
- Needing to be right; and
- Living trapped in the past or worried about the future.

The ego thrives on drama. Most people will claim that they want peace, yet part of us secretly craves conflict, be it a battle or an argument. It is the part of you that fires up to defend something no matter how trivial, seeking an argument rather than a discussion. Nothing strengthens it more than needing to be right, to win rather than to understand. This is one of the many dangers of a strong identification with one's ego. It loves an echo chamber, yet you learn nothing by only talking to those who agree with your opinions.

Growth comes from having an open mind, from accepting that you might be wrong. A growth mindset is the willingness to discover that the pieces you're missing may be held by others. The ego, however, often expresses itself through a *victim mindset*: a persistent belief that the world is out to get you, that nothing is in your control, and that all negative events in your life are solely the result of others' actions.

While a growth mindset expands your view of the puzzle, a victim mindset narrows it, cutting you off from the very pieces you need to grow. It is one of the most damaging manifestations of the ego. Despite being deeply flawed, many people cling to this mindset, often because it's socially reinforced. In many instances, it is not only condoned but actively encouraged. It is one of the strongest bars of many people's personal prisons. It's not hard to see why, either.

At its core, a victim mindset is a form of avoidance. It avoids asking the hard questions, and more importantly, it avoids the uncomfortable truths. Playing the victim is comfort food for the mind. If nothing is ever your fault, then you never need to change, trapping you in the smallest version of yourself. The challenge, as we'll see in the coming chapters, is that your thoughts often lead to a self-fulfilling prophecy. In the words of Henry Ford, "*Whether you think you can or think you can't, you're right.*" Start believing you have no control, and you'll gradually relinquish the control you *do* have.

Recognising this, and the other manifestations of your ego, is crucial in understanding your map. Until you can spot when your backseat driver is taking over, you're not consciously steering your life. You're simply along for the ride.

Lucid living

Throughout this chapter, we've explored the idea of awareness. Mindfulness strengthens it, meditation cultivates it, and recognising the ego requires it. The moment you become aware of a pattern, thought, or belief, you create space between yourself and it. Rather than being unconsciously driven by it, you gain the ability to observe it and choose your response. Few phenomena illustrate this more clearly than *lucid dreaming*.

A lucid dream occurs when you become aware that you're dreaming while the dream is still unfolding. Most dreams feel completely real in the moment. No matter how strange the events become, you rarely stop to question them. In a lucid dream, however, something remarkable happens. You suddenly recognise that what felt like reality is nothing more than a dream. With that awareness, you are no longer merely a passenger. You become a conscious participant in your own dream, often gaining the ability to influence or direct it at will. You may be asleep in reality, but you're wide awake within your dream.

A similar pattern plays out in our waking lives. Just as we rarely question a dream while we're in it, we rarely question the stories, assumptions, and habits that underpin our waking lives. We assume we're in the driver's seat, yet many of our thoughts, reactions, habits, and decisions arise automatically from conditioning, old beliefs, and an unchecked ego. We move through our days responding to familiar patterns without ever noticing they're there.

Just as lucid dreaming is becoming conscious in your dreams, *lucid living* is becoming conscious within your waking life. It's recognising the stories your ego tells you. It's noticing the beliefs that shape your decisions. It's catching yourself reacting automatically and choosing a different response. You move from being a passenger in your own life to actively steering it. By recognising your backseat driver, you reclaim the wheel.

Your ego is not the enemy. It isn't something you can destroy or escape, even if you tried. It's part of being human. That same voice that can trap you in conflict can also push you to grow, succeed, and take pride in yourself. The danger only arises when you can't tell who's really driving. When you over-identify with the ego, the real driver falls asleep at the wheel. The backseat driver takes over, dictating the entire journey. Give it too much control and it slips into the unhealthy patterns we explored earlier.

The solution is not to reject the ego, but to *integrate it*. As we grow and develop, so too does our ego. To reject it is to reject part of ourselves. Instead, the goal is to recognise your patterns and catch the ego in action. Learn to work with it, and the annoying voice in the backseat starts to feel more like a co-pilot.

You can choose to stay asleep at the wheel and hope for the best. Or you can wake up, take the driver's seat, and start steering towards a life you consciously choose. As always, the choice is yours.

◇

EXERCISE 2

Catch your ego

Over the next week, begin actively observing your ego. The goal is to recognise your egoic patterns and behaviours in real time. Once you can see it clearly, you create separation from it. You begin to see the sky through the clouds.

A practical way to do this is to keep a note on your phone. Each time you notice one of the patterns below, mark it down. This includes internal thoughts, not just what you say or do.

Defensiveness: When do you feel the urge to defend yourself? If you catch it in the moment, pause and ask: "*What exactly am I defending?*" Often, it's not the situation, but your self-image. The need to be right is one of the clearest signs that your ego has taken over.

Playing the victim: Notice when you fall into a victim mindset. This includes when you complain, blame others, or focus on what's outside your control. The underlying implication is that you've been wronged or are powerless.

Comparison: Watch when you compare yourself to others, whether feeling superior or inferior. This often shows up when scrolling social media or observing someone else's success. Comparison is one of the ego's primary ways of measuring self-worth.

Seeking validation: Notice when you look for praise, recognition, attention, or credit. The ego relies on external acknowledgement to reinforce its identity. When you catch this, see if you can simply notice the urge without immediately acting on it.

Lack of presence: When do you find yourself stuck in the past or preoccupied with the future? Reflection and planning both have their place, but when they dominate your attention, it's often a sign the ego is pulling you away from the present.

At the end of each day, complete a short audit.

- Which patterns appeared most often?
- Did you notice any recurring situations, people, or triggers?
- Were you able to recognise the patterns in the moment, or only afterwards?
- In moments where you noticed your ego clearly, did you experience any sense of separation from it, even briefly?

You may be surprised how often these patterns appear once you begin paying attention.

CHAPTER 2

WAKE UP THE DRIVER

Kids often struggle to tell the difference between stories and real life. As adults, we'd like to think we've outgrown such naivety, yet still we are repeatedly fooled. The only difference is it's no longer the bedtime stories told by our parents, but the stories we tell ourselves.

The greatest storyteller of all time

A backseat driver's defining trait is unsolicited commentary. Our ego is no different, providing us with constant chatter and stories as we journey through life.

We are all the product of these stories. They influence how we see ourselves, and in turn, how we see the world. They guide our choices, filter our options, and set the boundaries for what we believe is possible. Some of our stories are obvious, playing on repeat in our head. Many more lie below our conscious awareness yet nonetheless continue to influence our behaviours and decisions. They're powerful because we believe them, and dangerous because we rarely question them.

So why do we keep falling for them? Simply because we don't recognise them for what they are. Kids believe in Santa because no one tells them it's a story. We believe our own stories just as blindly as children believe in fairy tales. It's what makes our ego so effective. It crafts narratives so quickly that you rarely notice where the facts end and the story begins.

Imagine that the company you work for goes bankrupt. You arrive at work only for your boss to inform you that your role has been made redundant. Almost immediately, your mind begins to race. "*It's going to take ages to find a new job! People will think less of me now that I'm unemployed. I'm going to struggle as I don't deal well with change.*"

Did you see what the ego did there? None of those thoughts are facts. If it cannot be proven to be true, it is merely a story built on assumptions. The only facts are that the company went bankrupt and your role was made redundant. Your ego then extrapolates those facts into a complete story, using your underlying beliefs to fill in the blanks. This happens automatically. It is not malicious, nor is it deliberate. It is simply a built-in survival mechanism of the ego. Your sense of self has just been disrupted, forcing the ego to quickly construct a narrative to restore it.

To loosen the grip of these stories, you first need to see them. When you begin to observe your thoughts, you create space to pause and assess. This space lets you separate the facts of a situation from the stories your ego weaves in response. This is where mindfulness can be invaluable. It improves your awareness of your thoughts, allowing you to catch your stories in the very moment your ego starts telling them. It's remarkable how a mere awareness of the storyteller can lead to immediate detachment from its tales. Like seeing the man behind the curtain, the illusion is instantly shattered.

The next time you notice yourself reacting strongly to a personal story, place it outside of you. Picture it printed on the pages of a book. Imagine someone else reading it aloud, word for word. In doing so, you may already notice a change in how the story feels, as if it somehow holds less weight. When it's spoken in someone else's voice, the story becomes less personal. It allows you to listen closely and really pay attention. Which parts are grounded in observable fact? Which parts are based on assumptions or interpretations?

When you distil a story down to the facts, it allows you to react calmly and objectively. Stories may be emotive, but the facts are always neutral. They leave room for interpretation. It is the narrative layered on top that drives the emotional reaction, locking you into a fixed perspective. Remove that layer, and you regain the ability to choose how you respond.

Look for black swans

Once you become aware of your stories, you can start to question them. Does your ego have a point? Is there some truth behind its claims? The fact that we even need to ask leads to a more fundamental question: why are we so quick to believe it in the first place? Why do we afford our ego such credibility when its conclusions are built on remarkably little evidence?

Imagine a scientist running two small experiments, observing the same result, and then declaring they've discovered a universal law. We wouldn't accept a conclusion from such a small sample size without further testing. Yet that's exactly what we let our ego get away with all the time. It takes a limited set of experiences and generalises into broad conclusions about how the world works. Possibilities become certainties. Hypotheses become absolute truths.

To challenge this, we can borrow a principle from mathematics and logic. If someone claims something is always true, you don't need to test every possible case to disprove it. You need only to find a single counterexample where it doesn't hold.

Take swans as an example. For centuries, Europeans *knew* that all swans were white. This wasn't considered a belief. It was accepted textbook knowledge, an unquestioned fact reinforced by every swan they had ever seen. That is, until explorers reached Australia. Imagine their shock when they encountered a black swan. Had there not been multiple witnesses, the claim would likely have been dismissed outright. One single bird is all it took to shatter a belief that had gone unchallenged for generations. That is the power of a black swan, a single counterexample that exposes the limits of our assumptions.

Black swans offer a useful way to expose the false certainty of your ego. Many stories rely on absolutes like *always* and *never*. These words create the pretence of certainty though it's rarely justified. More often, they're the result of extrapolating a narrow slice of experience into a sweeping conclusion about reality. Sometimes your ego forgets about the counterexamples that prove the story false. Other times, like the early Europeans, you simply haven't experienced or seen enough to know that it isn't always true.

Think back to the earlier redundancy example. Will *every* person really think less of you if you don't have a job? You can probably name people in your life who respect you regardless of your employment status. Some may even respect you more for having the courage to walk away from security in pursuit of something better.

Is it *universally true* that you can't handle change? You may not *enjoy* change, but that's not the same as being unable to cope with it. Think back to times you've adapted, learned, or endured difficult situations. Perhaps it was a breakup, a career change, a big move, or a setback that you navigated successfully. Each one is evidence to be held up against the claims of your ego.

Awareness helps you notice the stories, while black swans dissolve their power. You don't need to completely disprove a belief to loosen its hold. One counterexample is all it takes to show that a story isn't universally true. Each one you find reminds you that your ego is not predicting the future or revealing hidden laws of the universe. It's simply presenting guesses with unwarranted confidence, based on incomplete data. When you learn to look for the exceptions, the ego's authority begins to crumble, and with it, the limits you impose on who you can become.

The subtle power of words

Once a story cracks open, even slightly, you create room to rewrite it. Rather than letting the ego write its tales unchallenged, you can step in as an editor. If unhelpful stories win out, it simply means that your ego's version of the truth is more compelling than your own.

Stories are built from language. If you change the language, you change the meaning. Change the meaning, and you change how you respond to it. This is what practices like *neuro-linguistic programming* (NLP) aim to explore. They focus on how language, thought patterns, and behaviours interact to form your subjective experience.

If a victim mindset is the poison, reframing is one possible antidote. Instead of seeing yourself as a passive receiver of external events, you learn to reinterpret those events, influence your emotional state, and choose your response. Some aspects of NLP are contested, but there's nothing mystical about this particular idea. At its simplest, it is about altering the language you use to influence how you interpret and experience the world.

Let's look once more at our redundancy example. Your initial story of ruin and disaster could be reframed into one of opportunity and growth. Maybe now, you can finally look for that job or career path you'd always wanted to explore. Perhaps this change will give you the time and space to explore a hobby you've always dreamed of. Even if you take a similar job elsewhere, the experience will be an opportunity to expand your network, skills, and future options. You'll meet new people, some of whom might become lifelong friends, or perhaps introduce you to new interests. The possibilities are endless, yet your thoughts act as blinders, filtering which ones you notice.

This works through a simple feedback loop. Experiences give rise to thoughts. Thoughts drive emotions. Emotions affect actions. Our actions then determine our experiences. Reframing is powerful because it lets you intervene at the start of the loop. By adjusting how you interpret the initial event, you influence everything that follows.

Reframing doesn't require sweeping philosophical shifts. It can start with a single word. Consider the difference between describing something as a *problem* or a *challenge*. Problems weigh you down. They trigger complaining, avoidance, and a sense of powerlessness, providing the perfect breeding ground for a victim mindset. This powerlessness leads to inaction, reinforcing the very situation you fear. Your thoughts create a self-fulfilling prophecy.

Call that same situation a challenge, however, and your entire outlook changes. It implies effort, but also capability and agency. You feel engaged rather than defeated, inviting curiosity to search for a solution. You take action as a result.

One word is all it took to alter your emotional state and with it, your behaviour. Over time, these small linguistic shifts compound into different choices, different actions, and ultimately a different life. Pay close attention to the words you habitually use. They don't merely describe your experience – they actively help to create it.

Harness your built-in navigator

While the language you use is important, there is another system that determines what you even notice in the first place. In deciding what gets through and what gets discarded, it directly influences the data from which your ego can build its narratives. This mechanism is known as the *Reticular Activating System* (RAS).

The RAS is part of the brain's filtering system for the overwhelming flood of sensory data you encounter every second. Some estimates suggest your senses receive millions of bits of information per second, while conscious awareness handles only a tiny fraction. In other words, most of what your brain processes never becomes part of your conscious experience. So how does it decide what makes the cut?

The answer is simple. *You do.* Your RAS brings to your awareness what *you* signal as important. It works like a social media algorithm, surfacing what it thinks you want while hiding the rest from your feed.

Think about the last time you were considering something new, like getting a dog. Suddenly, you start seeing them everywhere. They're on footpaths, in advertisements, and even in passing conversations you might previously have ignored. That's your RAS in action. Nothing you've observed is new; you haven't somehow manifested it into existence. You're simply noticing what was already there, now that your attention has been directed towards it.

By filtering your attention in this way, it acts like your internal navigator. It scans the road ahead, choosing which signs, turns, hazards, and opportunities to highlight, and which to completely ignore. But like any navigator, it can only work with the map it's been given. If that map is filled with old beliefs, outdated assumptions or stories you've never questioned, you can find yourself veering off course without ever realising.

Keep telling yourself the world is out to get you, and your RAS will actively look for examples where that's the case. It will highlight every perceived slight. Neutral glances will be misread as hostility. Every coincidence will be misinterpreted as proof. Focus instead on possibilities or solutions and you get a different result entirely. Your RAS begins solving the problem itself, flagging options, ideas, and possible connections that you've previously overlooked. It's yet another mechanism by which the mind can create a self-fulfilling prophecy.

It's also why practices like gratitude and visualisation are so powerful. When you regularly focus on specific types of experiences, you signal to your mind that they are important. Simply recording three things you're grateful for each day trains your mind to prioritise those experiences, bringing more of them into your awareness. It's how you update your algorithm.

This is where reframing and your RAS begin to work together. The way you interpret events determines the meaning you assign to them. That meaning then trains your attention. If you consistently interpret situations through a negative lens, your mind starts scanning for evidence to support it. You notice more of what confirms the story, which in turn reinforces the way you interpret future events.

The reverse is also true. Change the interpretation, and your attention begins to follow. Over time, this creates a feedback loop. Your interpretations influence what you notice, and what you notice strengthens your interpretations.

There is, however, an even deeper layer to this process. It's not just how you interpret events or what you notice, but also what you expect to happen next.

Don't stop believin'

One of the most remarkable tools at your disposal is belief itself. To many people, the idea that belief can influence outcomes is, well, unbelievable. Yet the placebo effect is one of the clearest demonstrations of its power. It occurs when measurable physiological changes take place in the body in response to the expectation that a treatment will work. For example, someone taking a sugar pill, while believing it to be a therapeutic drug, can experience improvements consistent with that belief.

This effect cuts both ways. The nocebo effect describes the opposite pattern, where negative expectations can produce negative outcomes. If you expect side effects, your body can generate them. This has important implications for how risks, prognoses, and even life expectancy are communicated.

This is not a fringe phenomenon. The placebo effect is significant enough that rigorous clinical trials often need to account for it. Some of the participants receive a placebo instead of the active treatment, allowing researchers to isolate its impact. This ensures that the results of the trial aren't driven purely by the expectations of its participants. In some areas, particularly pain, mood, and sleep, placebo responses can account for a significant proportion of the observed improvement. In rare cases, they can approach, or even exceed, the specific effect of the treatment itself.

Even more remarkable is that this effect can persist even when people know they are taking a placebo. Measurable changes can still occur even in the absence of any active treatment. In these cases, belief *itself* becomes part of the treatment.

When you combine NLP, the RAS, and the placebo effect, a consistent pattern begins to emerge. Your thoughts do not simply sit in the background. They influence what you notice, how you act, the opportunities you seize, and even aspects of your physiology.

Of course, there are still limits to this. Belief cannot override physical reality. This is not about convincing yourself that everything is possible. You cannot think your way out of every constraint, nor should you try. What this does highlight is that your brain is constantly predicting, filtering, and regulating based on the beliefs you hold. It is those beliefs that influence your thoughts, ultimately driving your perception, decisions, and responses.

The goal, therefore, is not blind optimism or forced positivity. Simply "thinking positive thoughts" is often ineffective because it fails to address the beliefs that produced those thoughts in the first place. You need to go to the source. By examining and updating your beliefs, you begin to generate thoughts that work with you, rather than against you.

Are you awake yet?

By now, you should be starting to wake up. You've peeled back the layers of your own mind, exposing your ego's stories and the assumptions that crumble under a single black swan. By reinterpreting events with NLP, directing your attention with your RAS, and understanding the role belief plays in influencing your outcomes, you begin to take the wheel. Yet here, a new challenge quickly surfaces.

With this awareness, it's easy to assume that if you can change your thoughts, you can control your life. Surely, with enough clarity, discipline, or effort, you should be able to influence outcomes exactly as you intend. This is where things start to break down.

No matter how skilled a driver you become, there are forces on this journey you cannot control. You may steer your car, but you don't control the road. You can't dictate the weather, the traffic, or the behaviour of other cars, yet you must navigate through them all the same.

The real challenge, then, is learning where your control ends and where it truly begins. In the next chapter, we'll explore how true power comes not from controlling everything, but from mastering how we respond.

◇

EXERCISE 3

Question your stories

Your next goal is to become more aware of the stories running through your mind.

Each day, capture at least five moments where you notice a strong thought, reaction, or internal narrative. Write each down as it appears. If it goes beyond what can be objectively observed, treat it as a story rather than a fact.

Examples might include:

> *"This always happens to me."*
> *"They must think less of me."*
> *"I'm just not good at..."*

For now, simply focus on noticing and capturing them.

Step 1 – Separate fact from fiction

At the end of the day, review what you wrote. For each example, ask yourself:

- What are the objective facts of the situation?
- What assumptions, meanings, or interpretations have I added on top?

Strip it back to what can be directly observed. Everything else is part of the story.

Step 2 – Look for black swans

Now challenge the story. Is it always true, or can you find a counterexample? You don't need to disprove the story entirely. You just need one exception to prove that the story is not an absolute fact.

Step 3 – Reframe the narrative

Once your attachment to the story weakens, you can rewrite it in a way that is more balanced, accurate, and useful. When reframing your stories, consider the questions below:

- How else could I view this situation?
- What is a more balanced or constructive way to describe it?
- What opportunities or alternatives might I be overlooking?
- How might my past experiences be influencing how I interpret this?

Avoid forced positivity. Aim for something grounded and believable instead.

Step 4 – Keep it brief

You don't need to dive deeply into every example. Spend just a few minutes on each one. The goal is to build consistency and awareness over time. As you become more conscious of your inner dialogue, you'll notice which stories hold the greatest influence over your thoughts, emotions, and behaviour.

Each time you question a story, you create space between what happens and how you respond. That space is where your real control lies.

CHAPTER 3

YOU CONTROL NOTHING... AND EVERYTHING

One of our greatest challenges in life is learning the difference between what we can and cannot control. It's not that we lack control entirely, but that we tend to look for it in the wrong place. We pour energy into areas where we have limited influence, while overlooking the one place where our power actually lies.

We like to believe we're steering our lives more than we are. We plan, optimise, negotiate, and persuade, convinced that with enough effort, we can bend outcomes to our will. It's the same instinct that drives athletes to cling to pre-game rituals, or gamblers to place their trust in lucky charms. These behaviours are not rational strategies so much as psychological comforts. They create the feeling of control in a world that is largely indifferent to our intentions.

If we pause and take an honest look, the limits of our influence become difficult to ignore. Zoom out far enough and it's negligible. We live on a tiny rock hurtling around a star, a mere grain of sand drifting through a cosmic ocean. Everywhere we look, we're surrounded by galaxies that neither know nor care that we exist. Zoom in to Earth and it's not much different. We can't control the weather, the wildlife, or even the traffic lights. Then there are the other eight billion people on the planet. We can barely influence those we know, let alone the vast majority we'll never even meet.

None of this should be surprising. After all, it would be unreasonable to assume we could exert any level of control at a global scale, let alone a cosmic one. Yet when we narrow the lens further and examine our own individual lives, we see the same pattern emerge. Our influence over events, outcomes, and other people is revealed to be far smaller than we would like to admit. The difference lies not in the scale of our influence, but in our expectations. Nobody would realistically expect control over the cosmos, but our own lives? Surely, we should have more of a say.

This cognitive bias, known as the *illusion of control*,[3] leads us to overestimate how much influence we truly have. Like many mental shortcuts, it exists for *efficiency* rather than *accuracy*. By relying on past experiences and familiar patterns, the mind forms quick judgements that feel certain and authoritative. The issue is that these judgements are not grounded in objective reality so much as in memory, habit, and belief.

It takes only a single moment of honest reflection for the curtain to slip. When it does, we begin to see that much of what we believed we were managing was never fully ours to command in the first place.

Breaking the illusion

Have you ever experienced the loss of a loved one, or a life-changing illness or accident? It's in moments like these that our control over the external world is revealed to be painfully insignificant. What once felt stable and predictable now feels fragile and uncertain. Our belief that life is within our control is

[3] Ellen J. Langer, "The Illusion of Control," *Journal of Personality and Social Psychology* 32, no. 2 (1975): 311–328.

exposed as nothing more than a story. A single, unexpected event is enough to unravel it. Life reveals a black swan, and with it, the illusion of control slips.

These moments, while deeply painful, also carry the potential for profound insight. When the illusion fractures, a different way of seeing the world becomes possible. We notice how much time and energy we've spent fighting battles we were never going to win in the first place. Every hour spent stressing over things you can't influence is an hour stolen from the things you can. Trying to control the outside world is as pointless as trying to empty the ocean with a bucket. As the saying goes, "*Worrying is like a rocking chair – it gives you something to do but gets you nowhere.*"

Letting go of this illusion may look like resignation. "*If I can't control anything, why bother trying?*" This couldn't be further from the truth. Letting go is not giving up. It's reclaiming agency. It's getting up out of the rocking chair and redirecting our energy where it will lead to real outcomes. We reclaim our power by refusing to exhaust ourselves on battles we can't win, in favour of those we can. Yet even after making this change, a more subtle habit can still undermine our best intentions.

Maybe so, maybe not

We tend to label events as *good* or *bad* almost instantly. Psychologists refer to it as the *affect heuristic*.[4] It's another mental shortcut, designed for speed, not absolute truth. This snap judgement is yet another attempt at control, hidden within our stories.

---

[4] Paul Slovic, Melissa L. Finucane, Ellen Peters, and Donald G. MacGregor, "The Affect Heuristic," in *Heuristics and Biases: The Psychology of Intuitive Judgment*, ed. Thomas Gilovich, Dale Griffin, and Daniel Kahneman (Cambridge: Cambridge University Press, 2002), 397–420.

The issue with this tendency is that we judge an event long before we understand its place in the bigger picture. A setback can feel catastrophic until it becomes a turning point. A victory can feel triumphant until it unravels into something far more painful. We cling to these premature judgements as if they were objective truth. In reality, they're nothing more than guesses made in the moment.

The parable of the Chinese farmer illustrates this perfectly. As the story goes, one day one of the farmer's horses runs away. His neighbours lament his misfortune, but the farmer doesn't react. Instead, he simply responds, "*Maybe so, maybe not. We'll see.*" Later, when the horse returns, bringing with it several wild horses, the neighbours now celebrate his good fortune. Again, the farmer replies, "*Maybe so, maybe not. We'll see.*" When his son snaps his leg taming one of the new horses, the neighbours lament his bad luck. Once more, the farmer says, "*Maybe so, maybe not. We'll see.*" A few weeks later, soldiers come to conscript all able-bodied young men for the army. His son is spared due to his injury, and so the neighbours exclaim, "*What tremendous luck!*" The farmer repeats, "*Maybe so, maybe not. We'll see.*"

The lesson here is that no event can be objectively labelled as good or bad. It's not that events lack consequences, but that we are in no position to judge them in isolation. Only time reveals how things unfold, with none of us living long enough to see the full story. Yet despite lacking all the pieces, we continue to label events with confidence, mistaking fragments for the full picture.

Even if we somehow *did* have all the information, events are not inherently good or bad to begin with. The universe is not conspiring for or against you. Events do not come with built-in meaning. We supply the meaning when we label them. It is the labels that we place on events that determine how they impact us, not the events themselves.

The parable of the farmer teaches us the wisdom of neutrality. While he may appear to be indifferent, he is acting from a place of humility. By accepting how little we can truly understand in the moment, we begin to see the futility of judging events. When you stop rushing to judge every experience, you recover the energy once spent on prediction, anxiety, and mental storytelling. You stop letting old stories decide your future.

Neutrality frees us from judgement, yet even as we loosen our grip on labels, another burden remains. Just as we must learn to let go of judgement, we must release the invisible baggage we carry with us through life.

Let go of your baggage

There is a famous Buddhist story about two monks travelling together. While walking, they come across a woman standing by a fast-flowing river. Unable to cross alone, she asks the monks for assistance. Without hesitation, the older monk lifts her up, carries her across, and gently sets her down on the other side. The younger monk is shocked. Their vows strictly forbid touching a woman, but he remains silent.

The monks continue their travels in silence for an hour. "*How could he break his vow so casually?*" the young monk wonders, but still, he says nothing. Another hour passes, then another. Finally, the young monk can stand it no longer. "*Why did you carry that woman when we vowed never to touch women?*" The older monk calmly replies, "*I put her down hours ago. Why are you still carrying her?*"

We all carry far more than we need to, whether it's old stories, emotional wounds, or unchallenged beliefs. Some may once have served us, but now they only weigh us down. Awareness shows us what we're still carrying, long after the moment has passed.

Letting go doesn't mean forgetting. Forgetting would only doom us to repeat our past mistakes and fall into the same traps. It's about acceptance. By realising that you can't change the past, you are consciously choosing not to let it limit your future.

The farmer teaches us to let go of judgement. The older monk teaches us to let go of what we no longer need to hold on to. Together, they show that much of our suffering comes not from life itself, but from the stories and baggage we attach to it.

The paradox of control

This brings us to the paradox at the heart of personal freedom. While you control almost nothing externally, by choosing your internal response, you control *everything*. Zoom out, and your control over the world is staggeringly insignificant. Zoom in, however, and your control over your inner world is far greater than you might imagine.

The external world will always extend beyond your control. Events unfold, outcomes arise, and other people will continue to act as they please. What remains is your ability to choose what you do in response. You can choose how you interpret events, how you respond to outcomes, and how much you let the behaviour of other people affect you.

As we saw earlier, it is the meaning you assign to an event that determines your emotional response. Those emotions result in the behaviour and actions that go on to influence your future outcomes. Your inner world acts as a filter through which every experience is processed. Your *stories* become your *reality*, and only *you* have the power to rewrite them.

This is why two people can live through the same event and walk away with entirely different lives. The circumstances may be shared, but the interpretation is not.

The last human freedom

History offers us countless examples of this truth, perhaps none more profound than Viktor Frankl. In *Man's Search for Meaning*, Frankl wrote:

> *"Everything can be taken from a man but one thing: the last of the human freedoms – to choose one's attitude in any given set of circumstances, to choose one's own way."*

Frankl didn't come to this realisation in the comfort of an office. It was forged by his lived experience, through surviving the horrors of Auschwitz. Prisoners had their clothes, their identity, and their dignity stripped away, along with every external freedom we take for granted. They had no say in the meagre scraps of food they received, when or how long they slept, how long they worked, or whether they would live to see another day. They were told when to stand, when to march, and when to be silent. Any opposition was met with swift and brutal retaliation.

None of this unimaginable suffering was within their control. Yet despite an environment of complete powerlessness, Frankl discovered the one freedom that no one could strip away – the ability to choose his internal response.

Stephen Covey, author of *The 7 Habits of Highly Effective People*, later explored a similar idea through the concepts of the circle of concern and circle of influence. This points to a deeper principle known as the *locus of control* associated with psychologist Julian Rotter. In simple terms, your locus of control refers to where you believe control over your life sits. When it sits outside of us, we live as passive reactors, at the mercy of the world around us. When we instead shift it inwards, we become conscious responders.

Mindfulness helps us locate the space between an event and our subsequent reaction. Through awareness, we can choose our response and reclaim our inner freedom.

> *"Between stimulus and response there is a space, and in that space lies our freedom."*[5]

The power of surrender

To gain internal freedom, we must first let go of the illusion of control. For some, like Frankl, the illusion is violently shattered, but it need not be that way for us all. Clinging to control is comforting, but it also distorts the boundary between what we can influence and what we must accept. The serenity prayer captures this beautifully:

> *"Grant me the serenity to accept the things I cannot change, the courage to change the things I can, and the wisdom to know the difference."*[6]

Wisdom is the doorway, and the illusion of control is the gatekeeper. Awareness is the key. Notice where you are attached to particular outcomes or trying to force events in a certain direction. Pay attention to when you instantly label experiences as good or bad, and the emotional reactions that follow. See if you can remove this judgement entirely, instead simply observing experiences, without feeling the need to assign labels. When viewed through a lens of neutrality, experiences begin to affect

---

[5] This quote is often attributed to Frankl, although its true origin is uncertain. In the foreword to a book about Frankl's principles, Covey explains that he came across the line in a library book and felt it reaffirmed Frankl's teachings, but he "did not note the name of the author so has never been able to give proper attribution."

[6] Adapted from Reinhold Niebuhr's "Serenity Prayer". See Elisabeth Sifton, *The Serenity Prayer: Faith and Politics in Times of Peace and War* (New York: W. W. Norton, 2003).

you differently, shining a light on your internal power that has always been there.

Note that there is an important distinction here between accountability and acceptance. Acceptance is about *reality*. Accountability is about *agency*. Acceptance does not mean admitting defeat, while accountability does not mean taking the blame. It is simply shifting your locus of control inward, accepting what you cannot control, and taking responsibility for what you can.

For those who have experienced severe trauma, this can understandably be confronting. You're not asked to pretend that everything is "meant to be" or to force meaning onto suffering. Acceptance may not ease the pain, but it does reclaim your power. It says, "*I cannot change what happened, but I can choose who I become because of it.*" It is the same freedom Frankl glimpsed when everything external was stripped away and the only territory left to govern was the inner world.

It's about choosing your internal power over a story that says the world is against you and you're powerless to change it. You stop burning energy fighting the world and instead invest it in building your life. Over time, automatic reaction is replaced with intentional response. You stop resisting what is and begin moving through it instead.

◇

EXERCISE 4

How much control do you really have?

Start by writing down the five biggest challenges in your life right now. Don't overthink it; just go with what immediately comes to mind. The ranking isn't important here. The goal is to identify what's consuming your mental bandwidth.

Step 1 – What's in your control?

For each challenge, consider what is actually within your control. For example, suppose one of your challenges is a boss who constantly micromanages you. If you reflect on it, you'll notice:

There are some things that you can change directly. You could improve how you communicate, set clearer expectations, or proactively provide updates. You might even identify behaviours of your own that are contributing to the situation.

There are some things you can influence but can't directly control. You can build trust, improve the relationship, and have conversations about working styles. These may reduce the micromanaging, but they don't guarantee it.

There are some things you can't change at all. Your boss's personality, tendencies, or management style may simply be what they are, regardless of anything you do.

Now apply that same thinking to your own list of challenges. For each one, ask yourself:

- What can I do about this directly through my own actions?
- How can I influence the outcome, even if I can't control it?
- Which parts are completely outside my control?

Step 2 – Where is your energy going?

Review your answers. Look at each challenge and consider where your time and mental energy are being spent.

- Are you acting on the parts you can change?
- Are you thoughtfully influencing what you can?
- Or are you repeatedly focusing on the parts that won't move despite your efforts?

Pay attention to where energy is leaking. This might include overthinking, frustration, complaining, replaying conversations, or trying to force outcomes. These behaviours *feel* active, but they rarely create meaningful progress. This is where many people get stuck.

Step 3 – Reallocate your energy

Now make a conscious adjustment.

Be deliberate about where your actions can lead to change. Double down where you can directly determine results. Where influence is possible, use it, but accept the uncertainty that comes with it. Most importantly, begin letting go of the areas where nothing will change regardless of how much energy you invest.

Remember that even when a situation is outside of your control, you can still choose your response. Every hour spent on what you can't control is taken directly away from what you can.

CHAPTER 4

LIFE ON AUTOPILOT

Understanding where your control lies fundamentally changes how you move through life, yet even with that awareness, another challenge remains.

Have you ever driven somewhere, only to discover on arrival that you can't recall the journey?

It's an unsettling thought. Were you not paying attention? Look closer, and the answer is more nuanced. Some part of you clearly must have been. You followed traffic, obeyed signals, navigated turns, and arrived safely. You completed the trip competently, just without conscious awareness of the process.

This phenomenon is known as *highway hypnosis* and it's how most of us move through our entire lives. Technically, we're functioning, but rarely with full awareness. Instead, we live on autopilot, often with little conscious recollection of how we arrived where we are. Like the ego, the autopilot itself is not the issue. It's a feature, not a flaw. The problem only arises when we fail to calibrate it.

The danger of drifting

Aviation offers a devastating illustration. In 1983, Korean Air Lines Flight 007 ended in tragedy. A failure to engage the intended navigation mode placed the aircraft on the wrong course, causing a gradual drift from the intended flight path. At first, it was barely noticeable. After 30 minutes, the aircraft was only 11 kilometres off course.[7]

By the next waypoint, however, it was 110 kilometres off course. Then 190. Then 300. Over five and a half hours, that tiny navigational error compounded into a deviation of more than 500 kilometres, redirecting the plane into restricted Soviet airspace. The military interception that followed cost the lives of all 269 people on board. A small drift, left unattended, became one of the deadliest catastrophes in aviation history.

The problem was not the system. The autopilot had done exactly what it had been programmed to do. It was the failure to set it correctly that led to disaster.

Our lives follow a similar pattern. Small misalignments, left unexamined, compound over time. The trajectory drifts gradually at first, until eventually you find yourself wildly off course. The solution is not to discard the autopilot, but to consciously recalibrate it. To do that, you first need to understand how it operates within your body and your mind.

Your body is on cruise control...

Let's begin with the physical body. The nervous system is commonly divided into the *somatic nervous system* (SNS) and the *autonomic nervous system* (ANS). The SNS governs voluntary movements, while the ANS regulates involuntary functions like breathing, heart rate, and digestion.

---

[7] International Civil Aviation Organization, *Destruction of Korean Air Lines Boeing 747 on 31 August 1983: Report on the Completion of the ICAO Fact-Finding Investigation* (Montreal: ICAO, 1993).

The ANS is, by design, an autopilot. Take breathing as an example. Take a moment to try the following exercise:

- Inhale for four seconds
- Hold for four seconds
- Exhale for four seconds
- Hold for four seconds
- Repeat for 20 cycles

This technique is known as *box breathing*. On the surface, it looks trivially easy, yet many people find it surprisingly difficult to make it to 20 without losing count. Instead, thoughts arise and compete for your attention, oftentimes winning. You get distracted, forget what you're supposed to be doing, and lose count. Yet despite that momentary lapse, your breathing continues anyway. The moment your conscious control slips, the ANS steps in and takes over.

This simple exercise reveals two important dynamics. First, many automated processes can be brought under conscious influence, but only temporarily and with effort. Second, the moment that effort fades, control returns to the underlying system.

This is a necessary limitation. Without this automation, we'd be overwhelmed. Many people struggle to complete 20 box breathing cycles. Imagine if it were every breath instead, as well as every heartbeat, and every other involuntary process. We'd be paralysed by our basic biology. The ANS is more than just a convenience, it ensures our very survival.

Perhaps more surprising is that even the supposedly voluntary movements governed by the SNS are also largely automated. Most movements are not micromanaged. When you go for a walk, you don't consciously coordinate each muscle contraction required to do so. The execution is automatic.

We underestimate the complexity of apparently simple tasks like walking because we do them effortlessly all the time. It's only when something disrupts the system that we realise how little of the underlying process we truly understand. This lack of conscious awareness is why it's so challenging to relearn how to walk after a severe injury.

What this reveals is that the distinction between *voluntary* and *involuntary* is less absolute than it appears. In practice, the ANS and SNS operate as an integrated system, with control existing on a spectrum depending on context and attention. You can intervene, but only up to a point. While attention is present, you exert influence. When it fades, as it inevitably does, control defaults back to automation, even for those actions you consider to be voluntary. Your body is not so much a system you fully control, but one you intermittently steer.

...and so is your mind

This same pattern also plays out in your mind. With your brain consuming roughly 20 per cent of the body's total energy, it's no surprise that it relies on similar shortcuts. Without a mental autopilot, we'd be cognitively paralysed.

It's not just small habits, like sitting in our favourite seat or ordering the same lunch. Your thoughts, behaviours, judgements, biases, and beliefs largely run on autopilot too. Even speech is largely automatic, with words often spilling out before you've consciously decided what to say next.

Thoughts behave much like breathing, arising continuously and automatically. Yet just like the breath, our thoughts can be consciously observed or influenced. Comparing the two, a spectrum of increasingly conscious control emerges:

Level of control	Breath	Thoughts
Automatic	*Unconscious rhythm*	*Egoic thinking*
Passive observation	*Observing the breath*	*Mindfulness*
Active intervention	*Controlled breathing*	*Directed thinking*

Automatic is your default level of control: the autopilot that allows you to function. Your breathing is handled by the ANS, while your thoughts are largely steered by ego, habit, and learned patterns. With awareness, you move into passive observation. Just as you can notice the breath without trying to change it, you can observe your thoughts without engaging with them. With conscious effort, you enter active intervention. You can deliberately control your breathing through techniques such as box breathing, or deliberately steer your mind towards creativity, problem solving, or focused work.

As with the body, the mind can't remain in these higher states indefinitely. Rather, they are active states you rise into and inevitably fall out of. Just as the ANS resumes control of breathing, the ego resumes control of thought. Habitual stories, fears, assumptions, and learned patterns take over.

With practice, you can spend more time operating in these higher states, but you must always revert to autopilot. The goal, therefore, is not to eliminate it, but to ensure it is aligned with where you actually want to go. That raises two practical questions: what is your autopilot currently doing, and once you're aware of it, how do you calibrate it?

To answer either, you first need to see what's running in the background.

Check your malware

A useful way to understand your internal autopilot is to imagine your brain as a computer. In fact, much of our computing language already draws on this analogy: the central processing unit is the *brain* of a computer, while RAM serves as *memory*.

Computers are powerful tools, but not without limitations. Over time, they accumulate background processes. Some are essential, others irrelevant, while some are outright harmful. Open *Task Manager* on a sluggish machine and you'll see dozens of obscure processes you never intentionally installed. Buried among the legitimate programs is *malware*, malicious software that covertly siphons resources for its own purposes, degrading performance in the process. Worse still, it hides in plain sight, often running under names you'd never think to question.

The mind works in much the same way, accumulating background programs over time. Some come from parents, teachers, or friends. Others are absorbed from culture, advertising, or even sheer repetition. Some are recent, while others have been operating since your childhood.

Many of these background programs are useful, automating your actions and behaviours in ways that serve you. Many more are not. They accumulate not through deliberate choice, but through a lack of scrutiny. They take root each time you blindly accept an idea without questioning its source, its accuracy, or its usefulness. Like malware, most are hidden. They embed themselves within seemingly harmless stories, later manifesting as your habits and behaviours. Operating in the background, they erode your agency and constrain your potential, often without you ever realising.

Imagine the freedom that comes when these hidden programs are removed. Clear malware from a computer and it feels like a new machine. In the same way, you can reclaim capacity once you stop running mental software you never approved of in the first place. Think of the clarity that emerges when intrusive stories, inherited beliefs, and outdated scripts stop consuming your bandwidth.

The challenge, of course, is that you can't delete a program you don't know is running. You must open your internal *Task Manager* and inspect what's operating in the background. Only then can you decide what stays and what must be removed.

◇

EXERCISE 5

Observe your autopilot

The aim of this exercise is to build awareness of the automatic processes operating beneath your conscious attention. To do this, we'll begin with a few simple practices.

Step 1 – Box breathing

Once per day, practise the box breathing technique we explored earlier. Set a timer for five minutes and count your cycles. The goal is to notice the difference between consciously directing your breath and the moment your attention slips and automatic breathing resumes.

Each time you notice your attention has wandered, simply observe that transition without judgement. Notice how the ANS resumes control, then gently return to your conscious breathing pattern.

Step 2 – Observe a routine activity

Choose a simple activity you already perform automatically. This could be walking, showering, or even making a cup of coffee.

For the duration of the activity, remove as much external input as possible. That means no phone, no music, and no distractions. Your task is to observe the physical automation underlying the activity. As you complete the activity, pay attention to:

- Each of the individual steps involved;
- How much of the activity happens without conscious instruction; and
- How often your attention drifts away from the present task.

This exercise reveals just how complex most activities really are. When broken down, even the most basic tasks still require dozens of individual steps and micro-movements. Despite this complexity, each activity continues automatically, even without conscious awareness.

Step 3 – Observe your mental autopilot

At least once a day, whenever you remember to do so, pause briefly and bring awareness to your thinking. Your task now is to observe the cognitive automation that underlies your current mental activity. Pay attention to:

- The number of individual thoughts, assumptions, or interpretations running in the background;
- How much of your thinking is running without conscious instruction; and
- How often your awareness slips from observing the process itself.

Notice that what feels like a continuous stream of thought is often an automated process running beneath awareness. Think of this as opening *Task Manager* and seeing what's running. You're not trying to close down any programs yet, only recognising that they exist.

CHAPTER 5

DESTINATION UNKNOWN

An autopilot is only useful once you have the coordinates to guide it. It might seem odd that we're only just now looking at your destination. Isn't that where you're supposed to start? Perhaps, but starting there can lead you in the wrong direction. Many people have a clear destination, yet clarity isn't the issue. The real question is ownership. How certain are you that the path you're on is one you've consciously chosen?

Say you want to be rich. Have you ever stopped to consider why? Does that desire genuinely come from you? Or has it been subconsciously absorbed from culture, social networks, and advertisements designed to convince you that material success is the path to fulfilment? Do you truly want the things you chase, or have you simply been conditioned into believing you should? To choose a destination that is truly yours, you first need to establish what is actually important to you.

Your inner compass

For any journey, it helps to have a guide.

Our core values are what help us navigate along the way. These fundamental beliefs guide our decisions and our behaviours. They represent what is most important to us, influencing how we set and pursue goals. Far from abstract labels, they're deeply ingrained principles that give our life meaning and direction. They show up in how we spend our time, what we tolerate, and what we walk away from. They serve as our compass, helping us determine which roads are truly worth taking.

Living in alignment with your core values brings meaning, reward, and fulfilment, both personally and professionally. Fall out of alignment, however, and you're likely to feel stuck, dissatisfied, or uneasy. Your wheels may still be in motion, but the direction has been lost.

To live by your values, you must first understand them. Our values are largely learned from our parents, peers, and culture. While many of these influences serve us well, we often adopt them without examination. As a result, we may cite the values we believe we *should* hold, rather than those we actually do. Someone may claim honesty as a value yet avoid difficult conversations or withhold constructive feedback. Another may say they value health yet consistently sacrifice sleep for late-night partying.

So how do you identify and define the values that are truly yours? The answer lies in your awareness. Begin by reflecting on what genuinely matters to you. Look back on the moments in your life when you felt the strongest emotions. Those moments that brought you real joy? You were likely in harmony with your values, acting in service of them. Those times you felt frustrated or angry? Chances are your values were being ignored, compromised, or subordinated, either by yourself or others.

Our emotions are one of the most powerful tools we have for uncovering our values. Instead of treating emotions as inconvenient, see them as messengers. Ask yourself what they're trying to tell you. When you suppress or dismiss them, you shut out the very feedback that could help you understand what's happening beneath the surface. It's like your mind holding up a bright neon sign saying, "*This is important!*" yet you turn away to avoid the glare, missing the message entirely.

Start paying attention to how you feel in the choices you make and how you spend your time. If you claim to value money over family, yet feel uneasy about long nights at the office, that discomfort is worth exploring. It may be a sign that your stated value doesn't match your lived one. Conflicting emotions when making decisions are often cues that you may be acting outside of your core values. It's your internal compass needle twitching, warning you that you've veered off course. Notice these moments and reflect on what your subconscious may be trying to tell you.

Once an emotion catches your attention, explore it further by asking why it's there. The first answer is only the starting point. To understand what's really driving it, you need to keep digging.

Find your real why

The *Five Whys* is a problem-solving technique developed by Sakichi Toyoda and later used in the Toyota Production System to get to the root cause of a problem. Toyoda, a Japanese inventor and industrialist, said that "*...by repeating 'why' five times, the nature of the problem as well as its solution becomes clear.*" Applied to self-examination, it becomes a powerful tool for uncovering the underlying motivations and needs behind our beliefs, statements, and desires.

Say, for example, that you want to be more productive with your time. Using the *Five Whys* might look like this:

Why do I want to be more productive? *To achieve more.*
Why do I want to achieve more? *To feel a sense of accomplishment.*
Why do I want a sense of accomplishment? *Because it makes me feel good about myself.*
Why do I want to feel good about myself? *Because I don't feel good enough right now.*
Why do I feel like I'm not good enough? *Because others have done so much more than me.*

At the bottom, an underlying cause emerges. It wasn't really about productivity at all. It was about feelings of inadequacy arising from constant comparison to others. With that insight, you can realign your focus. In this case, obsessing over efficiency won't help as it doesn't address the underlying issue. A more effective approach might involve redirecting your attention away from external comparison and towards personal progress. You compete only with yourself, not everyone else. Instead of watching others' journeys, you focus on your own. After all, you only get the one. Why spend it following someone else's path?

Choose your own adventure

Understanding your values is critical for the simple reason that this journey will end for each of us. We can't pursue every single endeavour, explore every road, or visit every landmark. Infinite paths exist, yet we have finite time to explore them. The roads we leave unexplored will vastly outnumber the ones we get to travel.

An honest understanding of your core values allows you to navigate each fork with intention, choosing paths that are deeply meaningful. Without that clarity, it's easy to drift. Distracted by detours, you can find yourself chasing goals that look impressive but feel hollow once achieved. Apparent victories can become empty successes when you realise they came at the expense of the things you truly value. You don't want to reach the end of the road only to realise you've been travelling towards the wrong destination.

Oliver Burkeman's *Four Thousand Weeks* offers a sobering reflection on the finite nature of human life. He reminds us that our time is limited to roughly four thousand weeks, and that this constraint should fundamentally change how we live. Rather than fearing missed opportunities, he encourages us to embrace the joy of missing out.

> *"It is the thrilling recognition that you wouldn't even really want to be able to do everything, since if you didn't have to decide what to miss out on, your choices couldn't truly mean anything."*[8]

In other words, it is precisely our choice to leave some roads unexplored that gives meaning to those that we do. While we may agonise over making the right choice, the real tragedy is avoiding choosing at all. Delaying or avoiding decisions costs you time. If it takes you too long to decide between two paths, you may lose the opportunity to explore either. This refusal to choose is still a choice, albeit one that most people don't realise they're making. I should know; I was one of them.

The only path you can ever take

For most of my life, I suffered from crippling analysis paralysis. I knew my time was limited, yet I wanted to explore every road. When forced to choose, I agonised over each decision, leaving me stuck and unable to commit, wasting precious time in the process. You'd think that knowing I didn't have all the time in the world would instil some sense of urgency, forcing me to choose *something*. Yet somehow, this only paralysed me further. Rather than risk getting a big decision wrong, I clung to smaller, safer decisions that I could more confidently get "right".

There were two big traps with this. First, by focusing on the decisions I was confident in, I wasn't expanding my confidence elsewhere. Second, and more importantly, I was avoiding the big decisions entirely. I chased small goals at the expense of meaningful ones, consumed by minor choices while avoiding the pivotal ones that could have moved me forward.

---

[8] See Oliver Burkeman, *Four Thousand Weeks: Time Management for Mortals* (London: The Bodley Head, 2021).

The change for me came from a single realisation: there is no *right* decision, only *the* decision. Remember the lesson of the farmer. We can't know for sure whether a choice is right or wrong without the fullness of time. When a fork appears, all you can do is choose a path using your values to guide you. Then, for better or worse, you must own that decision.

All too often, the fear of making a mistake keeps us stuck, paralysed by the thought of choosing the wrong path. Yet it's pointless. Mistakes are inevitable. Trying to avoid them not only prevents action but also stops you from learning. After all, mistakes are what lead to successes. They teach us what doesn't work. Thomas Edison, after countless failed attempts to develop a practical light bulb, is said to have remarked, "*I have not failed. I've just found 10,000 ways that won't work.*"

Do not take this, however, as an excuse to *repeat* mistakes. Making a mistake once is a learning opportunity but repeating it is a choice. Edison didn't simply try the same design over and over. He tried different ones. Every failure brought him one step closer to success. This doesn't just apply to your own mistakes either. As the saying goes, a smart person learns from their mistakes, but a wise person learns from the mistakes of others. It's better to avoid mistakes we can reasonably predict, either through our own experiences or the experiences of others.

This works both ways. When we share our mistakes openly, we help others learn from them. Each mistake shared becomes another warning sign placed clearly on the road ahead, making the journey safer for those that follow. Sharing our mistakes also cultivates humility, reminding us that no one is perfect. Humility, in turn, fosters deeper compassion and empathy, both towards ourselves and others, strengthening the very bonds that make us human.

Notice how this ties back to our stories and framing. When viewed in this way, mistakes are no longer something to fear. They become opportunities for growth rather than evidence of failure. Remove the fear of choosing the wrong path and you begin to choose with confidence. With every decision, you either win or you learn.

Yet even under this reframing, mistakes can still carry weight. For those burdened by past decisions, consider this: your life today is the result of every choice you've made and every experience you've had. Change any one of them, and the person reflecting on it now would not be the same. It's easy to imagine a different path, but that version of you exists only in theory. The reality is that you could only make decisions based on who you were and what you knew at the time.

That doesn't mean every decision was perfect. It simply means that each one played a role in determining who you are right now. Regret often comes from judging past decisions with present awareness, but that perspective didn't exist when the decision was made.

We can't change the past, but we can learn from it to guide what comes next. After all, the front windscreen is far wider than the rear-view mirror. Don't fixate on what's behind you when the road ahead is still open and full of possibility. Now, with your compass in hand, you're ready to explore it.

Once you've chosen a destination that's truly yours, the next step is to calibrate your autopilot.

◇

EXERCISE 6

Define your core values

In this exercise, you'll identify the values that resonate most strongly with you.

Step 1 – Categorise your values

Start by working through the list of values in the following table. As you read through them, sort each into one of three categories: always important, sometimes important, or rarely important.

Don't overthink this. Make a quick judgement and move on. If a value feels unclear, skip it rather than overanalysing it. Note that this table is not comprehensive. These values are simply suggestions to get you started. If something meaningful to you is missing, add it to your own list.

Achievement	Creativity	Health	Money
Adventure	Curiosity	Honesty	Purpose
Authenticity	Discipline	Impact	Recognition
Autonomy	Efficiency	Independence	Religion
Balance	Empathy	Influence	Resilience
Belonging	Excellence	Knowledge	Respect
Career	Fame	Leadership	Responsibility
Challenge	Family	Learning	Security
Community	Freedom	Legacy	Sexuality
Compassion	Friendship	Love	Spirituality
Competence	Fun	Loyalty	Stability
Contribution	Growth	Mindfulness	Wisdom

Step 2 – Rank them

Now focus on the values in your *always important* category. Your task is to organise these into a clear hierarchy. If two values came into conflict, which one takes priority?

Work through the list until you've narrowed it down to your top five. If everything feels important, that's the point. You're being forced to choose.

Step 3 – Test your direction

This step is about your intended direction, not your day-to-day behaviour.

Write down a small number of outcomes you are actively pursuing or believe you want. These might relate to your career, finances, health, relationships, or lifestyle.

For each one, ask yourself:

- Which of my top values does this serve?
- If I achieved this, why would it matter to me?
- Would this still feel meaningful without status, comparison, or external validation?

If you struggle to link a goal to your values, treat that as a signal: it may not truly be yours.

If a goal conflicts with your values, acknowledge the trade-off explicitly. Every path comes at the cost of another. You are not trying to perfect your direction here. You are simply testing whether the path you're on aligns with what is genuinely important to you.

Step 4 – Audit your behaviour

Now assess whether your behaviour aligns with your stated values.

At the end of each day, review how you spent your time and attention. This is not about what you intended to do, but what you actually did in practice. Ask yourself the following:

- Where did my time and energy go today?
- Which of my top values were reflected in my actions?
- Which values were neglected or overridden?
- If a stranger observed my day, what would they conclude I value most?

A quick sense-check is enough here. The purpose is not to judge yourself or immediately change your behaviour. You are simply trying to build an accurate picture of the gap between your stated values and your lived behaviour.

Step 5 – Reassess

After a week or two, revisit your top five values. Do they still feel accurate? Or do your behaviours and emotional reactions suggest that you're being guided by different values entirely?

CHAPTER 6

CALIBRATE YOUR AUTOPILOT

Now that you've defined your destination, the question becomes whether your autopilot is actually taking you there, or somewhere else entirely.

This is where the gap between intention and outcome begins to appear. The challenge is that it is rarely visible in the short term, only becoming obvious over longer time horizons.

"Rome wasn't built in a day."
"A journey of a thousand miles begins with a single step."
"From tiny acorns do mighty oak trees grow."

Outcomes rarely manifest in a single moment. Instead, they are nurtured gradually, through repeated actions over time. This is why we tend to overestimate what we can achieve in a week yet underestimate what we can achieve in a year. While the first step is undoubtedly important, the real power lies in the thousands that follow.

Isolated actions don't determine who you become. Nobody became a bodybuilder from one workout, nor obese from a single snack. Treating yourself to dinner at a fancy restaurant won't break the bank, but eating out every night? That's a different story. It's your habits, compounded over time, that ultimately make or break you.

The challenge of ingrained habits

Most of us are well aware of this yet continue with poor habits regardless. Why would we choose to sabotage our future selves like this? Perhaps we simply don't realise the harm our bad habits cause, or the benefits of adopting better ones. While this may be true for some, a lack of awareness is often not the real culprit. You could probably list several habits that serve you, and many more that don't.

The real challenge lies in the mismatch between how a habit feels in the moment and its eventual long-term payoff. Healthy long-term habits often demand temporary discomfort or sacrifice, while unhealthy ones offer comfort or relief instead. Smoking is a classic example. The instant relief of nicotine far outweighs the grave, but distant, long-term health consequences. Exercising or investing, on the other hand, take time and effort. Despite the enormous long-term benefits, they can feel unrewarding in the short term.

This same principle applies to our habitual thought patterns. A victim mindset can provide momentary relief from responsibility, yet inevitably leads to suffering when those same thoughts result in a self-fulfilling prophecy.

It takes discipline and self-control to consistently prioritise long-term outcomes over immediate gratification. As if this weren't challenging enough, a powerful cognitive bias known as *temporal discounting*, closely related to *present bias*, makes it even harder. It pushes us to prioritise immediate rewards over future outcomes. The further away the payoff, the stronger the bias becomes.

This bias is deeply hard-wired into our brains. For most of human history, survival was short-term. Predators, famine, and disease meant the future was never guaranteed. Calorie-dense food was a windfall, not a liability. Our dopamine system evolved to favour immediate rewards because immediate rewards kept us alive. In that world, valuing the present over the future made sense. In today's world, it often works against us. Society has evolved far quicker than we have. We're still running on hardware designed for immediate survival despite most modern rewards taking years or even decades to materialise.

A strong mind, body, and bank balance are built slowly over time, often with behaviours that require you to push against your own wiring. Follow your wiring blindly and you'll sabotage all three. Worse still, by the time you realise it, the damage is often already done.

The good news is that we're living in the best conditions humanity has ever experienced. Less than a century ago, most people lived in conditions we would now consider inhumane: short lifespans, high child mortality, and little access to medicine, electricity, or even clean water. Today, even the world's poorest have greater access to food, shelter, healthcare, and technology than most of humanity ever has. Yet that very comfort that defines our modern lives has introduced a new challenge.

The comfort trap

Meaningful change is most likely to occur when the discomfort of our current situation outweighs the discomfort of doing something about it.

Take your health for example. It's easy to neglect for years. Diet and exercise seem too hard compared to the relative comfort of a sedentary lifestyle and eating as you please. Over time, however, your body starts to speak up. Pain, fatigue, stiffness, and illness begin to creep in. Eventually the balance tips. Diet and exercise still require effort, but now the alternative seems even worse.

When movement becomes easier than stagnation, change becomes possible.

Today, life is comfortable enough that many people rarely feel compelled to act, leaving them in a state of bored unfulfilment. This creates an interesting paradox. A terrible job can sometimes be a better catalyst for change than a merely mediocre one. While a toxic workplace may be miserable, the discomfort is often impossible to ignore. A mediocre job, by contrast, can be just tolerable enough to endure indefinitely. You may dislike it, feel unfulfilled by it, and know you're capable of more, yet never feel enough urgency to do anything about it. It isn't bad enough to force action, yet it isn't good enough to be fulfilling.

This is why comfort can be so seductive. It doesn't need to make you happy; it only needs to make you comfortable enough to stay put. Discomfort, by contrast, creates pressure. When the pain of staying outweighs the pain of change, action becomes far more likely.

Comfort has become a modern liability because the rules of the game have changed. Our brains are still wired for survival in a world where it's virtually guaranteed. The challenge now is not merely to survive, but to *thrive*. To do this, you must master your habits. As the familiar saying goes:

> *"Watch your thoughts, they become your words; watch your words, they become your actions; watch your actions, they become your habits; watch your habits, they become your character; watch your character, it becomes your destiny."*

The irony of YOLO

Before we dive into one of the most powerful habits you can develop, we must first address the popular *you only live once* mindset, or YOLO. While this philosophy sounds empowering in the moment, it often ends up undermining your future.

YOLO suggests that since life is finite and the future uncertain, we should maximise our enjoyment right now. It urges us to seize what's available today rather than pursue future rewards that may never arrive. On the surface, it makes a compelling case. *Live in the moment. Enjoy your life. Make the most of your limited time.* These all sound perfectly reasonable. In reality, YOLO is simply present bias dressed up as wisdom.

The trap lies in the underlying assumption that the future is beyond your influence. Why bother planning for something you believe is out of your hands? In this way, YOLO can become a thinly veiled excuse to avoid responsibility for what comes next. It encourages overindulgence in the present, rewarding impulsive and short-sighted choices. Over time, it devalues your future, steadily eroding your willingness to take ownership of it – yet another self-fulfilling prophecy in disguise.

Left unchecked, this way of thinking can lead to a full-blown victim mindset. People with a victim mindset see their past and present as beyond their control. YOLO rounds out the trifecta by saying the future is off limits too. Why eat well if tomorrow doesn't matter? Why save for the future when today is the only day that counts? YOLO becomes the rallying cry of your backseat driver. It offers a convenient justification to turn off the GPS and hit the gas, without ever glancing at the map.

This is the great irony of the YOLO mindset. It is exactly *because* you only live once that the decisions we make for our future are so important. Global life expectancy more than doubled over the 20th century.[9] Do you want those extra years spent with health

[9] Global life expectancy at birth: 32 in 1900, 66 in 2000, and 73 in 2023. See Our World in Data, "Life expectancy", https://ourworldindata.org/life-expectancy.

problems or financial struggles, simply because you prioritised short-term indulgence now? Your future is far longer than the present moment, meaning every choice now has an outsized impact later. Rejecting YOLO is not about denying pleasure or giving up joy. It's about multiplying it over time.

Still, YOLO isn't entirely negative. It can have you saying yes to experiences you might otherwise pass up. It can open doors to exciting opportunities and memorable adventures. Besides, there's little point reaching the end of your journey with tanks full of unspent fuel, having barely travelled any roads. But YOLO must be conscious and deliberate, not the seductive voice of the backseat driver tempting you into every detour. As always, awareness is key. If YOLO resonates with you, try applying the *Five Whys* to uncover what's really driving it. You may be surprised by what you find.

The incredible benefits of an extra marshmallow

This tension between living for the now and planning for the future was famously illustrated in the Stanford Marshmallow experiment. Children were offered a choice: eat one marshmallow immediately or wait a short while and receive two. The results were compelling. Researchers found that children who were able to wait were more likely to have better outcomes later in life.[10] This skill, choosing a greater future reward over an immediate temptation, is known as *delayed gratification*.

Delayed gratification is, in effect, the opposing philosophy of YOLO. Where YOLO rationalises present bias, delayed gratification rejects it. People who adopt this mindset weigh

---

[10] Later research suggests this relationship is more complex, with family background, socioeconomic status, and environmental trust also playing a role. See Tyler W. Watts, Greg J. Duncan and Haonan Quan, "Revisiting the Marshmallow Test," *Psychological Science* 29, no. 7 (2018): 1159–1177.

future outcomes more clearly, allowing them to make better decisions today. Smoking becomes harder to justify when you understand its long-term cost. Investing feels more rational when its future value is more obvious. Training and nutrition become more compelling when you recognise the payoff will be a healthier, more capable life for years to come.

Advocates of YOLO would argue that delayed gratification leads to a life of deprivation, a joyless existence devoid of pleasure. They couldn't be further from the truth. Short-term sacrifices unlock far greater rewards in the future. What might be misinterpreted as missing out in the short term is simply a conscious decision to play the long game instead. It's choosing to optimise your return across the entire journey, not just the next few kilometres.

Ironically, it is the YOLO mindset that produces the poorer outcome. Its rewards arrive quickly, but they are small and fleeting. The costs take longer to appear, but they accumulate with far greater interest. What feels like a gain in the moment often proves to be an expensive trade when viewed over time.

Understanding how your current habits and behaviours affect your future allows you to design the life you want to live. The beauty of delayed gratification is that it can very quickly become a virtuous spiral. New habits may feel uncomfortable or awkward at first, but as rewards accumulate, they become easier to maintain. Eventually, the behaviours themselves can become enjoyable.

Ask someone who's stepped into the gym for the first time about the experience, and they'll likely describe it as painful or overwhelming. Speak to anyone who's been going to the gym for years, however, and they wouldn't miss it for the world. It makes their day. The energy, vitality, and sense of accomplishment they feel is enough to keep going. The same is true for eating well, investing wisely, or cultivating helpful patterns of thinking.

Delayed gratification also develops complementary traits such as patience, impulse control, discipline, and willpower. Together, these further compound the benefits over time. Quite simply, it is one of the most powerful tools available to keep your autopilot calibrated for the long haul.

Cultivating greatness

The vast literature on habit formation is clear evidence of the pivotal role they play in influencing our lives. Once you understand the power they hold, the first step is simply to notice what you're actually doing. Using your core values as your compass, you can then determine which habits move you towards the life you want, and which pull you away. With a clear destination, it becomes easier to introduce supportive habits and let go of those that no longer serve you.

Awareness of your ego deepens this understanding. It reveals *why* your habits exist: the thoughts, emotions, impulses, and stories that sustain them. Mindfulness research suggests that when we observe these stories more objectively, our ability to self-regulate and delay gratification increases.[11] By pausing long enough to observe your internal narrative, you create the distance needed to reframe it.

Rewriting your stories about the future weakens the pull of present bias. "*The future is uncertain*" becomes "*The future is mine to create.*" "*I won't see the benefits for years*" is reframed as "*This will benefit me for years to come.*" By doing so, your evaluation of short-

---

[11] Kirk Warren Brown and Richard M. Ryan, "The Benefits of Being Present: Mindfulness and Its Role in Psychological Well-Being," Journal of Personality and Social Psychology 84, no. 4 (2003): 822–848.

term comfort versus long-term reward becomes more grounded. A mindset of delayed gratification begins to take root on its own.

Once you're clear on the changes you want to make, a range of tools can help you make them stick. Children in the marshmallow experiment discovered some of these instinctively. Looking away from the marshmallow, covering their eyes, or distracting themselves all worked to reduce temptation. James Clear's *Atomic Habits* expands on these ideas, explaining how habits form and offering practical methods for recalibrating your automatic behaviours.

Like any navigation system, your autopilot requires periodic recalibration. Before you can adjust it, you need to understand the patterns currently guiding it.

◇

EXERCISE 7

Correct your drift

It's time to check your autopilot and see if it's taking you in the right direction. Over the next week, your task is to bring greater awareness to your habits.

Step 1 – Identify your habits

Start with a quick reflection.

Think through a typical day from the moment you wake until the moment you go to sleep. What do you do repeatedly, often without thinking? Do you get straight out of bed in the morning, or reach for your phone first? What do you do before sleep? Habitual ways of thinking are just as important as behaviours here. If it's something you're consistently doing, write it down. Focus on patterns, not one-off events.

Once you've completed this, spend a day with these habits in the back of your mind. Notice anything you missed and add it to your list if needed.

Step 2 – Categorise them

For each habit, ask yourself whether it is moving you closer to the life you want, or further away. Categorise each one according to whether it is:

- **Aligned:** Supporting your values and goals;
- **Misaligned**: Working against them; or
- **Neutral:** Having no meaningful impact either way.

Which category do most of your habits fall under?

Step 3 – Calibrate

Now calibrate. Start small and allow momentum to build over time.

- Pick one misaligned habit to reduce or remove;
- Choose one aligned habit to strengthen, or one new habit to introduce; and
- Commit to both for at least four weeks.

Habit formation does not happen overnight. You need to be consistent. It is far better to work on one or two at a time until they become automatic than to overhaul everything at once.

If nothing changes, your current habits will continue to compound in the same direction. If you make a few small adjustments and stay consistent, where might you end up instead?

CHAPTER 7

THE PATH TO FREEDOM

So far, we've been on a journey through the hidden architecture of your mind. Part One has exposed the mental mechanisms driving your behaviour, while equipping you with tools to examine and recalibrate them.

The simple act of asking why, not once, but repeatedly, has revealed what truly lies beneath your habits and decisions. In doing so, the jigsaw of your inner world has begun to take shape. You've met your backseat driver, recognising just how many decisions it has been making on your behalf. With its patterns exposed, its influence is harder to ignore. You've seen how mindfulness trains your awareness by creating distance from your thoughts. Stories that once felt unquestionably true have been exposed by the presence of a single black swan.

In understanding the power your mind holds in creating your reality, you've learned to shift your locus of control inwards. Time and energy are no longer wasted attempting the impossible. Accountability for the internal world has replaced frustration with the external one.

The extent to which your life runs on autopilot has been revealed, demanding intentional recalibration. Values have emerged as the only compass capable of guiding you to a destination independent of society's expectations. Habits have proven to be your incremental superpower, the mechanism through which your repeated actions compound into results over time. You've seen how delayed gratification amplifies their effect, while a YOLO mindset often undermines it.

Each insight, tool, and observation across your inner and outer worlds has been laying the groundwork for what comes next. Together, they form a system that can be applied across any domain. A system that leads, inevitably, to freedom.

The Freedom Framework

It's time to introduce the system that ties it all together: **KADI.**

Knowledge, Awareness, Direction, and Implementation.

These four steps must be applied in sequence. Miss one and progress stalls. Reorder them and much of your effort may be wasted. Most failures to produce meaningful change can be traced back to a breakdown in one of these four elements. Let's examine each in turn.

Knowledge

Knowledge defines the terrain. To pursue any goal, you must first understand the external world you're operating in. Knowledge represents the rules of the game, the constraints, and the mechanisms governing the systems you interact with. It tells you what is possible, what works, and what doesn't. It's the road rules, the fuel requirements, and the basic operation of the vehicle. It can be taught, studied, and refined over time.

Knowledge alone, however, does not create change. It doesn't alter behaviour, build consistency, or generate momentum. Instead, it helps prevent wasted effort by ensuring you're not fighting physics or reinventing the wheel. Without it, progress relies more on luck than effort or intention.

The purpose of Part One has been to provide you with the knowledge of your mind, the features of your inner map. These are not instructions to follow blindly, but principles that make awareness possible in the first place.

Knowledge only becomes useful, however, when you apply it.

Awareness

If knowledge is understanding the road, awareness is understanding the driver. It is the act of directing attention inward, towards your own lived experience. In doing so, you develop a detailed map of your internal landscape: your habits, patterns, stories, emotional triggers, and the influence of your ego. No book can provide this for you. Knowledge can tell you what to look for, but awareness is the act of actually seeing it for yourself.

Awareness cannot be applied, however, if you don't first understand what it is. This is why knowledge must always come first. Without an understanding of awareness itself, thoughts feel like reality, the ego is experienced as identity, and habits and behaviours remain beyond scrutiny. You cannot change what you cannot see.

Awareness must first be recognised as a capacity that can be deliberately trained. Once this knowledge is internalised, it becomes your responsibility alone to act on it. This is the linchpin of the system, the point where genuine accountability becomes unavoidable. Awareness reveals why knowledge is so often misapplied, selectively ignored, or never acted on at all. Without it, behaviour repeats, mistakes compound, and progress feels inexplicably out of reach.

Awareness is what allows you to leverage knowledge into change.

Direction

All the knowledge and awareness in the world mean nothing without a destination. Direction is the act of consciously choosing where you are going and, more importantly, why. An enduring *why* does not come from ambition, fear, or external validation. It emerges from your values.

Direction must follow awareness, for destinations chosen without awareness are rarely truly your own. They are inherited, imposed, or driven by ego, rather than purpose or intention. Awareness allows you to distinguish what you genuinely want from what you've been conditioned to pursue.

We've seen how values serve as your compass. Awareness is what allows you to read it clearly. Without direction, however, a map and compass offer little value. They only become useful once you've chosen where you want to go.

Implementation

This is the practical layer of the system that puts everything in motion. It's the habits, routines, and structures you put in place that move you inexorably towards your destination, regardless of what life throws at you. This is where you set your autopilot.

Implementation must come last in the system. The sustained effort required to achieve any goal is only possible when it's in service of something that you genuinely value. Progress requires work, and work is not always easy. Willpower can get you started, but it's a finite resource and an unreliable long-term strategy.

When your actions are in service of your values, work becomes sustainable. You replace fleeting external drivers with powerful intrinsic motivators. Showing up stops feeling like discipline and starts feeling like self-respect.

Without implementation, your intentions remain unrealised. It's only by consistently putting in the work that your actions can compound into your visions for the future.

The system as a whole

Each step of KADI serves a distinct function. Knowledge gives you the tools. Awareness shows you how to use them. Direction clarifies what is worth building. Implementation is picking up the tools and getting to work, brick by brick, day after day, regardless of conditions. This order is deliberate, with each step enabling the next.

Without knowledge, effort is blind and progress relies on luck. Without awareness, knowledge fails to translate into behaviour. Without direction, awareness produces insight without purpose. And without implementation, direction gives you a destination, but no means to reach it.

With the sequence complete, change depends less on motivation or circumstance. It becomes consistent, repeatable, and, over time, increasingly inevitable.

This is *The Freedom Framework*.

Governing principles

A system can work perfectly in theory yet still fail in practice if it's applied poorly. For KADI to work as intended, it must be governed by the principles of *accountability* and *control*. These are not additional steps in the sequence, but rather conditions that will determine the quality of the results you achieve.

Accountability

For this system to work, responsibility must sit with you. Only you can observe your internal patterns, choose a direction that reflects your unique values, and implement the behaviours required to move consistently towards it.

Accountability means owning outcomes, not just intentions. It's taking pride in progress, but also responsibility for mistakes. It's recognising the role your conscious and subconscious behaviours have played in creating your current reality, without placing blame on circumstance, luck, or other people. It's taking ownership of your future, recognising that you're the only one in charge of actively building it.

Most importantly, accountability means taking action. It is not enough to simply understand this system. You need to implement it.

Control

At all times, your effort must remain focused on what is in your control. The effectiveness of KADI is directly limited by how much time, attention, and emotional energy you waste trying to control what lies outside your influence. Every attempt to manage the uncontrollable only diverts resources away from the areas of your life that actually respond to your efforts.

This system requires you to consciously shift your locus of control inwards. It's recognising that you cannot control outcomes, other people, or external circumstances, but you can always control how you interpret, respond, and act.

Apply your efforts only where your actions can genuinely make a difference. Let go of everything else.

KADI

A practical sequence for creating lasting change

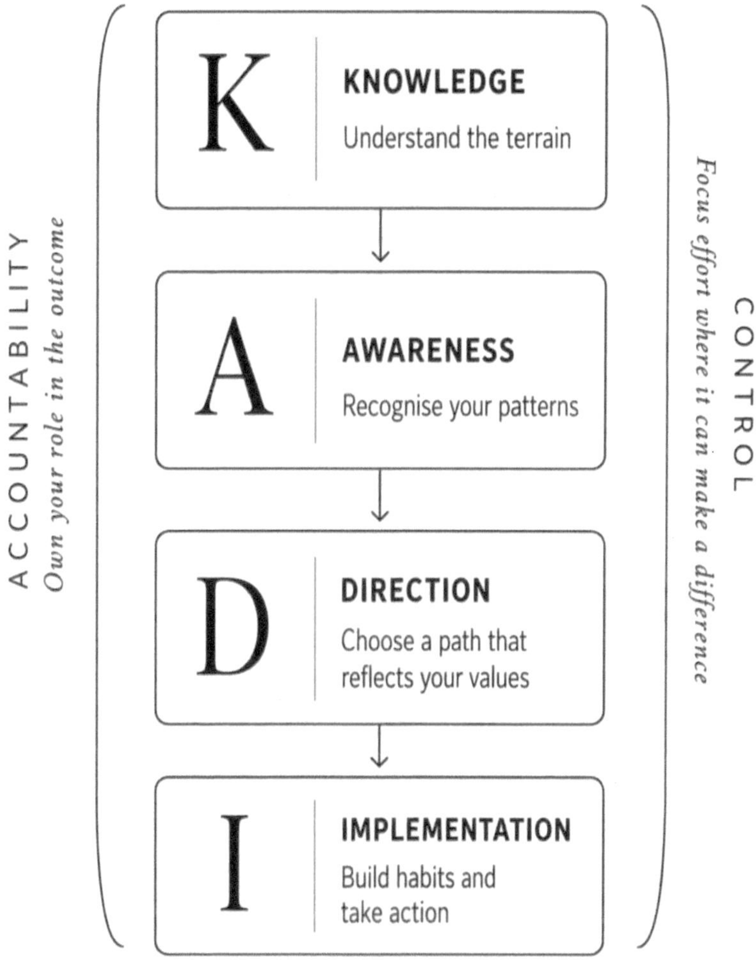

Putting it all together

KADI defines *how* change happens. Accountability and control determine whether it happens at all. Accountability keeps you in the driver's seat. Control keeps your attention on what you can meaningfully steer. When KADI is followed in sequence and supported by these principles, freedom follows as a natural outcome.

Mental freedom comes first. Understanding your inner landscape allows you to see clearly, choose deliberately, and act without being governed by unconscious patterns. Without this, your sense of choice is often an illusion. Apply the same system to your health, and physical freedom expands. Energy, resilience, and capability increase, opening up more options in how you live. Apply KADI to money and financial freedom becomes progressively more attainable, reducing constraints on how you spend your time and structure your life.

Mind, body, and money. Three radically different domains, yet all can be liberated by the same system.

With the knowledge gained in Part One, you now have the tools to reclaim your inner world, the foundation upon which everything else is built. Parts Two and Three apply this same framework to health and finance. The sequence and principles remain consistent across each domain, as do the outcomes. That is, so long as you're prepared to take responsibility for creating them.

◇

PART TWO

Your Vehicle

A map can help you plan out and navigate your dream journey, but without a working vehicle you're not going to make it very far. Part One focused on ensuring you have the prerequisite navigational tools for the journey ahead. Part Two ensures you'll have the physical means to explore it.

Your body is uniquely your own, the vehicle that carries you through life. You might be able to repair or even replace certain parts, but eventually, it'll fail for the last time and your journey will end. How well you care for it determines not only how far you travel, but also the comfort of the ride.

In the chapters ahead, we'll look at the three pillars of caring for your vehicle. First, we'll explore your overall health and wellbeing. This is the foundation, like regular servicing over the journey. Next, we'll examine nutrition and the role it plays in supporting your body's function and recovery. Finally, we'll explore exercise and training, ensuring your vehicle remains capable, resilient, and able to go the distance. Even a high-performance sports car filled with premium fuel will deteriorate if left idle for months on end.

Each pillar has its own benefits, but together they create a powerful feedback loop. Good overall health enhances your energy. Combined with diet, this supports a higher level of activity. A higher level of movement and activity then reinforces your overall health.

Ultimately, these chapters are about recognising that you are the only one responsible for maintaining your vehicle. When you take that responsibility seriously, through attention, effort, and consistency, your map transforms from a static plan into a living journey. You gain the ability to travel further, move with purpose, and fully experience the path you've chosen. Neglect it, and you'll limit your ability to explore your map, no matter how much you've planned the route.

This part of the book doesn't assume that health should be your highest priority. It simply recognises that, regardless of what you value, your physical condition acts as a multiplier on your ability to pursue it. A higher level of health generally makes most things easier to do, while the converse is true for poorer health.

These chapters explore what it means to only have one physical body to carry you through life. How you treat it today has consequences tomorrow, many of which are not obvious until it is far too late. The purpose here is to make those connections clearer, allowing you to make more informed decisions about how you choose to manage your health.

◇

CHAPTER 8

THE ONLY VEHICLE YOU'LL EVER HAVE

With your inner map uncovered, it's time to turn your attention to the one vehicle that'll carry you through the journey: your body. How you look after it will determine how far you can go, and what roads you're able to travel. Treat it with care and you'll find the journey far more manageable. Neglect it, and every step becomes harder than it needs to be.

This part of the book is about learning to respect that vehicle. Using KADI, we begin with knowledge. We'll examine the core pillars that determine performance and longevity. From there, it's up to you how far you want to take it.

The objective here isn't to achieve some elite physique, or exceptional physical standard. It is simply to maintain your vehicle well enough that it doesn't become the limiting factor along the way. When your health is accounted for, your attention is free to focus on the journey instead.

Nobody wants to live forever

I mentioned earlier the irony of YOLO in a world where life expectancy has more than doubled over the 20th century. Let that sink in for a second. Modern humans have existed for roughly 300,000 years. For the majority of that time, average life expectancy at birth hovered around 30 years. We now expect to live past 70. To put this into context, imagine compressing all of human history into a single 24-hour day. For 23 hours, 59 minutes and 30 seconds, nothing changes. Then, in the final moments, life expectancy more than doubles.

The trend isn't showing any signs of slowing either. Average lifespan continues to climb as our tools improve at an accelerating pace. Medical science is advancing. Nutrition is better understood. We are mapping the genome, developing new therapies, and using gene-editing technologies such as CRISPR to directly modify DNA. Artificial intelligence is speeding up discovery across just about every field in biology and medicine. We're building better repair tools while simultaneously deepening our understanding of how the body functions.

As these capabilities improve, so does our ability to extend and maintain our life. Where does it end? One hypothesis is the *longevity escape velocity*, the point at which each new breakthrough extends our lifespan by more than the time it takes to develop it. Imagine if it took ten years to discover a technology that added 15 years of life. Those extra years buy enough time to discover the next breakthrough, which adds even more. In theory, continued discoveries begin to outpace ageing itself, creating a kind of functional immortality.

To many, this sounds like science fiction, and perhaps it is. Whether or not it eventuates, the direction of the trend is clear. Even if progress were to stop today, your body is expected to last far longer than it once did. This is what makes modern behaviour so difficult to justify. YOLO made far more sense 100 years ago when you could die tomorrow from the common cold. Today, abusing your body just means driving twice the distance in a car you've never bothered to maintain. Advances in longevity haven't just tipped the scales in favour of delayed gratification; they've thrown them out the window.

Yet despite living longer than ever, our overall health is arguably the worst it's ever been. We've doubled our lifespan but also our waistlines. Over 2.5 billion adults are now overweight, and almost one billion are obese.[12] Depression is one of the leading causes of disability worldwide.[13] Chronic disease is now the norm, not the exception.

We possess greater knowledge and more advanced medicine than any generation before us, yet most of our time is still spent treating symptoms rather than preventing illness in the first place. We've become excellent at repairs, but terrible at maintenance. We've been handed the tools to tune our vehicle for the long haul, yet instead we continue to drive it into the ground. Why? It's not because we lack the tools or capability. We lack appreciation.

When something feels replaceable, we neglect it. When we don't value it, we cut corners or put other things first. Excuses become easy. Somewhere along the way, we started treating the most valuable, sophisticated machine we will ever have as something disposable. Recognising this tendency in yourself is the first step towards changing it. This isn't just a physical body. It's your one and only ride to carry you throughout this life.

The normal trap

Part of the difficulty in valuing our body stems from our inability to accurately judge its condition.

Your awareness of your health is heavily biased by whatever you're feeling right now. Think about the last time you recovered

[12] World Health Organization, 'Obesity and overweight', 1 March 2024, https://www.who.int/news-room/fact-sheets/detail/obesity-and-overweight
[13] World Health Organization, 'Depressive disorder (depression)', 31 March 2023, https://www.who.int/news-room/fact-sheets/detail/depression

from a cold or flu. You feel amazing. The congestion is gone, the sore throat has disappeared, and your energy is back. Of course, you're no healthier than you were before. It's simply the comparison to how you felt yesterday that makes "normal" feel so good.

The same thing happens with aches, tightness, and other minor issues. At first, they demand attention. Over time, however, they fade into the background. If nothing changes, you stop noticing them altogether. It's only when things improve or deteriorate that they come back into focus. This highlights that your perception of health is relative, not absolute. You notice sharp contrasts, but gradual changes slip by undetected.

That's assuming you can even assess yourself objectively in the first place. Consider how you feel right now. On a scale from zero to ten, how would you rate your overall health? Now ask yourself, do you honestly know what either end of that scale feels like?

A true zero is more than just a bit tired or run down. It's a medical crisis, a body that can't function without intervention. Thankfully, most of us will never experience it. Yet a true ten is just as rare. Imagine a body operating in perfect harmony. Deep energy, clear focus, fast recovery, and no chronic pain. Every system tuned to optimal conditions. How many people have genuinely felt that?

Without experiencing either extreme, you have no reliable reference point. Your baseline could be a three and you'd have no idea. It's like living with a mild cold your entire life and assuming that a sore throat is normal. You've never known any better, so you normalise the disease. This is exactly what most people tend to do. They believe they're operating at full capacity without ever having left first gear.

Part of the reason for this is biological. Both your body and mind are designed to adapt to your current conditions, regardless of whether they are optimal. In physiology, this appears as *homeostasis*, the body's drive to maintain equilibrium. Cut your sleep for a week and you'll feel exhausted at first, but your body soon begins to compensate. Stress hormones rise, alertness is artificially elevated, and performance is stabilised just enough to keep you functional. You feel better than you did at the start even though you're still operating well below capacity. The sleep deficit hasn't disappeared, it just doesn't feel as extreme.

Psychologically, a similar process takes place. The mind adjusts rapidly to whatever state the body settles into. This is known as *hedonic adaptation.*[14] A sudden onset of pain can be uncomfortable at first, before it eventually becomes accepted as normal. The converse is also true. Even optimal health can quickly feel unremarkable, once your mind has come to expect it.

Together, these mechanisms mean that we're exceptionally good at normalising our current state, but remarkably bad at evaluating it. This is *the normal trap*. These mechanisms don't push you towards optimal health. They simply anchor you to whatever baseline you're willing to accept. Neglect your health, and that baseline drifts lower without you realising. Energy crashes are accepted as part of getting older. Mental fatigue gets blamed on a busy week. Chronic injuries become just a side effect of training. What should be treated as your body's early warning signs get dismissed as normal instead.

If it weren't for these tendencies, you'd respond differently. You'd investigate the cause and attempt to correct it. Instead, expectations adjust downward. Because the body is remarkably

---

[14] See Shane Frederick and George Loewenstein, "Hedonic Adaptation," in Well-Being: The Foundations of Hedonic Psychology, ed. Daniel Kahneman, Ed Diener and Norbert Schwarz (New York: Russell Sage Foundation, 1999).

resilient, you're not immediately punished for it either. Problems accumulate gradually, like a faint rattle in an engine that you quickly learn to ignore. Months, or even years later, something finally gives. It can feel sudden at the time, even though the signs were there all along.

It's easy to fall into this trap because it's entrenched in the stories you've built to justify it. Every story you carry has the power to become self-fulfilling. Health is no different. Tell yourself you have a weak immune system, and you stop looking for ways to strengthen it. If you think you have low energy, you won't expect anything more. Over time, these stories solidify into your sense of identity. But your stories about your health aren't diagnoses. They're conclusions you've drawn from a distorted baseline.

Raising the bar

For years, this is exactly how I operated. I woke up groggy, dragged myself through the morning, crashed mid-afternoon, then inexplicably came alive late at night. I'd stay up gaming until two or three in the morning, sleep poorly, then repeat the cycle. I used caffeine and sugar to combat the constant brain fog, and medications to mask every illness. I was managing symptoms, without ever addressing the underlying cause.

None of it felt alarming because I had explanations for all of it.

"I'm just not a morning person."
"Everyone gets tired in the afternoon."
"I just have a weak immune system."
"This is just part of getting older."

These weren't facts. They were rationalisations. Each one lowered the standard I held myself to, removing the need to change.

By conventional standards, I looked healthy. I trained four or five times a week. I ate reasonably well. I didn't smoke and barely drank. Yet I was constantly fatigued, forever getting sick, and full of lingering aches and pains.

The turning point for me was recognising that the issue wasn't my body, but the stories I'd accepted about it. Once I stopped treating fatigue, brain fog, and constant illness as normal, my standards lifted. I started listening to the warning signs my body was presenting, rather than covering them up. I began to change my behaviours in response.

I improved my sleep. I prioritised recovery. I started viewing food as fuel first and pleasure second, no longer abusing it as a comfort. None of this required extreme willpower or discipline. Instead, these changes emerged naturally from a simple decision that I would no longer accept feeling mediocre.

Gradually, everything began to change. My energy stabilised. I rarely got sick, and when I did, recovery was much faster. As I write this, my health is the best it's ever been. Approaching 40, I'm stronger, leaner, and fitter than I was in my twenties. The surprising part is that I was more restrictive and obsessive back then. My habits and routines now are far more sustainable than anything I followed in the past. This was simply the natural result of working on my map. By rewriting my stories, I had removed the limits they imposed.

More importantly, I began to view my body in a different light. It was no longer just a vehicle to get me from A to B, but my most valuable asset. That mindset fundamentally changed my relationship with my body.

Think about those people who treasure their car, treating it as their prized possession. They keep it meticulously clean, service it regularly, and drive carefully on the road. They pay attention to small issues and fix them early, before they can turn into bigger problems. They don't do this out of obligation. They do it because they want to, because they truly value it.

Valuing your body begins with recognising that it's the only vehicle you will ever have. Once you fully internalise this, caring for it stops being a chore. It becomes part of your identity.

But I didn't choose this vehicle...

Have you been paying attention to your backseat driver while reading this? Did you notice any inner commentary? "*Sounds good in theory, but reality is different.*" "*My body just isn't built that way.*" There may be some element of truth to those stories, but they're also incomplete.

It is true that you didn't choose the vehicle you were given for this trip. Some people start with a Porsche, others a hatchback. Some bodies are naturally stronger and recover faster. Others require more maintenance and break down sooner. Not every vehicle is suited to every road.

None of this changes the fact that regardless of your ride, you can improve the quality of the drive. Maintenance and respect for your vehicle matter more than the badge on the hood. A well-maintained sedan will outperform an abused and neglected sports car. This isn't about pretending limits don't exist. It's about recognising that most of us have no idea where those limits actually are. Our beliefs often set the ceiling long before our biology does.

Consider how much influence you already have. Regular physical activity significantly reduces cardiovascular risk. Smoking dramatically increases the likelihood of many diseases. Sleep, nutrition, stress, and training directly affect energy, recovery, and resilience. Even gene expression can be influenced.

Through epigenetic mechanisms, lifestyle factors can influence how certain genes are activated or suppressed. The more we learn, the more control we discover we have.

Take *Tummo meditation*, for example. In studies of experienced practitioners, researchers have observed deliberate increases in body temperature, including reports of practitioners generating enough heat to dry wet sheets in cold conditions.[15] Through breath control and mental focus, they can influence systems typically considered automatic. It's an extreme case, but it highlights an important point: the boundary between what we can and can't influence is more flexible than it appears.

Even then, control is only part of the picture. What you can influence is one thing, but what you can build is another. Through sustained training, discipline, and adaptation, even an average starting point can be developed to an exceptional level. Strength, endurance, pain tolerance, coordination, and resilience can all be pushed far beyond what feels normal.

Consider Alex Honnold. By all accounts, there is nothing particularly unusual about him. He doesn't have an extraordinary build or any obvious physical advantage. Find out what he does, however, and you'd be forgiven for mistaking him for a different species.

Honnold is a climber who specialises in free-soloing, ascending sheer rock faces without ropes or safety equipment. A single mistake means instant death. At 40 years old, in front of millions of viewers, he climbed the 500-metre skyscraper Taipei 101 in under 90 minutes. Without any safety gear, he smiled and

---

[15] Herbert Benson et al., 'Body temperature changes during the practice of g Tum-mo yoga', *Nature* 295, 1982, pp. 234–236.

laughed, as high winds pushed against him hundreds of metres above the ground.

Yet that was nothing compared to his defining feat. In 2017, Honnold became the first person to free-solo El Capitan, an almost kilometre-high wall of uninterrupted vertical granite. It's widely considered one of the most demanding physical and psychological feats ever accomplished. No protection and no margin for error. Just precision, strength, and absolute psychological control.

He didn't reach that level overnight. This took years of deliberate practice, meticulous preparation, and progressive exposure to risk. Step by step, he expanded what his body and mind could tolerate until he achieved something almost beyond comprehension.

Honnold's accomplishments, while remarkable, are not isolated. There are countless examples of people pushing their physical and mental limits to the extremes. Amar Bharati, an Indian sadhu, kept his arm raised for decades, a position most people couldn't tolerate for more than a few minutes. Shaolin monks spend years conditioning their bodies to withstand impacts, tolerate pain, and perform feats that appear impossible.

At one end, you have individuals demonstrating unexpected levels of physiological control. At the other, you have individuals systematically expanding their physical and mental capacity to almost superhuman levels. Each example illustrates that the difference between *impossible* and *possible* is often nothing more than a belief left unchallenged.

This is why your map must always come first. If you accept the limits imposed by your current beliefs, you'll never challenge them. If you assume decline is inevitable, you'll accept it prematurely. Tell yourself, "*This is the best I can be*", and that story will define who you become.

While your vehicle is not without limits, it's your map that ultimately determines how close you get to them. You may not have chosen your vehicle, but your starting point matters far less than what you do with it. You don't need a supercar to achieve exceptional performance. The key is learning to use what you've got to its full potential.

Until you test your limits properly, you won't know what you're capable of. But to do that effectively, you need to understand what you're actually working with. Your body isn't something to be trained in isolation. It's part of an integrated system.

Become one with the machine

Professional racers often talk about the connection they feel with their vehicle. As Gilles Villeneuve put it, "*The car and I are like one. I feel everything it does, every vibration, every movement, like it's part of my own body.*" The vehicle is treated as an extension of themselves, as a partner rather than a tool. In the words of Barry Sheene, "*You don't just ride a motorcycle, you live it. The machine and the rider are one heartbeat.*"

While the driver and vehicle may be separate, on the track they move as a single unit. Without the vehicle, a driver is stranded. Without the driver, a vehicle is nothing more than dormant machinery. In much the same way, you are inseparable from your body. It is not just something that carries you through life. It's also the only way you will ever experience the drive. Every thought, emotion, and action is filtered through it. You don't just live *in* your body, you live *through* it.

It took Western philosophy a long time to recognise this. For centuries, the mind and body were treated as separate. Popularised in the 17th century by René Descartes, *mind-body dualism* argued that they were distinct substances. Modern neuroscience paints a very different picture, showing that the nervous, endocrine, and immune systems are in constant communication. Your thoughts influence your physiology, and your physiology feeds back into your thoughts.

Think of the last time you experienced heartbreak. That feeling wasn't confined to your head. It moved through your body. Whether it's a heaviness in the stomach, or an ache in the chest, grief quite literally hurts. The same is true for anxiety that ties your stomach in knots, anger that raises your blood pressure, or joy that makes your chest feel light and expansive. We tend to treat emotions as abstract, something that happens only in the mind. In practice, they imprint on the body. Your vehicle carries more than muscles and organs. It carries the residue of your experiences.

This connection influences how we respond to emotional events. When emotions are repeatedly ignored or suppressed, the underlying response doesn't disappear. It persists within the body. At first, the symptoms are barely noticeable, such as mild tightness or low-level fatigue. Over time, it becomes chronic and begins to take a physical toll. This is one way psychological strain can become psychosomatic, presenting as physical symptoms such as headaches, skin issues, or chronic pain.

When you trace these outcomes back, a consistent pattern emerges. The stress response doesn't come directly from the event itself, but from the meaning you attach to it. Something happens, you interpret it, and that interpretation drives the emotional response. When that response is negative, it creates tension that later settles into the body. Left unresolved, this manifests as physical symptoms over time. In other words, you can quite literally think yourself sick.

We've already seen this mechanism in action through the placebo effect. Expectations alone have been shown to alter hormone levels, neurotransmitter activity, and immune response. Your thoughts are far from passive. They are an active input into how your physiology operates.

This is what makes the connection between mind and body so powerful. The same pathways that allow stress and tension to accumulate can be used to support recovery and resilience. Change your interpretation of events, and you change your emotional response. Over time, this influences your behaviour as well as your underlying biology.

Once you understand this, the question is no longer whether your thoughts affect your health, but by how much. Your inner landscape sets the direction through your awareness, beliefs, and internal dialogue. From there, those patterns influence mood, behaviour, and eventually physical outcomes. Each layer builds on the one before it. This is why the work in these chapters isn't limited to the physical body. The mind and body form an integrated system. You cannot maintain one while neglecting the other. Truly caring for your vehicle means looking after both.

In the chapters that follow, we'll turn this into something practical. You'll look at the daily inputs that keep the system running well, from mental wellbeing through to physical health, nutrition, and movement. Applied consistently, these adjustments compound. Over time, they produce a vehicle that is more capable, more reliable, and far more resilient than most people ever experience.

◇

EXERCISE 8

Audit your health

Before we look more closely at how to care for your vehicle, take a moment to assess your current state of health.

Step 1 – How are you currently feeling?

Without overthinking, rate the following from zero to ten:

- Energy;
- Sleep quality;
- Focus and clarity;
- Mood; and
- Physical comfort (tightness, pain, niggles).

The goal is not perfect accuracy. You simply want a general sense of what your current baseline feels like.

Step 2 – Compare against your best

Can you remember a time when you felt noticeably better than you do now? Perhaps you had more energy, less physical discomfort, or were simply sleeping better. Take a moment to genuinely recall what that felt like. What has changed since then?

Now revisit your Step 1 ratings. Do they still feel accurate, or were they based on what you've gradually come to accept as normal?

Step 3 – Identify your stories

What explanations did you create to justify the change? Examples might include:

"I was a lot less busy back then."
"I was much younger."
"I didn't have as much stress."

Remember that your stories are not facts. Challenge them and see if they hold up under scrutiny.

Step 4 – Calculate the cost

Now connect your current health to the life you want to live. Consider your goals, priorities, and standards.

- Do you have the energy and stamina to pursue them properly?
- Are you showing up fully in your work, relationships, and daily life, or just getting by?
- How often are you slowed down by fatigue, illness, pain, or recurring minor issues?
- What parts of your life are being limited by your current state of health?

This is the real cost of your current baseline. Is your health strong enough to support where you're trying to go?

CHAPTER 9

STEADY AT THE WHEEL

We've now seen how the mind and body influence one another through multiple pathways. Optimising your overall health requires paying attention to both. Strength without steadiness or clarity without energy leaves you off balance. They aren't competing priorities, but complementary parts of the same system.

In this chapter, we move into the first stage of your regular service schedule by focusing on mental health. We begin with the innermost layer, because it sits upstream of everything else. Your thoughts, emotions, and internal narratives influence how every other part of the system performs.

You can have the best engine, the best suspension, and the sleekest design, but if the driver's grip is unsteady, the whole ride becomes unpredictable. Mental health is what allows you to steer through storms and navigate long stretches of challenging road. Neglect it, and even the strongest machine can feel fragile. Care for it, and you stay in control, no matter how bumpy the road may get.

We're all part of the jigsaw

We are social beings, wired for connection. For most of human history, our survival depended on belonging to a tribe. Isolation meant vulnerability, and vulnerability meant death. Modern society may have softened the penalties, but it hasn't diminished our core need for connection.

We still crave genuine, meaningful connection, and suffer when we go without. Strong social ties are associated with better physical and mental health, including a lower risk of early death. In contrast, isolation is associated with higher risks of depression and anxiety. Loneliness has even been compared to the health risk of smoking 15 cigarettes a day.[16]

The COVID pandemic made this reality impossible to ignore. Almost overnight, billions of people were cut off from their usual connections. The result was a surge in the rates of anxiety and depression. The World Health Organization reported a 25 per cent global increase in 2020, while *The Lancet* estimated tens of millions of additional cases worldwide. In Australia, services like Lifeline recorded record-breaking demand as people struggled with the weight of isolation.[17]

The pandemic made the cost of disconnection obvious. What's less obvious is that even now, with constant access to one another, the problem hasn't disappeared. Technology may have given us the ability to contact just about anyone, anywhere, at any time, but access is not the same as intimacy. We maintain hundreds of digital acquaintances, but fewer in-person relationships. Surveys in Australia and overseas continue to show that loneliness remains common, even in a highly connected

---

[16] Julianne Holt-Lunstad, Timothy B. Smith, and J. Bradley Layton, "Social Relationships and Mortality Risk: A Meta-analytic Review", *PLOS Medicine*, 2010; Julianne Holt-Lunstad, Timothy B. Smith, and Mark Baker, "Loneliness and Social Isolation as Risk Factors for Mortality: A Meta-Analytic Review", *Perspectives on Psychological Science*, 2015.

[17] World Health Organization, "COVID-19 Pandemic Triggers 25% Increase in Prevalence of Anxiety and Depression Worldwide", 2022; Damian F. Santomauro et al., "Global Prevalence and Burden of Depressive and Anxiety Disorders in 204 Countries and Territories in 2020 Due to the COVID-19 Pandemic", *The Lancet*, 2021.

world.[18] We've gained breadth, but lost depth, and it's the depth that nourishes us.

The solution isn't more connections, but higher-quality ones. Prioritise depth over quantity. Invest in real conversations, not just digital check-ins. Build or join communities around shared interests, values, or passions. Technology can help you find your tribe, but genuine nourishment comes from shared experiences, presence, and time.

Connection and belonging are more than just social preferences. They're mental oxygen. You rarely notice their importance until they're missing. When present, they provide a sense of value and place, anchoring you within something bigger than yourself. Without them, you're a single puzzle piece, disconnected from the broader picture.

Find meaning in the journey

Connection feeds naturally into purpose. It's not just about what you do, but why you do it. It's clarity of direction combined with the drive to move towards it.

Without purpose, you can still drive, but the journey feels aimless and hollow. With it, you're able to traverse even the roughest of roads. Obstacles and setbacks turn into part of the journey, rather than reasons to stop.

There are entire books dedicated to purpose and meaning. These are among the most fundamental questions of both our individual and collective existences. "*Why am I here?*" "*What am I supposed to do?*" These questions can feel heavy, but the answer

---

[18] Australian Psychological Society and Swinburne University of Technology, *Australian Loneliness Report*, 2018; Department for Digital, Culture, Media and Sport, *Community Life Survey 2020/21: Wellbeing and Loneliness*, 2021.

doesn't need to be grand. You don't have to find the cure for cancer or change the world to find purpose. It can be found in raising a family, supporting others, creating something meaningful, or contributing to a community. In Japan, some farmers dedicate their lives to cultivating strawberries so perfect they sell for hundreds of dollars. Your purpose simply needs to matter to you, offering a sense of meaning to your existence.

Research has shown that people with a strong sense of purpose live longer, maintain better health, and show greater resilience under stress.[19] It sharpens motivation and provides context for difficult times, allowing you to push through. In the words of Nietzsche: "*He who has a why to live for can bear almost any how.*"

If you're unsure where to start, use your awareness as a guide. Notice what activities give you energy rather than draining it. Are there topics of conversation that light you up, to the point you could talk about them for hours? Pay attention to where your natural curiosity pulls you. Identify your unique combination of strengths, and how you can best apply them. Purpose rarely comes from a single moment of clarity. More often, it emerges over time. By ensuring your daily actions are aligned with your values, patterns begin to appear, helping you define a path that feels meaningful.

There is no deadline here. Purpose can't be forced into place. Colonel Sanders was 65 when he franchised KFC, turning a lifetime of failed jobs into a global brand. Grandma Moses only started painting in earnest at age 78 after decades of doing just about everything else instead. So don't expect it to reveal itself right away. Try to force it, and you'll only create stress that turns the process against you instead.

---

[19] Randy Cohen et al., "Purpose in Life and Its Relationship to All-Cause Mortality and Cardiovascular Events: A Meta-Analysis", *Psychosomatic Medicine*, 2016.

Go easy on the nitrous

Stress gets blamed for almost everything. Headaches, sleepless nights, and a wide range of health issues are often traced back to it. While chronic stress does carry real consequences, stress itself is not the problem. The issue is how we're using the system.

When your ancestors faced a threat, their sympathetic nervous system activated instantly. Adrenaline and cortisol surged, heart rate spiked, and breathing quickened. Blood was diverted away from digestion and into muscles, allowing glucose to flood the bloodstream. The entire body moved into fight, flight, or freeze.

This system was highly effective when threats were life-or-death. It mobilised energy at lightning speed, sharpened focus, and gave us the best chance of survival. In that context, stress was like injecting nitrous into the system, a rapid burst of power to fuel our reaction to the threat. The problem is that your vehicle can't run on nitrous all the time. It's perfect for a short burst but run on it constantly, and you won't just waste fuel – you'll melt the engine. The stress response is a short-term survival tool, yet we're using it as a long-term operating system.

So why does this happen? After all, we're not in any *real* danger most of the time. We're not fighting for our survival or fending off wild animals, yet the system continues to activate. Emails, traffic jams, arguments, and overdue bills now trigger the same response that once helped us survive predators. You might think that the brain is overreacting, yet it's doing exactly what it's evolved to do.

Our brain is a prediction and protection machine, constantly scanning for both opportunities and threats. It does not treat them equally, however. The system is weighted towards detecting and prioritising potential danger. This is driven by a well-documented *negativity bias*, where negative events carry more weight than positive ones. From an evolutionary perspective, this makes sense. We react more strongly to danger than to reward, because ignoring a predator was far costlier than missing out on a berry.

When real threats are scarce, the system doesn't switch off. It recalibrates. The response is relative, not absolute. It doesn't look for big problems – it looks for your *biggest* problems. In the absence of any real danger, relatively small issues begin to register as significant threats. This means that, despite your best efforts, your brain will always find something to stress over.

The larger issue is the duration. The stress response is now staying active far longer than it was designed to. Modern "threats" typically persist, unlike many of the genuine dangers of the past. Facing a predator was a fleeting encounter, whereas a conflict with a colleague or partner can continue indefinitely. Instead of lasting seconds or minutes, stress is left running for hours, days, or even years.

Left switched on, the systems that once protected us begin to break us down. We burn out our engines and sacrifice our health, often over issues that pose no real threat at all.

Release the pressure

Stress can be managed, both in the moment and over time. While the response itself is automatic, your reaction to it is not.

Think of stress management like venting excess pressure from the system before it causes damage. The aim isn't to eliminate pressure entirely, but to use it effectively. Managed well, it becomes a source of energy you can channel into focus, growth, and performance.

So how do we vent this excess pressure? Reframing is one of the most effective tools available. Your ego tends to escalate situations by creating dramatic stories that amplify the threat. It can turn minor setbacks into catastrophes, convincing you that one awkward conversation or small mistake will somehow ruin your career.

Before reacting to these stories, pause and assess. Is this truly a threat, or just temporary discomfort? Is it actually dangerous, or is it your body treating a traffic jam like a predator? Will it still matter tomorrow? What about next week, or next month? This interrupts the escalation and restores perspective, turning mountains back into molehills.

Breathwork is another effective way to regulate the system. Slow, controlled breathing signals safety, moving the body out of fight-or-flight and back towards baseline. Practices like the box breathing we explored in Chapter 4 are simple, repeatable, and surprisingly effective. Mindfulness and meditation work in a similar way. By training your system to stay calm under pressure, they reduce the likelihood of overreacting to small triggers in the first place.

Movement is another powerful stress regulator. Physical activity burns off excess adrenaline, improves mood, and supports better sleep, all of which buffer against future stress. It doesn't need to be intense. A short walk, a few stretches between tasks, or even standing up to roll your shoulders can interrupt the buildup of tension before it becomes chronic.

Connection, play, and time in nature also help lower overall stress. Spend some time outdoors, share a laugh with friends, or simply do something purely for enjoyment. These moments remind your nervous system that life is safe, social, and full of small joys worth slowing down for. The key is choosing healthy outlets. Overeating, binge-watching, or constant distraction don't resolve stress. They're numbing strategies that mask it instead. It's the equivalent of putting tape over a warning light on your dashboard and hoping the problem goes away.

These strategies all help release pressure as it builds, but they're only part of the solution. Real resilience comes from tending proactively to your inner landscape. Earlier, we explored how your RAS acts as a navigator, filtering what you notice based on the signals you repeatedly feed it. When that system is trained deliberately, your attention is less likely to fixate on threats and more likely to settle on useful, constructive signals.

Develop a green thumb

Just like any system, what you feed into your mind determines how it operates, yet it's something we rarely stop to consider. A helpful way to frame this is to treat your mind as a garden. Every thought is a seed, and your attention is the water. What grows depends entirely on what you plant and what you choose to nurture.

If you constantly feed on negative inputs such as doomscrolling, gossip, or fear-driven news, you plant weeds in your garden. Left unchecked, they multiply and choke out anything positive. If, however, you choose to invest in positive practices such as journaling, gratitude, and reflection, you plant more constructive seeds. These seeds grow into resilience, optimism, perseverance, and perspective.

Mindfulness is the act of tending that garden. By observing it over time, you'll notice what is being planted and what is beginning to take hold. With that awareness, you can act accordingly by choosing which plants to water, which weeds to pull, and which seeds to introduce.

Be deliberate. Guard your garden from unwanted pests and invasive weeds. Nurture what strengthens you. Develop a green thumb and, over time, the mental environment you build will become the foundation of your resilience, clarity, and ability to thrive.

Align your wheels

Your mind and body function as one integrated system, each continually influencing the other. One ominous thought can raise your heart rate and create tension, while even a moment of gratitude or laughter can soothe the body and restore balance.

A healthy mind supports recovery, consistency, and discipline. A strong, active body, in turn, fuels clarity and resilience. They function like two wheels on the same vehicle. When one drifts out of alignment, the whole vehicle pulls off course. When both turn together, the vehicle holds its line, even on uneven ground.

This is why both mental and physical health require proactive attention. Too often, we treat our health as a last-resort fix, only addressing it once it has already started to fail. In reality, the goal is not to repair the system after it breaks down, but to keep it running smoothly in the first place.

In the next chapter, we'll turn to the physical side of the equation, the daily practices that keep your vehicle strong, capable, and roadworthy over the long term.

◇

EXERCISE 9

Run a system check

This exercise aims to bring awareness to the inputs and influences that affect your day-to-day experiences.

Step 1 – Observe your current patterns

Over the next week, pay attention to the following:

Connections: Who are you interacting with most often? Are they mostly in-person catch-ups, phone calls, or messages? Which interactions leave you feeling better, and which leave you flat?

Inputs: What content are you regularly consuming through news, social media, and conversations? Is it mostly constructive, negative, or neither?

Triggers: Are there situations that consistently create tension or frustration? Do you notice any recurring patterns?

Outlets: When these situations arise, how do you typically respond? Are your responses constructive, or do they tend towards numbing or avoidance?

Step 2 – Make small adjustments

Based on what you observe, make a few minor changes:

- Choose one connection to invest in more deliberately;
- Reduce or remove one consistently negative input and replace it with something more constructive;
- Choose one simple way to reset when tension builds; and
- Replace one numbing habit with a healthier outlet.

Commit to these changes for at least two weeks. Keep what works, adjust what doesn't, and repeat.

CHAPTER 10

A WELL-OILED MACHINE

No matter how sharp your mind or strong your will, a neglected body will hold you back. You won't get far in a vehicle that keeps breaking down. This chapter focuses on caring for your machine and building the foundation for your health.

Small, deliberate actions here compound faster than almost anywhere else. Think of these as high-leverage dials you can adjust to improve recovery, energy, and resilience. We'll cover training and nutrition next, but the foundation must come first. Get these right and everything else becomes easier and far more effective.

To go fast, you must go slow

We tend to assume that more effort leads to better results. While initially this is often true, past a certain point, that relationship no longer holds.

The body needs recovery and the mind needs downtime. Without both, more time and energy can produce worse results. In a culture that glorifies hustle, rest often gets mistaken for laziness. In reality, it's what allows you to sustain effort and perform at a higher level for longer.

As a self-confessed productivity geek with endless to-do lists, this took me years to accept. I still believed that if I could just push harder, focus longer, and squeeze more hours out of the day, I could somehow get on top of everything.

What's strange is that I already understood this principle in my body. I've always loved lifting weights. One of the first things I learned was that you don't actually build muscle in the gym; you're only creating the stimulus. Training creates micro-tears, breaking the muscles down. It's only during recovery that those tears repair and the body adapts in response. Without it, the body deteriorates instead. You can't simply train more to get faster results. This only leads to overtraining. More becomes less. Elite athletes understand this well, with recovery being just as important as the training itself.

What took me longer to realise was that the mind works in the same way. Reading *Four Thousand Weeks* forced me to confront the limits I had been trying to outrun.[20] I had always respected my body's need for recovery, but I hadn't given my mind the same courtesy. The answer wasn't to do more; it was to accept my limits and choose more deliberately.

Staying constantly "on" doesn't increase output – it only clogs the system. It's like running a computer with dozens of background processes open. Even the useful ones still consume resources. Clear the load and performance improves immediately. Stepping away can feel like slowing down in the moment, yet you return sharper, faster, and more focused.

Your mind can't simply be switched off on command. It takes a deliberate shift out of stress mode and into recovery. Mindfulness and breathwork both offer practical ways to reset your system. When you pair these practices with full-body

---

[20] For anyone caught in a productivity trap, Burkeman's book offers a sobering counterpoint. As he points out, being more productive, paradoxically, only makes you feel busier. *"American anthropologist Edward T. Hall once pointed out, time feels like an unstoppable conveyor belt, bringing us new tasks as fast as we can dispatch the old ones; and becoming 'more productive' just seems to cause the belt to speed up."*

relaxation, you give both the mind and body a signal that it is safe to slow down. You don't need hours either. Even ten minutes a day can noticeably calm your system, while longer guided sessions can deepen the effect.

These practices are powerful because they help create the conditions for recovery, but they are not the foundation itself. Even the most comprehensive restoration regimes will be limited if you don't prioritise the most important recovery tool at your disposal.

Vitamin S

Sleep is the greatest recovery lever you have available, enabling all the others. Matthew Walker, sleep researcher and author of *Why We Sleep*, puts it bluntly: "*The shorter your sleep, the shorter your life.*"[21] If sleep were a supplement, it would be the most effective one on the market.

Sleep is a fundamental biological process observed across nearly all life forms. Even organisms without brains such as plants have been observed to show sleep-like rhythms of rest and activity. While researchers may debate the exact reasons why we need sleep, they unanimously agree on its vital role in health, resilience, and longevity.

Adults need roughly seven to nine hours per night of quality sleep. On average, we're only getting about 6.8, with a third of adults living off fewer than six hours per night.[22] The short-term effects go far beyond simply feeling tired. A poor night's rest

---

[21] Matthew Walker, *Why We Sleep: Unlocking the Power of Sleep and Dreams* (London: Allen Lane, 2017).

[22] Robert Adams et al., "Sleep Health of Australian Adults in 2016: Results of the 2016 Sleep Health Foundation National Survey," *Sleep Health* 3, no. 1 (2017): 35–42.

impairs your judgement, making you more reactive and more likely to make poor decisions. After around 19 hours awake, you'll be as cognitively impaired as if you were legally drunk.[23]

Long term, the impact compounds. Chronic sleep deprivation is associated with worse metabolic, cardiovascular, cognitive, and immune health. Large-scale studies have even linked poor sleep with a higher risk of early death.[24]

The greatest danger, however, is the downward spiral it creates. When you sleep poorly, you start the next day depleted. Your energy drops, willpower weakens, and you take measures to compensate. You reach for caffeine, skip training, make poorer food choices, stay up late, and then end up sleeping even worse the following night. A single bad sleep can quickly become a self-reinforcing spiral.

Part of the challenge lies in how people think about sleep. It's often treated as a necessary evil, something that eats into the time available each day. "*Imagine how much more I could get done if I could just sleep for an hour or two less every night!*" Unfortunately, it doesn't work like that. Your body doesn't simply accept less sleep. It compensates in response.

Cut your sleep, and what you gain in hours is lost in quality. You might have a bit more time in the day, but your focus drops, your efficiency declines, and your decisions worsen. Extend your sleep, and the opposite happens. You think more clearly, act more deliberately, and get more value out of every waking hour. Sleep is not a price you pay each day. It's an investment in tomorrow.

---

[23] Drew Dawson and Kathryn Reid, "Fatigue, Alcohol and Performance Impairment," *Nature* 388 (1997): 235.

[24] Francesco P. Cappuccio et al., "Sleep Duration and All-Cause Mortality: A Systematic Review and Meta-Analysis of Prospective Studies," *Sleep* 33, no. 5 (2010): 585–592.

When you improve your sleep, the cycle begins to reverse. Better sleep improves energy, clarity, and consistency. This leads to better decisions, reinforcing the behaviours that protect your sleep. Over time, this becomes one of the simplest and most powerful virtuous spirals available.

To build it, there are plenty of evidence-backed levers you can apply to promote consistent, high-quality sleep. Some will be simple to integrate while others may require more discipline. As with any habit, focus on the low-friction wins first.

Leverage natural light: Spend ten minutes outdoors within an hour of waking. Natural light anchors your circadian rhythm better than any alarm clock. Indoor lighting averages 300 to 500 lux while outdoor sunlight ranges between 10,000 to 100,000 lux. It's no wonder you feel alive outside but sluggish under fluorescent tubes.

Dim artificial light at night: Blue light can suppress melatonin. Most devices now have built-in night mode or warm-light settings, making this an easy trick to implement. I personally set mine to run from sunset to sunrise on any device I may use, although it's best to cut devices altogether at least an hour before bed.

Respect caffeine's half-life: A coffee at midday leaves a quarter dose still active by the time you're trying to fall asleep. Swap to green tea or matcha, which also delivers calming L-theanine. Better still, reduce your dependence on caffeine or other strong stimulants altogether.

Engineer your sleep cave: Dark, cool, and quiet. Even small amounts of light can interfere with melatonin production. Use block-out blinds, or simply an eye mask to reduce any light entering your eyes. Target an optimal temperature of 15 to 20°C.

It's better to be slightly cool than to overheat. Make your room as quiet as possible or sleep with light earplugs.

Bed = sleep only: A major trap most people fall into is associating their bed with other activities. If you watch Netflix or work in bed, your brain learns to stay alert there. Reserve it for sleep and sex, nothing else. Link *bed* with *sleep* in your brain, and you'll fall asleep much faster.

Consistency beats weekend sleep-ins: Your body thrives on rhythm. Even moving your bedtime by an hour can disrupt your circadian clock. Stick to the same sleep-wake cycle, even on weekends. Give up the weekend sleep-in and you'll find you no longer need it as your sleep quality improves.

Wind-down rituals: Spend some time slowing down before bed with something calming rather than energising. Meditation, journaling, or reading under warm light all train your brain to anticipate sleep. Extend this even further into a routine and your mind and body will associate it with sleep, leading you to fall asleep quicker.

Naps as turbo boosters: NASA research on pilots found a 26-minute nap improved performance by 34 per cent and alertness by 54 per cent.[25] The key is avoiding longer naps that drop you into deep sleep. Experienced nappers also find it easier to fall asleep at night, especially if they've incorporated similar rituals and routines for both.

---

[25] Mark R. Rosekind et al., *Crew Factors in Flight Operations IX: Effects of Planned Cockpit Rest on Crew Performance and Alertness in Long-Haul Operations*, NASA Technical Memorandum 108839 (Moffett Field, CA: NASA Ames Research Center, 1994).

How to apply KADI

Before moving on, take a moment of honest reflection. As you read through these strategies, how many were you aware of? And of those, how many do you consistently implement each day?

Chances are you've heard of many yet practise only a few. Knowing isn't the same as doing. If your sleep isn't where you want it to be, the gap isn't information – it's implementation. If you truly value your sleep, why aren't you acting on it?

This is where you take responsibility by applying KADI. Knowledge comes first but, without awareness, you'll never notice the habits that undermine it. Without deliberate action, nothing changes. Start by observing your evenings without judgement. Notice your subconscious habits and behaviours. What do you do in the hours before bed? What about once you're in bed? Do you go straight to sleep, or scroll on your phone?

Next, examine alignment. Which of those behaviours actually align with what you claim to value? If sleep is important to you, it should be visible in your actions. If you find a behaviour that isn't aligned, investigate it. Use the *Five Whys* to trace it back to its source. There will always be a reason, whether it's distraction, comfort, or even a sense of identity.

From there, take deliberate action. Adjust one or two levers at a time. Make the changes small enough to execute consistently, but meaningful enough to move the needle. Then hold yourself accountable. This is the difference between knowledge and implementation. It's also where things tend to break down.

At this point, the issue isn't knowing what to do. It's understanding what's getting in the way. Answering that requires you to be honest about yourself, your values, and the stories you tell. Take smoking for example. If someone continues to smoke, it's not because they're unaware of the risks; the dangers have been well understood for decades. The real reason lies in the justifications they've built to explain the behaviour. "*I can't quit*" isn't a fact. It's a story, and stories can be rewritten.

Saying "*I've tried everything and nothing works*" is self-deception. It locks you into victimhood, bleeding helplessness into every other area of your life. For smoking, addiction is powerful, yes, but it's also beatable. Resources and methods exist, and many smokers do successfully quit, especially with the right support and repeated attempts. If you don't succeed at first, remember Edison's approach – you haven't failed, you've simply found what doesn't work. Success often sits just beyond a long line of "failures".

A better reframe might be "*I smoke, and I accept that this is likely to shorten my life and increase my risk of serious disease.*" It may be confronting, but at least it's honest. Importantly, it doesn't relieve you of your responsibility. Change remains a possibility. This is the power of KADI. It cuts through avoidance, exposes misalignment, and puts control back in your hands.

As you move through these chapters, apply the same approach to each lever. Notice where your habits clash with your values. Identify where you use stories to remove your accountability. Finally, take ownership of your ability to change them.

With that foundation in place, you can start layering in additional levers.

The overlooked levers

Good sleep is free, powerful, and irreplaceable, but it's not the only tool at our disposal. Once you've built a solid foundation there, you can start to expand beyond it. It's time to move on to some of the lesser-known levers that can improve your health, energy, and resilience.

This isn't a list of the most obvious health rules. Instead, these are often overlooked or underutilised levers that meaningfully improve how your system functions. Some of these you've probably never considered, but once you apply them, you'll wonder how you lived without them.

Get into nature

Some of the most powerful restoration comes from the simple act of stepping outside. We evolved under open skies, among trees, streams, and soil, yet many of us today spend the vast majority of our lives indoors. The *Biophilia Hypothesis* suggests humans are wired to thrive when surrounded by nature and other forms of life.[26] There is growing evidence to support this idea. Indoor plants reduce stress, absorb toxins like benzene and formaldehyde, and increase workplace productivity by up to 15 per cent.[27] Hospital patients with a view of greenery recover faster and need less pain medication.[28] *Shinrin-yoku*, or forest bathing, has been linked with lower stress, reduced blood pressure, and improved immune function.

Time outdoors helps set your circadian rhythm, enhances immunity, and reconnects you with your biological roots. Aim for three 20-minute outdoor sessions per week without your phone. Once per month, try to immerse yourself for a full weekend, be it

---

[26] Edward O. Wilson, *Biophilia* (Cambridge, MA: Harvard University Press, 1984); Stephen R. Kellert and Edward O. Wilson, eds., *The Biophilia Hypothesis* (Washington, DC: Island Press, 1993).

[27] Marlon Nieuwenhuis et al., "The Relative Benefits of Green versus Lean Office Space: Three Field Experiments," *Journal of Experimental Psychology: Applied* 20, no. 3 (2014): 199–214.

[28] Roger S. Ulrich, "View through a Window May Influence Recovery from Surgery," *Science* 224, no. 4647 (1984): 420–421.

camping, hiking, or simply unplugging in nature. Screens drain but trees restore.

Move!

The gym is incredibly beneficial for many reasons which we'll explore in later chapters. However, our biggest challenge isn't that we're skipping the gym – it's that we spend most of our lives sitting still. The average adult now spends between nine to ten hours per day seated. Office workers have it even worse, spending up to 75 per cent of their waking hours sedentary. Going to the gym helps to offset some of this, but research shows that sitting more than six hours a day raises mortality risk by up to 37 per cent regardless of workout habits. In other words, you can't out-train the side effects of spending your whole day sitting.[29]

The real answer is incidental movement. Throughout the day, look for small ways to keep your body moving. Do some stretches at your desk, take the stairs at work instead of a lift, and move wherever possible. Get creative with it. You can use a standing desk, walk while you work, or keep a small pedal bike under your desk and do five minutes of light pedalling every hour. The options are endless. For those times you do need to be seated, make a conscious effort to use a comfortable, ergonomic setup and change position regularly. You could even experiment with sitting on a fitball or stool, as these can encourage more active sitting rather than passive slouching.

---

[29] Aviroop Biswas et al., "Sedentary Time and Its Association with Risk for Disease Incidence, Mortality, and Hospitalization in Adults: A Systematic Review and Meta-analysis," *Annals of Internal Medicine* 162, no. 2 (2015): 123–132; Hidde P. van der Ploeg et al., "Sitting Time and All-Cause Mortality Risk in 222,497 Australian Adults," *Archives of Internal Medicine* 172, no. 6 (2012): 494–500.

An hour at the gym every day certainly helps, but it doesn't mean you can slack off for the other 16 waking hours of your day. Prioritise moving as often as possible.

Breathe better

Few levers are as simple or as overlooked as breathing. It is available to everyone and requires no money or special equipment. You need only your awareness. The way you breathe directly influences your nervous system. Rapid, shallow chest breathing tells your body you're under threat, keeping cortisol and adrenaline elevated. Slow, deep diaphragmatic breathing does the opposite, signalling safety and moving your body into recovery mode, lowering blood pressure and heart rate within minutes. Techniques like the box breathing we explored earlier are particularly effective. Your breath is the fastest dial you can turn to change your state from stressed to calm, wired to grounded, and restless to recovered.

Run diagnostics

You can't manage what you don't measure. Health checks turn guesswork into data. One of the biggest mistakes people make with their health is waiting until something breaks before they check the system. Just as you shouldn't drive your car for years without a service, your body deserves regular checks too. Routine blood tests and screenings can reveal nutrient deficiencies, hormone imbalances, inflammation, and even early signs of metabolic issues, often before the warning lights come on.

Preventive screenings like blood pressure, cholesterol, and glucose tests are inexpensive and can make an enormous difference if problems are caught and acted on early. Don't wait until something feels wrong before you start paying attention. Think of it as running system diagnostics. It may be inconvenient, or carry some costs, but it's well worth the investment. It's how you monitor your health and performance for the long run.

Minimise toxins

Your body is a detox machine, but it's not invincible. Every day it works overtime to filter what you eat, drink, and breathe. Give it a lighter load and it will run longer and stronger. Smoking is the worst offender, but there are plenty of others that you might be less aware of.

Take water for example. Your body is about 60 to 70 per cent water. The quality of what you drink directly influences performance, yet tap water often contains trace heavy metals, chlorine, and microplastics. A 2019 report by the World Wide Fund for Nature estimated that the average person consumes up to a credit card's worth of plastic each week.[30] A simple under-the-sink home filter can reduce chlorine, heavy metals, and up to 90 per cent of microplastics. It's also cheaper and more sustainable than bottled water.

Food is another major source of toxins. We'll explore this one specifically in the next chapters. Even the air inside your home isn't as clean as you might think, with some reports suggesting that indoor air can be two to five times more polluted than outdoor air.[31] NASA's *Clean Air Study* showed that common plants like peace lilies and snake plants can filter out volatile organic compounds, reducing airborne toxins by up to 87 per cent in 24

---

[30] World Wide Fund for Nature, *No Plastic in Nature: Assessing Plastic Ingestion from Nature to People* (Gland: WWF International, 2019), based on research by the University of Newcastle.

[31] United States Environmental Protection Agency, *The Inside Story: A Guide to Indoor Air Quality* (Washington, DC: US EPA).

hours.[32] As an added bonus, the greenery helps to lift mood and focus as well.

At this point, you might be feeling some helplessness seep in. If toxins can be found in our food, water, and air, then how can you avoid them? Well, you can't, at least not completely. They're everywhere in our modern life. As always, focus on what is in your control. Your job here is not to avoid them completely, but to reduce the unnecessary load. Toxins are like grit in your engine. A few specks won't break it, but day after day the build-up clogs, corrodes, and slows you down. The cleaner you can keep the system, the more energy your body has to thrive.

The liquid assassin

No discussion of tools to improve your health would be complete without addressing the one thing that actively impairs your ability to use them. It disrupts sleep, impairs recovery and judgement, and interferes with toxin removal. Unlike most toxins we face, this is one we willingly expose ourselves to. That toxin is alcohol.

I'm sure you know drinking isn't great for you, but the scale of its impact may still come as a surprise. Alcohol is particularly insidious because it's socially sanctioned. Its consumption is encouraged and ritualised, often enshrined in ceremony such as wedding toasts or birthday drinks. Imagine if we treated other harmful chemicals this way, toasting with a little asbestos or bonding over some arsenic.

It's a wolf in sheep's clothing. It may seem harmless enough, yet it's a potent toxin. It damages the liver, increases the risk of

---

[32] B. C. Wolverton, Anne Johnson and Keith Bounds, *Interior Landscape Plants for Indoor Air Pollution Abatement* (Washington, DC: National Aeronautics and Space Administration, 1989).

several cancers, and contributes to accidents, violence, and broader social harm. Worldwide, alcohol contributes to millions of deaths each year, placing it in the same league as smoking.[33] Yet while society has largely woken up to the dangers of smoking, we still give alcohol a free pass. We dress it up as celebration, sophistication, and even self-care. Its ubiquity, legality, and cultural acceptance are what make it uniquely dangerous.

So what is it exactly that makes it so harmful? Start with the liver, your body's frontline defence against many toxins. Much of what you eat, drink, breathe, and absorb eventually passes through this filter in one form or another. When you drink, the liver has to prioritise breaking down ethanol. While it's doing this, its ability to neutralise other toxins is compromised. Alcohol does far more than simply add to the toxic load; it places extra strain on the very system responsible for handling it. The organ designed to protect you from today's chemical barrage is weakened by the one toxin we willingly pour down our throats.

Even the process of breaking down the alcohol is harmful. Alcohol is converted into acetaldehyde, a compound far more toxic than the alcohol itself. It binds to proteins, disrupts enzymes, and inflames liver tissue. The damage sparks repair attempts, but when the injury is repeated, repair can turn into scarring. Layer upon layer of this scarring is what can eventually become cirrhosis. Over years, this leads to liver failure and leaves the entire body more vulnerable to the toxic load of modern life.

The good news is that the liver has a remarkable ability to recover, meaning that some alcohol-related damage can be reversed, especially in the earlier stages. Fatty deposits and mild inflammation can begin to improve within weeks of not drinking.

---

[33] World Health Organization, *Global Status Report on Alcohol and Health and Treatment of Substance Use Disorders* (Geneva: World Health Organization, 2024); World Health Organization, "Tobacco," fact sheet.

Even when scarring or fibrosis has started, the process can sometimes be slowed or partly reversed if you give the organ a long enough break. It's only once cirrhosis sets in that the damage becomes far harder to undo.

Total abstinence is ideal, but any meaningful reduction still delivers measurable benefits. Every day you don't drink is a day your liver can heal and strengthen its defences against the endless stream of chemicals, pollutants, and additives it faces. Ultimately, the healthiest habit will be the one that you can realistically sustain. Drinking less is always better than making no change at all. Try to include stretches of abstinence from alcohol. Longer breaks, weeks or ideally months at a time, allow your liver to reset, recover, and reclaim its role as your body's most important shield against toxins.

From maintenance to performance

We've now covered the foundational levers you need for good health, the essentials that keep your engine running and your system resilient. But basic care and recovery are still only one side of the equation. To truly improve your vehicle's performance, you need to nourish it properly and challenge it consistently. In the next chapters, we'll turn to diet and training, the two biggest levers for building energy, strength, and long-term health.

◇

EXERCISE 10

Build your foundation

In this chapter, we've explored the core levers that support overall health and performance. This exercise is about putting them into practice.

Step 1 – Choose your actions

Select two behaviours to implement immediately: one to improve sleep quality, and one from the additional levers covered in this chapter.

Step 2 – Make it specific

Define each action clearly. What will you do and when will you do it? Avoid vague intentions like "*I'm going to move more throughout the day.*" Instead, define it precisely. For example, you might say, "*Once every hour during my workday, I will get up and stretch for five minutes.*" Remove any ambiguity so it's easy to follow through.

Step 3 – Commit and review

Commit to both actions for at least one week. The aim is to start small and build consistency rather than optimising everything at once. At the end of each week, review what's working, keep what sticks, and build from there.

CHAPTER 11

YOU ARE WHAT YOU EAT

Most people are running a high-performance engine on the nutritional equivalent of contaminated fuel. Feed your body garbage such as highly processed foods and refined sugars and you'll sabotage the engine over time. Support it instead with a wide array of nutrient-dense foods and you'll start to see what your vehicle is actually capable of.

Nutritional education is often lacking, but lack of knowledge alone isn't the issue. Most people know they should eat better, yet few consistently do. The challenge is that food is far more than just fuel. It's identity, comfort, culture, habit, and often a way of avoiding emotions we'd rather not face. To nourish your body effectively, you need more than nutritional knowledge. You need awareness of your values, your habits, and the deeper *why* behind your choices. In other words, you need to revisit your map.

As always, we'll start with the knowledge by looking at the fundamentals. We'll cover the basics of energy and fuelling the body, then move into the awareness that actually drives behaviour. With the foundation built, we'll then move into practical strategies and systems, before addressing the myths that derail most diets.

What do we mean by fuel?

Earlier, I described money as the fuel for your journey through life. Here, we're narrowing the focus to one of the most important places that fuel is ultimately spent: sustaining the vehicle itself.

Food is the energy source that powers your body, much like petrol powers a car. In a practical sense, it is both biological fuel and a financial expense. Food powers the vehicle, while money funds the broader journey. One enables physical freedom, the other financial freedom. The better you manage both, the further you can go.

This overlap is intentional because food and money operate under surprisingly similar behavioural and mechanical principles. Both involve consumption, limits, trade-offs, habits, delayed consequences, and the constant tension between short-term gratification and long-term outcomes. The same lack of awareness that drives poor eating often drives poor spending as well.

Throughout this book, you'll see these parallels repeatedly. Learn to manage one form of consumption well, and many of the same skills transfer naturally to the other.

Fuel here is more than just a metaphor. The energy your body uses each day could, in theory, drive a small car 30 to 40 kilometres. The exact amount varies based on age, sex, build, and activity level. Some people's vehicles are veritable gas guzzlers while others use very little. Regardless of how much fuel you need, food is how you get it.

This energy is typically measured in *calories*. In technical terms, a calorie is the energy required to heat one gram of water by one degree Celsius. In nutrition, we're actually referring to *kilocalories* (1,000 calories), though the terms are used interchangeably.[34] For practical purposes, they mean the same thing.

---

[34] As an aside, the use of kilojoules avoids this odd vernacular problem. 1 calorie = 4.184 joules, and 1 kilocalorie = 4.184 kilojoules. Calories tend to be easier to work with however, as the numbers are smaller and more manageable.

At its simplest, your body consumes and burns energy. Every day, your body receives energy from the foods and beverages you eat and drink. This energy is then used by your body for everything from basic cellular activity to movement, repair, and organ function. Consume more than you burn and the excess is stored in reserve as fat. Burn more than you consume, and you draw from those reserves. "*Calories in versus calories out.*" It's a useful but incomplete equation, which we'll unpack in the next chapter. Calories matter, but not all calories are created equal.

For now, picture your diet as a fuel system. Imagine if your car could run on dozens of different fuels rather than just one. Some could get you hundreds of kilometres per litre, while others only a few. Some keep your engine clean while others corrode it slowly over time. Now imagine pouring random amounts of each into your tank every day. That's how most people fuel their most important vehicle.

The benefits of healthy eating

Before we get into the details, it's worth understanding what makes healthy eating so important. If you've ever improved your diet, you've likely felt the difference, but many people have never known anything else. As we saw earlier with the normal trap, we quickly adapt to our baseline, even when it's suboptimal. Diet is one of the clearest examples of this. What feels *normal* is often far from *optimal*. It's only when you make the change that you realise just how much better you can feel.

Eating well is about far more than just maintaining a healthy weight. Like sleep, it is a foundational lever that affects nearly every system in your body.

Energy and vitality: A well-fuelled body operates differently. You wake up with more energy, no longer dragging yourself through the day waiting for the next caffeine fix. With more energy, you naturally start to move and exercise more, reinforcing the cycle.

Hormonal function: Hormones regulate far more than most people realise, from energy and sleep to fertility and muscle mass. Food is one of the strongest levers you have to influence them. Stable blood sugar keeps insulin under control. Healthy fats support sex hormones. Micronutrients like magnesium and B-vitamins help regulate stress hormones. Disrupt this system with poor diet and you will feel it everywhere from brain fog to fatigue.

Sleep quality: By stabilising energy and hormones, a healthy diet promotes deeper, more restorative sleep. This, in turn, supports better dietary choices the next day. Conversely, research from the Mayo Clinic shows that if you sleep less than five hours, you'll consume, on average, an extra 550 calories per day.[35]

Longevity and healthy ageing: Poor diet is among the leading contributors to chronic disease worldwide, with dietary risk factors linked to an estimated 11 million deaths annually. [36] Improving your diet reduces your risk of heart disease, diabetes, cancer, and dementia, just to name a few. It also influences visible markers of ageing, including skin, hair, nails, and oral health. Good nutrition adds both years to your life and life to your years.

Recovery and resilience: Your body is a complex biological system with specific nutritional requirements. Give it what it needs, and you'll fight off disease more easily, recover faster, and bounce back more quickly from stress and injury. Deprive it of the

---

[35] Andrew D. Calvin et al., 'Effects of Experimental Sleep Restriction on Caloric Intake and Activity Energy Expenditure', *Chest* 144, no. 1 (2013): 79–86.

[36] Ashkan Afshin et al., 'Health Effects of Dietary Risks in 195 Countries, 1990–2017: A Systematic Analysis for the Global Burden of Disease Study 2017', *The Lancet* 393, no. 10184 (2019): 1958–72.

right resources and you'll experience slower wound healing, prolonged illness, and a greater susceptibility to infection.

Mental health: The gut and brain are more tightly linked than most people realise. Poor diet can disrupt this relationship, contributing to inflammation, mood swings, anxiety, and brain fog. Diets rich in whole foods are consistently associated with lower rates of depression, while highly processed diets are linked to worse outcomes. Eating quality food can literally improve how you feel.

In addition to improving your physical and mental health, a healthy diet directly influences your financial wellbeing. As we'll see in the next chapter, it's a common myth that eating healthy is expensive. Some of the biggest costs can come from preventable expenses arising from diet-related medical conditions. Doctors' visits, specialist appointments, medical bills, and expensive medications all add up to far more than the cost of a healthy diet. Eating well is an investment, not an expense.

What makes nutrition such a powerful tool is how these benefits compound. Eat well and you'll have more energy, meaning you'll move more, be more productive, and sleep better. This in turn improves mental health and decision making, leading to better food choices the next day. Over time, these effects work together to reduce illness, increase longevity, and even improve your financial position. Conversely, poor diet drives the opposite, leading to fatigue, illness, poorer decisions, medical bills, and a reduced lifespan. Your daily nutritional choices determine which spiral takes hold.

Why don't we just eat better?

Given the overwhelming evidence of the benefits of a healthy diet, you'd think the choice would be easy. The state of the developed world suggests otherwise. Diet-related conditions such as type 2 diabetes, fatty liver disease, and heart disease are now commonplace. In countries like Australia, roughly two-thirds of adults are classified as overweight or obese.[37] Globally, obesity has nearly tripled since 1975.[38] We are, quite literally, eating ourselves to death.

Despite consistently overeating, we are undernourished. We're drowning in calories yet starved of nutrients. The food supply is increasingly dominated by ultra-processed products, engineered to be shelf-stable, hyper-palatable, and addictive. Packed with additives, emulsifiers, and flavour enhancers, these foods are stripped of vital nutrients. They're cheap, convenient, and everywhere, crowding out the nutrient-dense foods our bodies actually need to thrive. In many developed countries, these foods now make up a substantial share of the average diet. For children, the pattern can be even worse, with packaged snacks, fast food, and sugary drinks crowding out more nourishing options.

Much of this probably isn't news to you. We all *know* we should eat better, but it's easier said than done. So what exactly makes eating well so difficult? The answer lies in three overlapping layers of environmental pressures, biological wiring, and internal drivers.

Environmental pressures: The modern food environment is stacked against you. Ultra-processed foods are engineered to sell and are often more heavily marketed than whole foods. Billions of dollars are poured into advertising campaigns that don't just sell food, but identity. At the same time, food literacy has eroded.

---

[37] Australian Bureau of Statistics, *National Health Survey: 2022*, released 15 December 2023.

[38] World Health Organization, 'Obesity and Overweight', fact sheet, 1 March 2024, https://www.who.int/news-room/fact-sheets/detail/obesity-and-overweight

Many people still assume fruit juice or muesli bars are automatically healthy, while whole foods like eggs, red meat, or natural fats are demonised.

Alongside this is the decline in cooking literacy. Just two generations ago, most families could prepare balanced meals from scratch. Today, convenience foods and takeaway dominate because they require no skills, no time, and no thought. When you're stressed, time-poor, or exhausted, the path of least resistance leads straight to packaged meals and drive-through windows.

Biological wiring: Even if you strip away marketing and convenience, we're still fighting our biology. For most of human history, the next meal wasn't guaranteed. Our brains evolved to seek calorie-dense foods and to overeat when food was available. Modern food companies exploit this wiring with scientific precision.

Products are designed at the exact "bliss point" of sugar, salt, and fat to override your body's natural fullness signals and keep you coming back for more. Hedonic adaptation then kicks in, with your taste buds no longer satisfied with anything less than the richest of foods. A fresh apple pales in comparison to a doughnut engineered with fat-sugar-salt ratios that don't even exist in nature. Left unchecked, your palate changes so much that real food tastes bland, even though it's exactly what your body needs.

Internal drivers: Finally, there's the most difficult layer, the reasons why we eat in the first place. Eating is rarely about physical sustenance, with food playing a much larger role in our daily lives. Habits, conditioned responses, and cultural expectations often dictate what, when, and how we eat. We reach for snacks when stressed, cookies when bored, or ice cream when lonely, but rarely as conscious choices. These internal drivers are difficult to untangle because they operate below awareness, reinforced over years of experience, rituals, and emotional associations.

When you combine these factors, it's clear why knowledge alone doesn't change behaviour. You're swimming upstream against an environment that pushes convenience, a biology wired to crave calories, and an inner landscape that ties food to comfort, culture, and habit. It's why willpower alone is rarely enough. Diet can be one of the hardest areas to master given how complex our relationship with food is. If you want to take control of your diet, the first step is to better understand this relationship by leveraging your awareness, not just of what you're eating, but why.

The hunger trap

Hunger is the most fundamental driver of eating, yet we often misinterpret what's really behind it. We tend to associate hunger with a genuine need for food, when often it is simply a desire. Experts have identified many different types of hunger, yet only one represents a true biological need. Broadly speaking, they fall into four categories:

Physiological hunger: Driven by a need for actual sustenance. Signs include stomach growling, hunger pangs, and a feeling of stomach emptiness. Note, however, that even true physical hunger can be misleading depending on the type of food you eat. A large bag of nuts can provide more than enough daily calories, yet it's unlikely to keep you feeling full for as long as its calorie load would suggest.

Emotional hunger: Driven by emotions, this includes comfort eating, celebratory eating, boredom eating, or distraction eating. It often feels sudden and specific, a craving for something in particular, rather than food in general. It rarely leaves you feeling truly satisfied, especially if the underlying emotions remain unresolved. Learning to recognise this pattern is crucial as it's the form of hunger most closely linked to overeating and other disorders.

Sensory hunger: Driven by smell, taste, and sight, this is largely a pleasure-based hunger. Examples include always being able to make room for dessert at the sight of a decadent cake, or the almost irresistible allure of a delicious-smelling bakery.

Associative hunger: Arises when you have created mental links between particular stimuli and eating. A common example would be habitually getting popcorn at the movies, even if you've just eaten. Most forms of hunger have an element of association attached (such as the bakery example above, or associating sadness with eating ice cream).

Given the diverse reasons we may experience hunger, we need to consider which one it is we're actually experiencing in any given moment. In modern societies, true physiological hunger is relatively rare. Much of what we call hunger is really craving, triggered by a complex mix of emotions, hormones, and associations.

There's nothing wrong with enjoying food, but confusing hunger with boredom, stress, or sadness keeps you repeating the same patterns without ever addressing the cause. If hunger can be triggered by so many different signals, you can't rely on it alone to guide your decisions. You need a way to pause, step back, and recognise what's actually driving the urge to eat.

Are you paying attention?

Mindfulness is much more than just a meditation technique. It's a way of living. In Part Three, we'll see how it applies to finances as well. Here, it's one of the most effective tools for regaining control over your diet and your health.

To understand mindful eating, consider the opposite. Have you ever had a "snaccident"? It's where you "accidentally" finish an entire bag of chips or block of chocolate without even realising. That's mindless eating. It happens every time you graze while scrolling on your phone, eat lunch at your desk while working, or finish a meal while barely noticing the taste. You've reverted to autopilot. Like highway hypnosis, you can eat an entire meal and not even remember doing so.

Mindful eating is switching off the autopilot. It's slowing down and fully engaging with the experience. Remove distractions by putting your phone down and turning off the TV, bringing your full attention to the meal instead. Notice the taste, smell, and texture of your food. Pay attention to your hunger and satiety as you eat. In this way, you turn your meals into mini-meditation sessions. By becoming fully present as you eat, food becomes more satisfying and you're far less likely to overeat.

At a deeper level, bring awareness to your behaviours and emotions around eating. Ask why you're eating in the first place. Is it true hunger, or is it boredom, stress, celebration, or simply habit? Observe how you feel before, during, and after meals. Notice any patterns that emerge. Do you snack when anxious? Perhaps you reward yourself with food? Do you feel guilty after eating certain foods? This layer is about recognising the drivers behind your choices, not just the food on your plate.

To develop mindful eating, start with mindfulness more broadly. Regular practice improves attention and awareness, which naturally carries over into how you eat. Even ten minutes of daily practice can sharpen your awareness enough to noticeably change your relationship with food. From there, apply that awareness directly. Something as simple as pausing for three breaths before eating creates a gap between impulse and action, allowing you to choose rather than react. Delaying gratification, even briefly, strengthens self-control. It's about reclaiming agency, eating because you decide to, not because a craving made the decision for you.

The goal here is not to strip away the joy of eating – quite the opposite. Most people find food becomes more enjoyable when they're fully present for it. The deeper aim is awareness. Once you can see your automatic habits, you can change them. Your choices move from reflex to intention. Each mindful meal strengthens your ability to pause, reflect, and act with purpose – the same skill that underpins every meaningful change in health and in life.

The final piece of mindful eating is examining your stories around food and diet. Do you believe "*carbs are bad*" or that "*breakfast is essential*"? What story do you hold about food itself? Is it fuel, comfort, reward, or perhaps pleasure? As with all stories, assess whether there is any truth in them, or whether they are conditioned beliefs. More importantly, are they serving you?

When you change the way you think about food, you change the way you consume it. Food stops being a drug for comfort and becomes a resource for thriving instead. The next step is to apply that same awareness to what you're consuming.

Watch what you eat

Developing awareness of your intake requires tracking it, at least in the short term. This becomes especially important when you consider how unreliable our estimates tend to be.

Hidden calories quickly add up. Sauces, salad dressings, and cooking oils can each add hundreds of calories without you noticing. As a result, we tend to heavily underestimate our daily intake. One study found that participants substantially under-reported their intake, reporting roughly half the calories they were actually consuming.[39]

The consequences of this estimation error do not surface immediately. Eat an additional 200 calories per day, or roughly a small handful of nuts, and you're unlikely to notice anything in the short term. Over time, however, that small surplus can gradually show up in your waistline. Extend the pattern over multiple years and it can lead to significant unwanted fat gain.

By bringing hidden calories into view, tracking helps prevent the gradual creep in bodyweight that might otherwise occur. In the next chapter, we'll cover how to do this in detail. It doesn't need to be perfect, but it should be complete. That means every food and every drink. Writing things down exposes what you're really consuming rather than simply what you remember.

When you do this, patterns quickly become obvious. You may think you snack occasionally until you see it recorded in detail. Two biscuits with each coffee might seem insignificant, until you realise you're having four or five cups a day. That's almost a pack of biscuits each day, often without you ever noticing. These small habits, repeated daily, add up faster than you'd expect.

Tracking also reveals behaviour. You might notice that Friday nights consistently lead to poorer choices after a long week, or that stressful days drive you towards snacks. We've already seen that eating is about much more than hunger. Logging your intake helps you connect food to mood, context, and routine, allowing you to identify the triggers behind your habits.

---

[39] Steven W. Lichtman et al., 'Discrepancy Between Self-Reported and Actual Caloric Intake and Exercise in Obese Subjects', *New England Journal of Medicine* 327, no. 27 (1992): 1893–98.

Over time, you also develop a clearer understanding of how food affects you physically. When your energy peaks or crashes, you can look back and see what preceded it. Every meal you record becomes useful data you can use to better fuel your body in the future.

There's also a psychological bonus known as *the Hawthorne effect.*[40] People tend to change their behaviour when they know they're being observed, even if they're the ones doing the observing. When you track your food honestly, your choices tend to improve. You pause before the third doughnut because you know you'll have to write it down. Sharing your log with someone else, be it a coach or a friend, magnifies this effect.

From awareness to strategy

By bringing awareness to your eating, you step out of autopilot and start making deliberate choices about what you put into your body. Awareness gives you visibility, but on its own, it isn't enough. The next step is to build systems that support better decisions consistently.

In the following chapters, we'll turn that awareness into practical strategies. You'll learn how to understand your food, cut through the myths, and build habits that make better choices easier to sustain. This isn't just fuel. It's what powers the most important vehicle you'll ever own.

◇

[40] James McCambridge, John Witton and Diana R. Elbourne, 'Systematic Review of the Hawthorne Effect: New Concepts Are Needed to Study Research Participation Effects', *Journal of Clinical Epidemiology* 67, no. 3 (2014): 267–77.

EXERCISE 11

Understanding your hunger

The goal of this exercise is to bring awareness to why you eat and drink.

Approach this with curiosity, even if it isn't something you currently struggle with. Awareness is a transferable skill. The better you understand the drivers behind your behaviour, the easier it becomes to change them as required.

As we'll see in Part Three, there are strong parallels between patterns of eating and patterns of spending. The awareness you build here will carry over into the financial chapters later in the book.

Your task over the next few days is simple. Before you eat or drink, pause briefly and notice what is driving the decision. Is it:

- Physical hunger or thirst;
- Emotion, such as stress, boredom, or comfort;
- Pleasure or craving; or
- Habit.

At the end of each day, take a moment to reflect. Which of these showed up most often? What does that suggest about your current patterns?

CHAPTER 12

WHAT ARE YOU REALLY CONSUMING?

Before you can build a healthy diet, you first need to understand what you're actually consuming. In this chapter, we'll explore how the body processes and expends energy, along with practical tools to track your intake and better understand what's in your food.

We'll start with the calorie, examining both sides of the energy equation, and build the basic skills you need to understand what's in your food. With this knowledge, you'll be able to steer your diet deliberately rather than letting cravings, habits, or marketing claims dictate your choices.

The energy equation

Before diving into practical tools, let's take a closer look at the energy equation.

As we've seen, bodyweight is largely influenced by the balance between energy consumed and energy expended. In simple terms, weight gain occurs when energy intake exceeds energy expenditure, while the reverse is true for weight loss.

While the principle itself is straightforward, the reality is far more nuanced than simply comparing calories in with calories out. To understand why, we need to take a closer look at both, as well as the relationship between the two.

Calories out

Your *total daily energy expenditure* (TDEE) is the number of calories your body burns in a day. It is made up of:

Basal Metabolic Rate (BMR) – ~60 to 70%: This is the energy needed to keep you alive at rest, including breathing, circulation, and basic cellular function. It is influenced by age, sex, genetics, and body composition, with muscle tissue requiring more energy than fat.

Non-Exercise Activity Thermogenesis (NEAT) – ~10 to 25%: All movement that isn't structured exercise, including walking, standing, fidgeting, and any other incidental movement throughout the day. NEAT can vary dramatically between individuals.

Thermic Effect of Food (TEF) – ~8 to 12%: The energy required to process food. Chewing, digesting, absorbing, and metabolising food all cost energy. Some foods require more energy to process than others, meaning TEF can be influenced by your dietary choices.

Exercise Activity Thermogenesis (EAT) – ~5 to 10%: This is the energy you burn during planned activity, such as training or sports.

It may surprise you to see that NEAT often contributes more than formal exercise. In other words, the calories burned through everyday movement often exceed those burned through planned training sessions. This helps explain why incidental movement is so critical for overall health and wellbeing – and why you can't out-train a sedentary lifestyle.

The low contribution from EAT reveals another important insight: exercise burns far fewer calories than most people realise. Thirty minutes on a treadmill typically burns around 200 to 300 calories, often less than the calories in that doughnut you may eat as a reward. Add in the hunger spike that often follows exercise, and it becomes clear why using exercise to compensate for overeating rarely works. It is usually easier to avoid excess calories than to try to burn them off through exercise. While exercise remains invaluable for fitness, strength, and long-term health, when it comes to body composition and weight management, diet is usually the more practical and powerful lever.

That brings us to the other side of the equation: the energy coming in.

Calories in

This is the total number of calories you consume each day. To understand this side of the equation, we need to look at a few key concepts:

Macronutrients: All food contains some combination of fat, protein, and carbohydrate. Protein and carbohydrates both provide four calories per gram, while fat provides nine. The calorie density of a food depends primarily on the ratio of these three macronutrients. Olive oil, being pure fat, contains around 900 calories per 100 grams, while celery (mostly water and fibre) is only about 16 calories.

Alcohol: Many people don't realise that alcohol itself contains calories, even before accounting for any mixers or carbohydrates in the drink. It's also surprisingly calorie dense – at seven calories per gram, alcohol provides nearly as many calories as fat.

Micronutrients: These are all the vitamins and minerals in our food, critical ingredients for good health. They provide no energy, meaning the amount of micronutrients in a food is unrelated to its calorie content. Foods like fruits and vegetables are considered *nutrient-dense* because they provide a high amount of micronutrients relative to their calorie content. Most junk foods are the opposite, with items like cake or ice cream containing relatively few micronutrients despite providing a large amount of energy.

Satiety: How filling a food is. Foods differ wildly in their ability to satisfy hunger. A boiled potato ranks among the most satiating foods, while croissants sit near the bottom. Satiety is an important consideration, as a diet that leaves you constantly fighting hunger is rarely sustainable. Feeling full makes it easier to maintain a lower calorie intake over time.

Absorption: Not every calorie you consume is fully absorbed. Highly processed foods are typically more completely digested, while whole foods are less so. For example, you absorb fewer calories from whole peanuts than the same weight of peanut butter. Even cooking methods can sometimes have an impact. Cooling rice or potatoes after cooking increases resistant starch, reducing the calories absorbed.

The take-home message here is that not all calories are equally valuable. Calories measure the energy in food and nothing else. They tell you nothing about nutrient density, fullness, or the broader effect a food has on your body. While 100 calories of broccoli and 100 calories of cookies contain the same amount of energy, their effects on satiety, nutrition, and overall wellbeing differ significantly.

Understanding calories in and calories out is useful, but the real value comes from understanding how you balance the two.

Balancing the equation

The goal is not always to keep the two perfectly balanced, but to align them with your objective. A calorie surplus promotes weight gain, a calorie deficit promotes weight loss, and a rough balance maintains your current weight.

One question that naturally follows is: "*How many calories do I actually need?*" The answer varies considerably from person to person. Factors such as age, sex, body size, muscle mass, occupation, and activity level all influence energy requirements. As a very rough guide, many adults will maintain their weight consuming somewhere between 1,800 and 3,000 calories per day, although individual needs can fall well outside this range.

This is why there is no universal calorie target that works for everyone. Rather than searching for the perfect number, start with a reasonable estimate and monitor the results. You'll never know your precise daily energy expenditure or calorie absorption, and even calorie intake can only be estimated. That's completely fine as you don't need precision to produce meaningful results. What you're really aiming for here is directional awareness.

Ultimately, it is not the exact calorie target itself that matters, but the results it produces over time. Your bodyweight and physique provide feedback on whether your intake aligns with your goals. For example, if your goal is fat loss and your weight is gradually increasing, you are likely consuming more energy than you burn. If your goal is weight gain and your weight remains unchanged, you may not be eating enough.

Note that while bodyweight is often the simplest metric to track, it should be considered alongside changes in body composition, performance, and overall appearance. The scales only tell part of the story. For example, a beginner resistance trainer may lose fat while simultaneously gaining muscle, resulting in little change in bodyweight despite a noticeable improvement in physique. Tracking multiple indicators over time provides a more complete picture of progress.

Just remember that daily fluctuations are normal, especially for bodyweight. Focus on the trend, not the individual readings.

Seeing through the marketing

Understanding the energy equation is one thing but applying it in the real world is another. You can only manage what you can measure, and that becomes difficult when you don't fully understand what you're eating in the first place. This is where you need to learn how to read food labels.

Packaged foods list ingredients, macronutrients, and calories, yet most people rarely stop to read them. Instead, they let marketing claims such as *low fat*, *high protein*, or *no added sugar* do the thinking for them. This is exactly what marketers are counting on. The useful information sits on the back. Start reading the facts on the nutrition label instead of relying on the marketing designed to get you to buy. Here's what you should start paying attention to:

Serving size: That small chocolate bar that no rational person shares with anyone? You may be surprised to discover that it contains two to three servings. Always compare the stated serving size with what you actually plan to eat or drink.

Ingredients list: Ingredients must be listed in order of their quantity. Consider *Nutella*. The first two ingredients are sugar and vegetable oil, while hazelnuts make up only 13 per cent. Despite many people thinking it's a healthy nut-based spread, it's really just sugar and oil with a hint of hazelnuts.

Calories per 100 grams: The calories per serving are highly misleading. Stick to calories per 100 grams instead. This allows for consistent comparison across products and quickly builds an understanding of calorie density. Just because something is nutritious doesn't mean it's low-calorie.

Macronutrient breakdown: This shows where the calories are coming from. Using the numbers per 100 grams makes interpretation simple. If a food contains 17 grams of protein per 100 grams, it is 17 per cent protein. This becomes useful later when structuring your diet.

Sugar: Listed under carbohydrates. Added sugars are widespread in highly processed foods, including those marketed as healthy. Learning to spot sugar on labels highlights just how much can be hidden in everyday products, often in foods you wouldn't expect.

Fibre: Also listed under carbohydrates. Fibre plays a key role in satiety and gut health, yet many diets fall short. Paying attention to fibre content helps you identify foods that are more filling and supportive of long-term health.

Sodium: While not inherently harmful, sodium is often overconsumed, particularly through highly processed and packaged foods. It tends to accumulate quickly across the day, making it worth keeping an eye on even when individual items don't seem excessive.

By making a habit of reading labels, you cut through the marketing and start building real food literacy. You begin to distinguish between the foods that genuinely support your goals and those that simply have compelling marketing.

The zero-calorie Tic Tac

Take *Tic Tacs*, for example. These tiny mints are made up of over 90 per cent sugar. They contain approximately 400 calories per 100 grams, not unusual for confectionery. What *is* unusual is that the package lists a serving as one single mint. At less than half a gram per *Tic Tac*, that's about two calories per "serve". In the US, food companies are legally allowed to round down anything below five calories to zero. This allows *Tic Tacs* to be labelled legally as zero calories per serving.

One *Reddit* user reported eating one to two packs per day believing they were calorie-free. They'd relied on the front-of-pack claim while failing to inspect the detail on the back. Those "zero-calorie" mints were actually adding between 400 and 800 calories daily, roughly the equivalent of a full meal. Over a year, that misunderstanding contributed to nearly 40 pounds (18 kilograms) of weight gain.

It's a clear example of why serving sizes and front-of-pack claims should not be taken at face value. If you rely only on what's printed in bold on the box, you can easily be misled. Always check the numbers per 100 grams, do your own quick maths, and sanity-check the outcome.

Record your intake

By now you understand the theory. The next step is to turn it into daily action. To do this, let's explore how to track your intake in a way that's accurate enough to be useful, but not so burdensome that you give it up entirely.

In the beginning, tracking can be challenging. It can feel like information overload, as you navigate through dense nutrition labels and long lists of ingredients. Logging takes effort and every meal can feel like homework. This is normal. Like any new skill, it requires some discipline to get started before it becomes routine.

To reduce this initial friction, approach the process with curiosity instead of resistance. I personally find it empowering to learn what's really in my food. It's nice knowing that I'll never be fooled by a marketing claim on a label. It can also be surprisingly eye-opening. Foods or meals I'd assumed were low in calories have often turned out to be quite the opposite. Conversely, others have turned out to be far more calorie-efficient than I'd expected, often becoming staples in my diet as a result.

To get started, choose a method that you'll actually use. Apps like *MyFitnessPal*, *Cronometer*, or *MacroFactor* are easy entry points. A simple spreadsheet can be just as effective, especially if you prefer more control and want to build your own database of unique recipes over time. However you choose to do it, begin tracking honestly for at least seven days. This provides a clear snapshot of your habits, highlights repeat foods, and exposes any hidden calories that might otherwise go unnoticed.

Aim for completeness, not perfection. Log everything you eat and drink, even if you have to estimate. When eating out, make your best guess and move on. Missing entries undermine the process far more than imperfect ones. Pay particular attention to liquid calories, especially alcohol, as these are easy to overlook and can significantly impact your total intake.

As you continue, patterns will emerge. You'll see where your calories are coming from and which foods contribute most to your daily intake. In doing so, you develop a more intuitive sense of the calorie density of different foods. This allows you to be more strategic with your tracking.

Calorie-dense foods are where small measurement errors have the greatest impact. Underestimating a heaped tablespoon of peanut butter, for example, can create a meaningful discrepancy. In contrast, low-calorie foods are far more forgiving and often don't require the same level of precision. As this awareness improves, your estimation becomes more accurate and efficient.

At the same time, your food literacy improves. You begin to recognise patterns in both your food choices and your behaviour. Within a few weeks, most of the foods you regularly eat will already be familiar, making tracking faster and less effortful.

With enough exposure, you may eventually rely less on active tracking and more on instinct, using your bodyweight and general awareness to stay on course.

That's ultimately the goal. You don't want to have to track forever or obsess over every calorie. Instead, the aim is to build your food awareness, improve accuracy, and prevent the small daily surpluses that accumulate over time. Used correctly, it's one of the most effective tools you have for managing your health, energy, and weight.

The opportunity cost of calories

When you first start tracking calories, it can be useful to consider the concept of *opportunity cost*. The true cost of any limited resource is not the price paid, but the opportunities forgone. The true cost of a new $1,000 phone is everything else you could have bought with that same money instead.

While the concept is most often applied to money, it can sometimes be less relevant there. There's no need to choose between options if you have enough money to afford them both. The same cannot be said for your time and your calories. You only get 24 hours in a day, and a finite number of calories you can consume without gaining weight. Saying *yes* to one option means saying *no* to another. Every calorie you consume uses part of your daily budget that could have been spent elsewhere.

This idea is powerful because it reframes diet from restriction to choice. "*I can't have this*" becomes "*Would I rather spend these calories elsewhere?*" It also highlights just how costly some foods really are. Would you still eat that decadent cake for 1,500 calories if you saw all the other things you could eat for the same calorie price? Your answer may still be *yes*, but at least now it's a conscious and informed decision.

This isn't about depriving yourself of enjoyment. It's about getting the most value from your limited calories. A highly calorie-dense food may be enjoyable in the moment, but it often displaces a larger volume of food that could provide more sustained satisfaction. In many cases, it's possible to find lower-calorie options that are just as enjoyable, but without the strict limits on quantity.

Liquid calories are one of the worst offenders here. A single can of soft drink contains around 160 calories and is often consumed in seconds. Three cans a day is nearly 500 calories that could have been spent on something more nourishing, filling, or enjoyable.

Thinking in terms of opportunity cost helps you align your daily dietary choices with your long-term goals. Instead of banning foods, you start asking whether they're the best use of your budget.

Next steps

Tracking isn't just about counting calories. It's about educating yourself on what you consume every day. With greater food literacy, you move away from eating on autopilot and begin making deliberate choices. You start to understand not just what you eat, but how it affects your body. That awareness helps you better manage your energy, performance, appetite, and weight.

In the next chapter, we'll move from understanding individual foods to structuring your overall diet. We'll cover the principles that support wellbeing, tackle common nutrition myths, and give you strategies to create a diet that fits your individual needs. With these tools, you can put your food literacy into practice, reclaim control of your diet, and manage your cravings with confidence.

◇

EXERCISE 12

Build your food literacy

For this exercise, you can choose the level of engagement that best suits you. Each level builds upon the previous one.

Low effort – Start reading packaging

Inspect the labels on anything you eat or drink. Pay attention to calorie density (calories per 100 grams), total calories per package, and the ingredients list. There is no need to track or record anything at this stage. The aim is simply to build awareness and improve your food literacy.

Moderate effort – Track your intake

Using the approach outlined earlier in this chapter, record everything you eat and drink for at least one week. The goal is to make your consumption visible and expose any hidden behaviours. You don't need to calculate anything here. This is only a record of your consumption, not an analysis.

Higher effort – Calculate your calories

Here, you build on the previous level by calculating your approximate calorie intake. This level is most relevant if you have a specific outcome in mind, such as losing fat or gaining muscle.

You can use any of the tools mentioned earlier, or another method of your choice. It is also useful to monitor bodyweight, ideally at the same time each day. Remember it's not the daily fluctuations that are important, but the trend over time.

This is not a short exercise. You'll likely need to continue for at least a few weeks before any meaningful trends emerge. By monitoring these trends, you will gain a better understanding of your true energy requirements.

CHAPTER 13

HEALTHY EATING IN PRACTICE

With the groundwork laid, it's time to explore how to build a healthy diet in practice.

Healthy eating is far simpler than most people realise. Trends come and go like fashion, but the fundamentals rarely change. Most new research refines the edges rather than rewriting the rules. You don't need to follow every headline or read scientific journals to eat well. A handful of proven basics will get you most of the results. From there, it's up to you how much you want to optimise your nutrition.

The Golden Rule

Of all the dieting advice, tips and hacks, there is one rule that stands above the rest: *Eat as many different types of healthy foods as you can.*

There are no true "superfoods". An apple a day won't keep the doctor away, at least not on its own. What you need is variety. Different foods bring different benefits, from unique micronutrient profiles to compounds that support long-term health.

Eating the same meal on repeat risks missing certain nutrients, while potentially overloading on others. These imbalances rarely show up immediately. They build in the background and often only surface years later, making the cause difficult to trace. It's why it's so important to be proactive with your nutrition. When used correctly, it becomes one of your most powerful preventative tools for preserving health in the long run.

To apply this rule in your daily life, aim for diversity across food groups. Fruits, vegetables, beans, legumes, fungi, meats, dairy, eggs, nuts, grains, seeds... the list goes on. Don't just tick off each group, rotate within them regularly. Try different fruits and mix up your vegetables. If you eat meat, use different cuts and include parts of the animal such as liver and other offal. This approach naturally fills nutritional gaps while having the added benefit of keeping your meals interesting. Once variety is in place, a few simple principles will make your day-to-day decisions even easier.

Principles for a healthy diet

Moderation is something you'll often hear when talking about diet. Simply put, the dose makes the poison. Cake isn't a health food, but one piece won't do any harm. Fruit is highly nutritious yet eating 20 pieces a day is likely to cause issues. *The Golden Rule*, by design, leads to moderation. Eating a diverse range of foods naturally means eating smaller amounts of each.

It's not just the quantity of what you eat that's important, but the quality. The closer a food is to its natural form, the more useful it tends to be. Whole foods come with fibre, greater satiety, and slower absorption. Compare an apple to processed juice. The apple fills you up, provides fibre, and takes longer to digest. The juice, on the other hand, is mostly sugar water with the fibre stripped away. One keeps you full, while the other makes it easy to overconsume.

The same applies to liquid calories more broadly, and it's why they tend to be such a pitfall in modern diets. Water should be your default. Soft drinks, fruit juices, and flavoured milks all deliver a hefty payload of calories with almost no satiety, making them incredibly easy to overconsume. Alcohol only compounds the issue. Gram for gram it contains nearly as many calories as fat, but without any nutritional value to show for it. Liquid calories should be treated as occasional indulgences, not daily staples.

Finally, don't overlook your fibre and salt balance. Fibre is essential for digestion, gut health, and satiety, yet most people fall short of their daily needs. Salt, on the other hand, is typically consumed in excess, largely through highly processed foods. While your body requires sodium for nerve and muscle function, consistently high intakes can contribute to elevated blood pressure, particularly when paired with inadequate fluid intake. Bringing intake back towards whole foods naturally improves this balance.

None of this is complex, so why does healthy eating still feel complicated in practice? Much of the confusion isn't accidental. It's often deliberately engineered. To take control of your nutrition, you'll need to learn how to cut through the noise.

The health confusion

At this point, it may sound like I'm just stating the obvious. "*The trick to having a healthy diet is to eat healthy foods.*" The difficulty is that most people aren't sure what "healthy" actually means.

It's not that people don't care about their health. If anything, the health industry is booming more than ever. The real issue is a gap in understanding, amplified by marketing that is disingenuous at best and deliberately misleading at worst. It's common to see people trying to "eat clean" while filling their cupboards with ultra-processed foods packaged to look healthy.

This is where the tools from the last chapter come into play. Marketing can mislead you into thinking that a product is healthy, but the ingredients list and nutrition label cannot. These labels can't hide the fact that the first ingredient is sugar, or that it's far more calorie-dense than it may appear. Now that you know how to read them, the responsibility falls on you. Companies know that healthy sells, but they can't force you to buy.

Knowledge helps, but it still needs to be applied critically. Not all information is published with honest intentions, particularly in the nutrition space. The infamous sugar-fat scandal is a sober reminder that even official guidelines shouldn't be blindly accepted.

Sugar vs Fat

Back in the 1960s, the sugar industry was facing growing scrutiny. Early studies were beginning to link sugar to heart disease, obesity, and other chronic illnesses. Instead of facing the evidence, the industry fought back. They funded Harvard researchers to publish studies that passed the blame from sugar onto fat. These papers, appearing in highly respected medical journals, downplayed sugar's potential role in disease while pointing the finger squarely at dietary fat as the enemy.[41]

The impact was enormous. For decades, public health guidelines, government policy, and consumer habits revolved around the idea that fat was the problem. Food manufacturers responded by creating low-fat products. When the fat came out, it was often replaced with sugar, refined starches, and additives to restore texture and flavour. Consumers thought they were

[41] Cristin E. Kearns, Laura A. Schmidt and Stanton A. Glantz, 'Sugar Industry and Coronary Heart Disease Research: A Historical Analysis of Internal Industry Documents', *JAMA Internal Medicine*, vol. 176, no. 11, 2016, pp. 1680–1685.

eating healthier, but in many cases, they were swapping beneficial dietary fats for processed fillers. These products became part of a broader shift towards highly processed foods, which has contributed to the obesity and diabetes epidemic we're still fighting today.

This wasn't simply an innocent mistake that was recognised in hindsight. It was deliberate manipulation designed to protect an industry's profits. It's a clear example of why you can't take marketing claims or even dietary guidelines at face value. Industries have powerful incentives to protect their profits, not your health. Sadly, the same playbook is still being used today. Products get marketed as plant-based, gluten-free, or low fat. These labels sound healthy, but are often ultra-processed junk food in disguise, loaded with refined oils, added sugars, and other harmful additives.

To protect yourself from this, you need to go back to basics. Focus on whole foods, read labels carefully, and don't take marketing at face value. Even new studies that contradict long-standing principles should be taken with a grain of salt. You don't need a PhD in nutrition to eat well. The fundamentals of a good diet are simple, timeless, and grounded in common sense.

Diet myths

With the foundation in place, we can turn our attention to some of the more common myths in nutrition. Some are deliberately exploited by marketers, while others are spread by well-meaning but misinformed sources.

If a myth sounds convincing, it's usually because it contains a grain of truth. Let's look at some of the more persistent myths:

Superfoods can save your diet: Foods like sardines, eggs, and berries are undeniably nutritious, but no single food can compensate for an otherwise poor diet. As the *Golden Rule* reminds us, real health comes from a diverse mix of nutrient-dense foods, not a single silver bullet.

The calorie confusion: People often assume that foods high in calories must automatically be "bad" while low-calorie options are seen as "good". Looking at calories in isolation is incomplete. Calories may influence body weight, but nutrients determine how well your body functions. Some foods provide both, such as eggs or fatty fish. Others provide mostly energy, like lollies and biscuits. A food's value isn't defined by its energy content alone, but by what comes with it. That's why it's better to think in terms of calorie quality instead. Look for foods that punch above their weight nutritionally, giving you maximum return on your calorie investment.

Sugar-free means healthy: This myth arises from the same calorie confusion. Because artificial sweeteners contain little to no energy, they are often treated as a free pass to consume otherwise unhealthy products. Others take the opposite view, treating them as dangerous chemicals simply because they are artificial. Neither position is accurate. Artificial sweeteners can help reduce sugar intake, but offer no nutritional value and may reinforce a preference for highly sweet foods. Removing sugar from an otherwise unhealthy product does not transform it into a health food. Often these products compensate with other ingredients, making label reading essential.

Fat is bad for you: Oversimplified thinking drives many other dietary myths. Many people avoid fatty foods under the mistaken belief that "*fat makes you fat*". More recently, carbohydrates have taken the blame instead. Both arguments ignore the underlying mechanism. Fat is more calorie-dense than protein or carbohydrates, and refined carbohydrates are easy to overconsume, but neither is inherently fattening. Weight gain comes from a sustained calorie surplus, regardless of whether those calories come from fat, carbohydrates, or protein. A more useful distinction is how foods are processed. Whole, minimally processed foods tend to be more satiating and harder to overconsume than highly refined alternatives, which helps explain our next myth.

Fresh is always best: This is a classic example of how a half-truth can turn into a hard rule. Freshness is not always related to quality. That "fresh" orange on the supermarket shelf may have been picked months earlier. Frozen produce, on the other hand, is usually picked at peak ripeness and snap-frozen, often retaining more nutrients than the limp broccoli that's been sitting in your fridge all week. They are also typically cheaper and more convenient, making them a powerful tool for anyone trying to eat well on a budget.

Healthy eating is expensive: This is perhaps one of the most persistent myths in nutrition. Healthy eating is often seen as expensive, yet many of the most nutritious foods are also among the cheapest. Oats, beans, tinned sardines, frozen vegetables, and seasonal fruit all provide high nutritional value at a low cost. This perception of cost is often driven by marketing and the positioning of health foods as premium products. You don't need exotic foods or ingredients to have a healthy and balanced diet.

Meal-timing is critical: There are even myths surrounding *when* you eat. While timing can influence behaviour, its physiological impact is often overstated. Eating late at night, for example, is frequently associated with weight gain, but the mechanism is usually behavioural rather than metabolic. Late eating tends to coincide with mindless snacking and higher overall intake. Similarly, breakfast is not inherently more important than other meals. Total daily intake and overall nutrition have a far greater impact.

The metabolic scapegoat: Finally, there are the stories people tell themselves. *"My metabolism just isn't what it used to be."* In reality, metabolism remains relatively stable throughout adulthood until around your sixties.[42] Even then, the decline is gradual. What usually changes are your habits. You're likely moving less and sitting more or eating differently. A slowing metabolism gets blamed for what is simply lifestyle creep sneaking in under the radar.

Many nutrition myths start as legitimate findings, then get stretched into rigid rules the evidence never supported. Once you understand the underlying principles, it becomes easy to spot the grain of truth while discarding the rest. Clear the myths first, then focus on what actually works.

Diet hacks

Learning to eat well takes time, but a handful of practical strategies can make the process far more effective and sustainable. Here are a few to get you started:

Cook and prep your meals: This is one of the most effective ways to take control of your diet. When you cook for yourself, you know exactly what goes into your food. It saves money, improves quality, and builds a valuable skill. Meal prepping takes it a step further, saving time, reducing decision fatigue, and keeping you consistent. Most importantly, it keeps you on track when life gets busy. Build it into your routine and it becomes easier over time. You'll likely end up with a personal library of meals you enjoy, along with a rough sense of their nutritional value.

Reframe how you think about food: Start linking nutritious foods with the benefits they bring, such as increased energy,

---

[42] Herman Pontzer et al., 'Daily Energy Expenditure Through the Human Life Course', *Science*, vol. 373, no. 6556, 2021, pp. 808–812.

improved health and long-term vitality. Over time, this changes your preferences, making these foods more appealing. You can also apply the same idea in reverse. Pay attention to how heavily processed foods leave you feeling, whether that's sluggish, bloated, or unsatisfied. You may find you no longer wish to habitually consume indulgent foods, reserving them for treats or special occasions instead.

Don't deprive yourself: Willpower is limited. Cutting out the foods you enjoy often backfires, leading to cycles of deprivation followed by binging. Aim for moderation over elimination, and sustainability over perfection. Approaches like cheat meals or relaxed days can work, so long as they don't become a free-for-all.

Reclaim your palate: Many people have adapted to foods high in sugar and salt, dulling their sensitivity to more subtle flavours. As you move towards less processed foods, your palate naturally readjusts. You can speed this up by reducing exposure to overly rich foods. What once seemed bland begins to taste better, while overly processed foods can start to feel excessive. Over time, you may find you need less to feel satisfied.

Out of sight, out of mind: Make your environment work for you. Don't keep junk food around "just in case" or because it's on sale. Skip the supermarket aisles stacked with snacks, or better yet, do online shopping so you don't get tempted in the first place. At the same time, make the healthy option the easy choice. Keep healthy snacks ready to grab for when hunger strikes.

Make it enjoyable: The more you enjoy the process, the more consistent you'll be. Treat healthy eating as something to explore rather than endure. Experiment with ingredients, adapt your favourite meals, and find versions that support your goals. With a bit of creativity, you can build a diet you genuinely look forward to.

Basics first, then optimise

Nutrition is a deep field, with many areas to optimise. For example, you may choose to experiment with nutrient timing or explore different fasting protocols. These approaches may offer additional benefits, but they are not mandatory for good health and are best treated as refinements. For now, focus on mastering the basics. By consistently applying the fundamentals in this chapter, you'll already have most of your bases covered.

While the fundamentals of good nutrition are universal, the way you apply them can be highly individual. Some people prefer higher carbohydrates, others higher fats. Some do well with structured meals, others with more flexibility. Try different approaches to discover what best suits your body, preferences, and lifestyle.

You might have noticed that supplements haven't been emphasised. While they can be useful in specific cases, they're largely unnecessary if your diet already covers a wide range of nutrient-dense foods. The supplement industry often relies on the same myths and shortcuts discussed earlier, selling the idea of an easy fix. Before reaching for a pill or powder, work on improving your diet first. If you're considering supplementation, use blood work to guide you rather than relying on marketing claims or guesswork.

With your nutrition sorted, your vehicle has all the quality fuel it needs. Now it's time to learn how to tune your machine for peak performance.

◇

EXERCISE 13

Make a healthy change

The previous two exercises focused on your awareness, helping you understand what you eat and why. Now it's time to take action by making one simple change to your diet.

Step 1 – Make a change

Select one healthy eating practice or diet hack from this chapter to implement. You might increase the variety of foods you eat, reduce liquid calories or added sugar, prepare more meals yourself, or eat more whole foods. Keep it small and specific. For example, your change might be "*I will drink one less can of soft drink each day.*" Then commit to it for at least two weeks.

Step 2 – Monitor the effects

During this time, pay attention to how you feel and function. Has your energy changed? Are you sleeping better? Have you noticed any difference in hunger, cravings, digestion, mood, concentration, or physical performance?

Some effects may be subtle or take longer to emerge. Look for patterns rather than judging individual days.

Step 3 – Review and build

At the end of the two weeks, review what happened. Did you notice any benefits? Was the change easy enough to maintain? If it feels sustainable, continue with it and consider introducing another change.

Over time, these small changes accumulate. The aim here is not to optimise every detail, but to gradually build the fundamentals of healthy eating into your everyday life.

CHAPTER 14

PERFORMANCE DRIVING

Nutrition provides the foundation for performance, but it's only one part of the equation. Even the best-maintained vehicle will deteriorate if it is never used. Parts seize up, joints stiffen, and the engine grows weak over time.

Exercise is how you realise your physical potential. We've already seen how important incidental movement is for your overall health, but it can only maintain what already exists. Training takes this a step further by building new capability entirely. It's how you progressively build strength, endurance, resilience, and long-term physical capacity.

Drive like your life depends on it

We are built to move. For hours each day, our ancestors walked, lifted, carried, ran, climbed, and hunted. Movement was mandatory for our survival. Today, survival requires little more than sitting at a desk, scrolling a screen, and occasionally walking to the fridge. Movement has become optional, and we're increasingly opting out.

This mismatch between our biology and our modern environment helps explain many of the health and physical-capacity problems we see today. Sedentary lifestyles are associated with higher risks of obesity, type 2 diabetes, cardiovascular disease, weaker bones, and declining physical function.[43] Many people now struggle with basic physical tasks such as carrying groceries, climbing stairs, or getting off the floor unaided. Weakness in later life is a major predictor of falls, hospitalisation, and loss of independence. Building strength is less about looking fit and more about maintaining physical capacity.

The challenge is that strength starts to decline far earlier than you'd think. Without intervention, muscle mass and bone density can begin declining as early as your thirties, with inactivity accelerating the process.[44] Simply put, if you don't use it, you lose it. The good news is that this process is highly responsive to training. You don't need to be an elite athlete to change this trajectory. You just need to put your vehicle to work. Modern life may not demand movement, but your body still does.

Life in a performance vehicle

Maintaining your vehicle helps prevent decline, but tuning it properly changes the journey completely.

Regular training builds a stronger, more resilient body. You experience fewer injuries and niggles and move with more energy each day. Cardiovascular health and metabolic function improve. Your immune system becomes more robust. Strong muscles stabilise joints and support posture, preserving your mobility and independence as you age. These improvements are among the most obvious benefits of training, yet its effects extend well beyond physical health. Training also sharpens the mind.

---

[43] World Health Organization, *WHO Guidelines on Physical Activity and Sedentary Behaviour* (Geneva: World Health Organization, 2020); F. C. Bull et al., "World Health Organization 2020 Guidelines on Physical Activity and Sedentary Behaviour," *British Journal of Sports Medicine* 54, no. 24 (2020): 1451–1462.

[44] Alfonso J. Cruz-Jentoft et al., "Sarcopenia: Revised European Consensus on Definition and Diagnosis," *Age and Ageing* 48, no. 1 (2019): 16–31.

During a hard set or sustained effort, your attention narrows. Distractions fall away, replaced by a clear focus on the task at hand. For many people, it's one of the few times they're fully present. In this way, training can offer similar mental benefits to meditation and support mental health more broadly. A single session can elevate your mood through the release of endorphins and other neurochemicals. In the short term, it can act as a natural reset button, a circuit-breaker from your day-to-day stressors. Over time, regular training builds a more resilient mind, improving sleep, reducing anxiety, and lowering the risk of depression.[45]

Beyond physiology, training builds useful traits. Progress requires consistency. It takes discipline and accountability to repeatedly put in the effort. As you set and achieve physical goals, you begin to generate momentum. By proving that you can follow through on difficult things, you build confidence in yourself. Over time, these traits work together to make training self-sustaining. Combined with the natural high from a good workout, this creates a virtuous spiral that keeps you coming back. Before long, training evolves from something you should do, to something you don't want to miss.

These effects are reinforced through the social element. We've seen how connection and belonging are vital for mental health. Training often provides both. Classes, clubs, and training partners turn it into a shared challenge. This improves your mental wellbeing while also making your workouts more enjoyable. It also helps keep you consistent, as you're less likely to skip a session when someone's expecting you.

---

[45] World Health Organization, *WHO Guidelines on Physical Activity and Sedentary Behaviour* (Geneva: World Health Organization, 2020); Felipe B. Schuch et al., "Physical Activity and Incident Depression: A Meta-Analysis of Prospective Cohort Studies," *American Journal of Psychiatry* 175, no. 7 (2018): 631–648.

Alongside these benefits, there's a practical upside that's easy to miss. Train consistently and you'll likely see a long-term financial benefit. While this may require some upfront investment in membership fees or equipment, these cost far less than managing avoidable health issues over time. Many cases of chronic pain and minor injury are associated with reduced strength, poor mobility, or general deconditioning. Building and maintaining physical capacity helps reduce that risk, along with the associated costs of treatment, time off work, and ongoing care.

A healthy body doesn't just change how you look. It determines how well you move, think, and handle the demands of daily life. Unlike your mind or your finances, however, your body will inevitably decline with age. Good training and nutrition can delay that decline considerably, but doing so requires ongoing discipline and commitment. You're going to need a motivation that holds up over time.

Find an enduring *why*

There are many different reasons why people begin their fitness journey. For some, it's freedom of movement. For others, it's strength and resilience. Sometimes it's simply wanting to look better in the mirror. That's perfectly fine too. What's important is having a strong enough *why* to get you started.

The catch is that these early motivations don't always last. In the beginning, progress comes quickly. You become stronger and fitter, your energy and mood improve, and your body can feel like it's changing right before your eyes. This honeymoon phase makes consistency easy because the gains are constant and measurable. But eventually, progress slows. Personal bests get harder to come by and the mirror stops changing. Motivations that depend on visible results or physical appearance begin to falter. This is where many people lose momentum.

At that stage, progress needs a new definition. Early on, it means growth. Over the long term, it means preservation. Maintaining your strength, mobility, and vitality year after year *is* progress against the natural course of decline. Every workout that keeps you capable is a victory over the gradual decline you'd otherwise experience.

When you view progress in this way, the timeline for your goals naturally stretches. You're no longer chasing results next month. You're investing in outcomes that won't be obvious for years or even decades. As the payoff moves further in the future, a mindset of delayed gratification helps you stay focused on the bigger picture.

That's why the people who get the best results aren't the most extreme. They're the most consistent. Training works a lot like investing. The ones who benefit most are those who stay in the game the longest. The longer you're able to keep showing up, the more the benefits compound.

That mindset fundamentally changes how you approach training. When you view it as a marathon, not a sprint, patience replaces ego. You prioritise technique, mobility, and recovery. You avoid the trap of pushing too hard only to burn out soon after. Progress means knowing when to press the accelerator, but also when to ease off the gas. It's how you keep your body working well for decades.

For this to work, your *why* needs to be durable. It has to hold up even when progress slows and novelty fades. Tie your motivation to something that lasts, and consistency becomes far easier to maintain. The end goal is to have a body that enables your life, rather than placing limits on it. Framed in this way, keeping your body functional becomes a lifelong investment rather than a short-term pursuit.

Test your limits

Showing up is the first step. The next is refusing to let your own assumptions define what's possible. The limits you accept for yourself set the ceiling on what you can achieve. Training your body also means challenging the limits imposed by your mind.

Most people don't realise how much of their potential is held hostage by belief. "*I'm not athletic.*" "*I'm too old.*" "*I'm just not built for that.*" Repeat these often enough and they become subconscious instructions, influencing your actions in response. As you train, pay close attention to your backseat driver. Question it. Your body is capable of far more than your stories would have you believe.

History offers plenty of examples. For decades, people believed that nobody could sprint 100 metres in under ten seconds, that the human body simply wasn't built for it. Then, in 1968, Jim Hines clocked the first sub-ten. Since then, hundreds have followed. We didn't suddenly evolve. Aside from minor changes in training and equipment, nothing fundamental changed about the human body. The barrier had never been physical. It was psychological.

When something is considered impossible, few people seriously attempt it. By proving the limit wasn't real, Hines shattered a widely held belief, and performance quickly followed. Training your body is no different. Don't accept limits you've never actually tested. Stop telling yourself what you can't do and start finding out what you can.

Your road, your vehicle

A final reminder that your vehicle is unique. Don't compare your progress, your genetics, or your physique to anyone else's. You're driving a different vehicle, with its own quirks and strengths. Someone else might have a turbocharged engine, but you might have better handling. The goal isn't to copy their journey but to understand your own machine.

When you stop racing others and start refining your own drive, training becomes more satisfying and sustainable. Build awareness, strengthen your *why*, stay consistent, and most importantly, run your own race.

◇

EXERCISE 14

Connect your capacity to your values

Reflect on the values you identified earlier (such as family, independence, career, adventure, or personal growth).

Now consider how your physical capacity interacts with those values. Ask yourself:

- In what ways do my strength, energy, or fitness make parts of my life easier?
- Are there situations where fatigue, lack of strength, or limited mobility make things harder than they need to be?
- Has my physical capacity been improving, declining, or staying roughly stable over time?
- If that trend continued, would it support the life I want to live in five, ten, or 20 years?
- What level of strength, energy, and capability would be required to live fully in alignment with my values?
- Is there a gap between where I am now and what that would require?

The goal here is to recognise the role your physical capacity plays in enabling or limiting how you live. For many people, this connection only becomes obvious when something starts to decline. This exercise is designed to surface that relationship earlier, while you still have the ability to influence it.

CHAPTER 15

TUNE YOUR RIDE

Now that you have a clear *why*, it's time to focus on the *how*.

Developing a body that is truly capable is like building a performance vehicle. Speed alone doesn't make a great car. Grip, handling, responsiveness, and reliability are all just as important. Fitness works the same way. It's the sum of your body's capabilities: how it moves, reacts, endures, and adapts.

To tune it properly, you need to understand what each system contributes.

Fitness bank accounts

Think of your overall fitness as a series of bank accounts. Each account represents a key aspect of your physical health. Every time you train a particular area, you're making a deposit. Each one improves what you can do today while also providing insurance against injury and long-term decline.

Strength is your *top speed*. It reflects your body's physical resilience and capacity to produce force. It builds bone density, stabilises joints, and supports how you move and handle load in everyday life. Studies consistently show that strength is one of the best predictors of longevity.[46]

---

[46] See, for example, Jonatan R. Ruiz et al., 'Association between Muscular Strength and Mortality in Men: Prospective Cohort Study', *BMJ* 337 (2008): a439; Darryl P. Leong et al., 'Prognostic Value of Grip Strength: Findings from the Prospective Urban Rural Epidemiology (PURE) Study', *The Lancet* 386, no. 9990 (2015): 266–273.

Power is your *quarter-mile acceleration.* It's strength expressed quickly, such as the ability to sprint, jump, or react with explosive control. Power is a hallmark of youth and vitality, and one of the first traits we lose with age. Training for power helps keep your nervous system sharp and your body more responsive later in life.

Endurance is your *tank capacity.* It's how long you can keep going. It supports cardiovascular health, lung efficiency, and even mental resilience. Whether it's climbing stairs, chasing your kids, or hiking mountains, endurance lets you keep going without running out of steam.

Flexibility and mobility are your *handling and steering.* They allow you to move freely and efficiently through life. Without them, everything feels stiff and effortful.

Balance is your *suspension system.* It reflects your ability to remain stable and centred. As we age, this system naturally dulls. Training balance keeps your stabilisers, reflexes, and coordination sharp, reducing the risk of falls and injury.

Recovery is your *pit stop.* It determines how quickly you can get back out on the track. It's far from passive and requires just as much investment as your training sessions. Improving your capacity to recover allows you to come back stronger, faster, and ready for the next lap.

Each of these accounts contributes to how your vehicle performs. You can prioritise some more than others, but none can be ignored indefinitely without consequence.

People new to training often focus on strength and power at the expense of mobility and recovery, areas that seem unimportant until something goes wrong. It's when something breaks down that people realise how essential these maintenance accounts are. Injury, fatigue, and burnout are all forms of debt.

These negative balances arise when you fail to make consistent deposits into the right accounts. Managed poorly, they'll sideline you entirely. When you can't train, every account starts to decline, not just those you've neglected.

Contribute to each account regularly and your overall fitness wealth will grow far more than if you focus on a single one.

Build your training program

No single approach can fill every account on its own. A balanced program simply ensures you're making deposits across each of them. You might lift weights for strength, add mobility work to keep your range of motion, mix in cardio for endurance, and include recovery work to recharge between sessions. The goal is to stay solvent across the board, building a resilient, capable body that performs well across all areas of life.

If you want a simple starting point, a week might include a few sessions to build strength, some form of cardiovascular work to support endurance, and regular mobility work to maintain your range of motion. Layered on top of that is daily movement and a deliberate focus on recovery through sleep, nutrition, and lower-intensity activity.

You don't need to overthink it. The most important thing is to start with something manageable and sustainable. Choose activities that fit your life and that you'll actually enjoy. A program you can consistently commit to will beat the perfect program you quit after a month. Just make sure you're not neglecting any account, and pay attention to those that start to run low.

Make it easy

Every meaningful change begins with a single deposit. It doesn't matter *where* you start; it matters *that* you start.

The initial goal is to make that first step as easy as possible. Get your gym clothes ready the night before, have a program ready to go, and block out time in your calendar as you would any other valued appointment. The more barriers you remove, the less likely you are to talk yourself out of going. If getting to the gym feels overwhelming, start smaller. Go for a walk, stretch for five minutes, or do a few push-ups at home. Building consistency is your first priority.

The early days will be the toughest. Physically, every movement feels harder than it should. The mental resistance is often even stronger. You're fighting against years of habits and a mind that's trying to negotiate why you shouldn't do it. This is all part of the process. It takes consistent effort to get the ball rolling, but once it does, each session becomes easier and more automatic.

The real challenge is to keep showing up long enough for this momentum to take over. That's when discipline turns into habit, and habit into identity. Consistency becomes sustainable. Every rep, every session, and every step becomes a vote for your future self: the stronger, steadier, more vibrant version of you that you'll one day become.

Above all, learn to enjoy the process. Fitness isn't a finish line you cross once. It's a lifelong pursuit of tuning, refining, and learning to drive your machine just a little better every day.

Time to hit the road

Across these chapters, you've looked at how to maintain your vehicle from multiple angles.

Your health sets the foundation, your diet provides the inputs, and your training builds capacity. Recovery is what allows all of it to work over time. These systems don't operate in isolation. Strength in one enables the others, while neglect in any area will spill over into the rest.

This is the reality of having a single vehicle. You don't get to step outside of it. You don't get to replace it when it starts to struggle. Every experience you have, and everything you pursue, is influenced by its condition.

This isn't about making health your highest priority. It's about recognising the role it plays in everything else. Whatever you value, your physical capacity determines how effectively you can pursue it. A well-maintained vehicle expands your options, while a neglected one gradually narrows them.

Once your vehicle is in order, there is one final layer to consider. Your physical capacity is undoubtedly important, but it's still only part of the equation. Capacity determines which roads you can handle, but not which ones are available to you in the first place.

It's time to turn our attention to your finances, the fuel that determines how far and how freely you can travel.

◇

PART THREE

Your Fuel

Now that you know how to read your map and care for your vehicle, it's time to turn your attention to the fuel you need for the journey. Without adequate fuel, even the best-laid plans can come to a standstill. Your choices become limited at every turn, while small detours can lead to major setbacks. Manage it well, however, and you remain free to choose the roads you wish to travel. In the same way, how we manage our finances plays a critical role in the freedom we experience on our journey.

It's a fascinating force, money. It touches almost every person on the planet, influencing our choices, shaping societies, and driving much of human behaviour. For better or worse, it remains one of the greatest motivators of the modern age. Yet despite its power, money itself is rarely our true destination; it is simply the fuel that helps us get there. What we really seek is what money can give us, whether it's possessions, experiences, or even the feelings that we believe it will provide. In truth, money is just the medium through which we trade our time, energy, and potential for the life we want.

In these chapters, we'll explore how to use that medium consciously, so money serves you rather than controls you. We'll begin, as always, with awareness. We'll uncover what financial freedom really means and the psychology that influences how we interact with money each day. We'll explore the dynamic relationship between money in and money out, and how investing the difference allows compound growth to work in your favour. At each step, we'll explore the small, consistent habits that slowly but inevitably determine your financial trajectory.

This part of the book is not about getting rich. It's about rediscovering what life can look like when you're no longer worrying about money all the time. Rather than accumulating fuel for its own sake, the goal is simply to have enough to travel in the direction your map and vehicle allow.

CHAPTER 16

WHAT MONEY MEANS TO YOU

Money and sex influence our lives more than we'd like to admit, yet we rarely talk openly about either. It's no surprise that financial literacy is lacking when asking someone their salary or what they paid for their house can be considered offensive. We avoid the conversation, and as a result, most people stay in the dark.

Open the conversation, however, and the first thing you notice is how differently we relate to money. To some, it slips through their hands as quickly as it arrives. Only rarely is it stored, saved, or even respected. To others, it's held tightly. Some even value it so highly that it's pursued at the expense of almost anything else. While each dollar may carry the same economic value, the meaning we attach to it varies dramatically.

How you value money depends on the relationship you have with it. We all have one, and it influences every financial decision you make, whether you're aware of it or not. It's not just about what you earn, spend, or invest. It's about what money *means* to you. For some, it represents security or freedom, while others see it as validation or status. Some view it as a source of pleasure and entertainment, while others associate it with uncertainty, conflict, or tension.

Recognising what money means to you is the first step in exploring your relationship with it. Without that awareness, you'll keep repeating the same financial patterns, regardless of how much money comes into your life.

Understand your money lens

As with all subconscious behaviour, it's important to understand how it's formed in the first place.

Each of us interprets the world through a unique lens built from a lifetime of experiences. This blend of beliefs, emotions, and assumptions acts as a filter that affects our perception, choices, and behaviours.

Money, as with all other areas of our life, is viewed through that same lens. It influences how you earn, spend, save, and invest. See money as scarce, and you'll hoard it like treasure. View it as abundant, and it starts to feel disposable. Believe money is dangerous or corrupting, and you'll inadvertently push it away. See it as a tool for freedom, and you'll treat it with respect and intention.

To understand how powerful this is, consider two people. Bob and Joe start from the same financial position. They earn the same salary, have the same net wealth, and even share the same long-term goal of early retirement. On paper, their paths should look identical, yet they can have completely different financial trajectories. How their journeys ultimately unfold will depend on the lens through which they view money.

Bob grew up believing that money equals security. His parents lived through tough times, so he learned to value saving, patience, and caution. To Bob, money offers peace of mind, a way to sleep at night knowing he's safe from financial hardship. As a result, he's careful with his money, invests prudently, and focuses on building a foundation of freedom. His goal isn't wealth for its own sake, but the calm that comes with not worrying.

Joe, on the other hand, learned that money equals status. Growing up, he saw wealth used as a scoreboard. His parents' friends compared cars and houses, with praise lavished on each new luxury purchase. Behind closed doors, there was talk of "keeping up". To Joe, money is validation, a reflection of self-worth. When he earns more, he spends more. After all, you can't receive validation for a bank balance nobody sees. Each pay rise justifies a lifestyle upgrade, a public signal of progress. He's not reckless, but he is trapped in an endless chase for more.

Fast forward ten years. Bob has built a solid investment portfolio, upgrading his lifestyle only when it felt safe to do so. Joe, on the other hand, upgraded his lifestyle at every opportunity, while failing to build the solid foundation needed to sustain it. Bob has broken free from the cycle, while Joe is running faster than ever, only one stumble away from collapse.

Same starting position, same opportunities, yet vastly different destinations. The truth is that it's not just your income or your bank balance that determines your trajectory, but also your mindset.

Where your money mindset comes from

Before addressing your money mindset, it helps to understand how it evolved in the first place.

From the example above, we see how both Bob and Joe's mindsets were moulded by their upbringing. The way your parents earned, spent, argued about, or avoided money leaves a lasting imprint. If it was spent freely, you'll likely do the same. If money was a source of stress, you may associate it with anxiety. If it was rarely discussed, you may view it as unimportant.

These early experiences are critical because they form your initial lens. Once that lens is in place, you're no longer experiencing things neutrally. Confirmation bias takes over, and you begin to seek out evidence that reinforces what you already believe, while dismissing anything that challenges it. Over time, those beliefs feel less like opinions and more like facts.

It's why early conditioning can be so persistent. Future experiences continue to mould your mindset, but they're filtered through what you already believe. In most cases, they'll only reinforce the existing pattern. It usually takes a significant or repeated experience to challenge and reshape that lens.

Your personality influences how this plays out in practice. How open-minded you are will determine how likely you are to allow your filter to even be questioned in the first place. People who are naturally more open-minded are more willing to question their assumptions and adjust their behaviour. Those who are more rigid tend to hold onto existing beliefs, even when presented with conflicting evidence.

Certain personality traits can also directly influence financial behaviour. Impulsivity makes it harder to delay gratification, placing more weight on immediate rewards. A high tolerance for risk can lead to bold investment decisions, while low tolerance can result in excessive caution or missed opportunities. Conscientious individuals tend to plan, track, and follow through, while others may struggle with consistency. Even traits like optimism and pessimism play a role, influencing whether you see opportunity or downside when making financial decisions.

Finally, there are the ever-present environmental and social factors. Friends, colleagues, and social circles create a reference point for what feels normal. If everyone around you upgrades their lifestyle as income grows, it's easy to do the same without ever questioning it. With financial education lacking, it's easy to lean on our closest connections for guidance, even though they might not know any better themselves.

Talking yourself out of freedom

Once our lens is formed, we begin to develop our stories about money. Like all our stories, these are far from harmless thoughts. They become internal rules that we subconsciously and unquestionably follow.

Earlier in the book, we explored the dangers of leaving these stories unchallenged. The difficulty, however, is recognising them in the first place. It's why we spent so much time on awareness earlier: to build the habit and train the muscle. Now as we explore your financial mindset, you can put it to good use by identifying the stories that are unknowingly influencing your financial journey in the background.

Some stories you'll have inherited. Expressions like "*money doesn't grow on trees*" or "*money is the root of all evil*" are often repeated, with many adopting them as a result. Others are more personal, developing over the years based on your financial experiences. "*I'm bad with money*" or "*I'll never retire early*" are two stories you'll often hear when talking about finances.

As with all our stories, they're rarely universally true. We've seen how black swans can readily shatter a long-standing belief. The more important consideration here, however, is not whether a story is objectively true, but whether it is useful.

A belief like "*money is the root of all evil*" isn't just philosophical. It influences your behaviour. You may find yourself with a moral aversion to money and, in doing so, subconsciously push it away. You're more likely to associate money with greed rather than agency, changing how you use it as a result. It can even change your financial goals, as wealth or even financial freedom can now carry negative associations.

In this way, your stories work behind the scenes to directly influence your actions. They place limits on what you believe is possible, what risks you're willing to take, and what outcomes you expect. Until you identify these stories, you're operating within boundaries you didn't consciously choose.

When emotion takes the wheel

We like to think our financial decisions are rational. In practice, they're often deeply emotional. It's why behaviours like *comfort buying* and *panic selling* exist. This is what makes your stories so important. They influence how you feel about money, and those emotions drive your behaviour.

A belief that money is scarce creates fear, leading to hesitation, excessive caution, or an unwillingness to invest. When success is measured by wealth, the need for validation emerges, often leading to overspending or lifestyle inflation. If you believe that early retirement is possible, confidence and direction arise, resulting in long-term consistent action.

These emotions tend to lead to patterns of financial behaviour. Some people treat money as a tool for enjoyment, spending to create experiences and maximise life in the present. Others avoid engaging with money altogether, using spending as a distraction from stress or uncertainty. Then there are those driven by scarcity, holding tightly to money and experiencing guilt even when spending is reasonable. These patterns aren't fixed identities, but they are signals. They show you how your mindset is expressing itself through behaviour.

When you put it all together, you can see how your money mindset creates a self-fulfilling prophecy:

Your *lens* determines your *stories*;
Your *stories* trigger *emotions*;
Your *emotions* drive *behaviour*;
Your *behaviour* produces *outcomes*; and
Those *outcomes* then reinforce your *lens*.

Changing your financial trajectory starts by interrupting this loop. The good news is that you already have the tools required to do so.

Rewrite your future

The solution isn't to ignore your stories, but to bring them into your awareness. Once they're out in the open, you can start to unpack them.

Think about how you adopted each story in the first place. Was it repeated so often that you accepted it without question? Did you inherit it from your parents or others close to you? Or did it form after a small number of experiences that you've assumed are universal truths? This is where you can break the illusion, separating fact from fiction by looking for black swans.

Ask yourself if there is any emotional charge underlying your stories. Notice how they play out in your day-to-day life, influencing your actions, or inactions. In doing so, you'll begin to recognise which of your stories are serving you and which are holding you back. The useful stories can be retained, laid out on the table to motivate you and hold you to account. For those that are secretly sabotaging you, reframe them instead. You can't ignore reality, but you can choose more empowering interpretations that serve you instead.

Consider the following stories you might hold, and how you might reframe them:

Limiting story	→	Empowering story
"I'm not good with money."	→	*"I can learn how to manage money wisely."*
"I don't deserve more money."	→	*"My income reflects how I create, communicate, and capture value, not how I feel about myself."*
"You have to get lucky to get rich."	→	*"I can create my own luck by preparing myself to act when opportunities arise."*
"I'll have to give up the things I love to save."	→	*"I can prioritise my spending so there is still room for the things that mean the most to me."*
"I'll never retire early."	→	*"I can make changes that will move me towards financial freedom."*

Notice that none of these reframes are delusional. They're simply replacing limiting beliefs with more useful ones. The change is subtle, but the impact is significant. By moving from victimhood to empowerment, you create agency, redirecting yourself away from limitation and towards a world of possibility.

Change your internal narrative and your external results begin to align. Think you'll never retire early? You'll never try. The journey is over before it even began. Believe that it's possible instead, and you'll start looking for how. This is why two people with the same salary, opportunities, and tools can end up in completely different places. They're not living different lives – they're living different stories.

◇

EXERCISE 15

Understand your money mindset

This exercise is about uncovering how your relationship with money was formed and how it continues to influence your decisions today. Take your time with this one. The insight you build here will underpin everything that follows in later chapters.

Step 1 – Identify your current patterns

Start by reflecting on how you currently behave with money:

- Do you tend to spend freely or hold back?
- Do you actively engage with your finances, or avoid them?
- What emotions do you associate with money?

Step 2 – Trace it back

Now consider where these patterns may have come from. Start with childhood:

- Was money openly discussed, avoided, or a source of tension?
- How did your parents typically behave with money? Did they tend to save, spend, struggle, or invest?
- Were there recurring messages or phrases about money that influenced you?

Next, consider key life experiences:

- Were there moments where money created stress, conflict, or uncertainty?
- Were there experiences where money created opportunity, freedom, or pride?
- Did any specific events significantly change how you think about money?

Step 3 – Identify your stories

List the beliefs you hold about money. Include anything you frequently think or say, directly or indirectly.

Treat this as an initial capture. Over the next few days, stay alert to additional beliefs or subtle patterns and add them as they appear.

Step 4 – Test your stories

Once you have a comprehensive list, begin to question each belief:

- Is this always true?
- Where did this belief come from?
- Is it helpful, or is it holding me back?

Separate the beliefs that serve you from those that are holding you back.

Step 5 – Rewrite what no longer serves you

Where a belief is limiting, replace it with one that is more useful and aligned with the life you want. Keep the new belief constructive, but realistic. You want empowering truths, not wishful thinking.

Step 6 – Connect it to your future

Finally, step back and reflect by asking yourself:

- How has my current mindset influenced my financial decisions so far?
- If nothing changed, where does my path lead?
- What would need to change in how I think about money to produce a different outcome?

Awareness is your starting point. Once you can see the pattern clearly, you can begin to change it.

CHAPTER 17

THE FREEDOM EXCHANGE

If your job stopped paying you tomorrow, would you still show up?

Some people would answer yes. They're the ones who genuinely love what they do, finding purpose, challenge, and connection in their work. They're also the minority. For most people, a job is simply a means to an end. Remove the paycheque and you remove the employee. Money means survival and work is how they get it.

This dependence on a paycheque means that we equate money with freedom, rather than the ability to choose whether we work at all. Instead of putting plans in place to build our freedom, we fantasise about winning the lottery. To many, it feels like the only option.

Part of this is because we're never really taught how money works, but it's also due to social conditioning. Paid work is treated as an expected part of life. It's baked into the language itself. We ask each other, "*What do you do for a living?*", as if living must first be earned. That phrase embeds a social contract, one that equates living with labour and worth with output. Our days become defined by the hours we sell for money.

Few people consciously agree to those terms. Unable to see another option, they rationalise it instead, trading five days of work for two days of rest until their late sixties. We create comforting phrases like *work-life balance* to make captivity sound sustainable. Deep down, we know this isn't true freedom. It's a coping mechanism.

The realistic escape

Winning the lottery offers money but rarely freedom. Without the skills to manage it, many winners end up worse off than before. True financial freedom is deliberately engineered, not accidental. It's built on understanding money and your relationship with it. It's what happens when discipline and intention are applied over time. Money, like the mind, is an excellent tool but a terrible master. Just as you can train your thoughts and strengthen your body, you can train your finances to serve you rather than control you.

People often assume that financial freedom means never working again, but that misses the point entirely. It means never *having* to. It's about changing work from a contract to a *choice*. It gives you the power to spend your time as you choose, rather than trading it out of necessity. Working a job you don't enjoy means selling the most precious resource you'll ever have. Financial freedom means never having to make that trade again.

Financial freedom is often mistaken for self-interest, yet its impact stretches far beyond the individual. When people aren't forced to trade time for survival, they can invest their energy in work that generates real value, whether that's for themselves, their communities, or society at large. The cure for cancer might lie in the mind of someone who never had the chance to study. The next great invention could come from a parent currently working two jobs just to stay afloat. By releasing ourselves from the shackles of financial dependence, we also unleash our potential.

Of course, freedom without direction can still drift into aimlessness. That's why you'll need a clear map and a reliable vehicle to ensure that your reclaimed time is well spent. Get your finances in order, however, and you create the space to invest more deeply in both. In this way, each individual freedom helps to build the others.

The deferred life

Few people would say they don't want financial freedom. The real challenge is convincing them that it's actually possible.

It requires setting plans in motion today that may not pay off for years, possibly decades. It's the ultimate exercise in delayed gratification. That's a hard sell in a world addicted to immediacy, and precisely why so few achieve it.

Everywhere you look, people are working harder, earning more and yet somehow no closer to being financially free. Many spend decades chasing the idea of retirement only to realise they were never living along the way. It's the script we've all been taught to follow. Go to school, get a qualification, and get a job. Then work 40 to 50 hours a week for several decades and hope there's something left of your body and spirit by the time you finally retire. That's assuming you even make it that far.

While retirement is often treated as a certainty, around one in ten Australians die before reaching it.[47] Globally, it's closer to one in five.[48] For these unfortunate people, the dream of "one day"

---

[47] Derived from Australian Bureau of Statistics. *Life Tables, Australia 2021–2023* (Canberra: ABS, 2024). Figure calculated using cohort survival probabilities to age 67.

[48] Derived from United Nations, Department of Economic and Social Affairs, Population Division, *World Population Prospects 2024* (New York: United Nations, 2024). Figure based on global life table survival probabilities to approximately age 65–67.

never arrives. Yet even for those who do retire, the years spent in good health are often fewer than people imagine. Australians live into their eighties on average, but healthy life expectancy is only around 71 years for men and 73 years for women.[49] This means that many people spend at least part of their retirement managing chronic illness, disability, or reduced physical function.

For countless people, living is deferred until it's too late. The real tragedy is that this isn't the product of fate. It is the result of unconscious choices, unnecessary consumption, and a culture that encourages both.

We often equate success with our finances. Everywhere you look, the clear message is that more is better. Who's earning the most? Who's driving the latest car? Who's got the highest net worth? We've turned personal finance into a public sport, a constant comparison game that nobody can win because the goalposts keep moving. What we're not taught, however, is what this truly costs us.

Hidden behind this pursuit is the freedom we pay in exchange for it. Consumerism has become a form of modern-day servitude, with every purchase tightening the invisible chains tethering us to our jobs. By equating success with being rich, we've lost sight of what it truly means to be wealthy. We rarely measure success by inner peace, contentment, or purpose. You won't see Forbes publish a *Top 100 Most Fulfilled* list because we're celebrating the wrong things. The poorest person can feel rich in meaning and connection, while the richest can feel empty and enslaved. When wealth becomes a scoreboard, we lose the point entirely. We're left chasing the wrong goals.

---

[49] Australian Institute of Health and Welfare, *Australia's Health 2024* (Canberra: AIHW, 2024).

The rat race rebellion

Still, something is changing. A rebellion against consumer captivity is taking place, with people across the world waking up to the trap. Movements like FIRE (*Financial Independence, Retire Early)* have become rallying cries for those who refuse to spend their best years in service of someone else's dream. The core message is that money should serve you, not the other way around. Money is reframed from something you chase to something you harness. Wealth is redefined from accumulation to liberation.

FIRE advocates aren't chasing millions for status or extravagance, but autonomy. They understand that true freedom isn't measured in dollars, but in how you spend your days. It's not about quitting your job or going off grid. It's about waking up to the reality that the rat race is *optional.* It's the conscious choice to stop trading your time for money, instead building systems that give it back. It's choosing life now, not later.

It's not hard to see the appeal, especially for younger generations who've grown disillusioned with the promises that once defined success. They've seen their parents work themselves to the bone for a house, a mortgage, and a retirement that often never came. They've watched housing affordability crumble, the cost of living climb faster than wages, and the retirement age get pushed further out. The deal has changed and people aren't happy with the new terms.

FIRE offers a different approach. It begins with recognising the biggest trap that keeps us stuck in the rat race to begin with.

Hop off the treadmill

The issue with chasing more is that it's a race that never ends. There's always something newer, shinier, or bigger to pursue. It's an ever-receding horizon, a finish line that seems to only move further away the closer you get. We may dress this up as ambition, but for most people, it's just a more subtle form of captivity.

It's often our emotions and stories about money that keep us trapped. A thirst for more is often driven by *if only* thinking. "*If only I had a bigger house, then I'd be happy.*" "*If only I earned more, then I would be secure.*" You chase the next carrot that you think will bring you joy, only to quickly realise that it's temporary. A pay rise feels euphoric. A new car is exciting. Before long, however, they become the new normal and you're left chasing the next upgrade.

This cycle is known as the *hedonic treadmill.* As your standard of living rises, so do your expectations. Lifestyle creep sets in. You run faster, but remain stuck in place, convinced that the next lifestyle upgrade will finally be enough. It rarely is. Satisfaction often remains stubbornly out of reach, because a thirst for more can never be quenched.

So how do we avoid this trap? One option is to hop off the treadmill entirely, by recognising that the happiness it offers is merely an illusion. It doesn't mean abandoning ambition or refusing to grow. It's about being mindful of why you're pursuing something in the first place. By grounding your ambition in purpose, the pursuit *itself* becomes meaningful. Joy is found in the process, not the promise of happiness attached to the outcome.

Practising gratitude is a powerful tool to interrupt the cycle of wanting by reminding you of what you already have. You don't need to seek happiness in consumption when you're already content.

Ultimately, the most important thing is to stop chasing a horizon you can never reach. To do this, you need to determine when enough is enough.

Enough

In economics, "utility" refers to the satisfaction or happiness we get from a product or experience. Economists have found that many goods and services follow a pattern of *diminishing marginal utility*. In other words, the more you consume, the less you enjoy each additional unit. Think of a bag of chips. The first few taste incredible. Keep eating, however, and the pleasure begins to fade. By the end, you're no longer eating out of enjoyment or even hunger. You're just finishing the pack because it's there.

Your money works the same way. Studies have repeatedly found that beyond a certain point, additional income adds little to happiness.[50] In *Your Money or Your Life*, Joe Dominguez and Vicki Robin describe this as your *Fulfilment Curve.*[51] When you have very little, small improvements have an outsized impact. Securing food, shelter, and safety dramatically lifts your quality of life. Once those basics are covered, however, the gains shrink. Comforts may make life easier, but they're not nearly as transformative. Push further into luxuries, and the returns shrink again. They cost the most yet add the least. Eventually, what felt like a reward can start to feel like a burden. That car you once

---

[50] See, for example, Daniel Kahneman and Angus Deaton, 'High income improves evaluation of life but not emotional well-being', *Proceedings of the National Academy of Sciences* 107, no. 38 (2010): 16489–16493; Andrew T. Jebb et al., 'Happiness, income satiation and turning points around the world', *Nature Human Behaviour* 2 (2018): 33–38.

[51] Vicki Robin and Joe Dominguez, *Your Money or Your Life: Transforming Your Relationship with Money and Achieving Financial Independence*, revised ed. (New York: Penguin Books, 2018).

loved becomes another expense to protect, maintain, and worry about. The curve turns negative. More becomes less.

If having more first lifts your happiness, but eventually erodes it, the obvious question is where to stop. The answer lies not in abundance, but in *enough*. Defining what this means to you frees you from the illusion that happiness is always one purchase or promotion away. The goalposts stop moving and you can finally feel content with what you have.

Everything has a price

We tend to think of money in terms of what it can buy rather than what it *costs*. The true price of every dollar is the slice of your life spent acquiring it. The challenge is that we grossly underestimate the conversion rate.

Say you're paid $240 for an eight-hour workday. On paper, that's $30 per hour. But that's just the hours spent in the office. Once you factor in getting ready, commuting, and the time you need to mentally decompress after work, you're probably closer to ten hours. Now subtract your costs. Tax, transport, and other work-related expenses quickly add up. Once everything is deducted, you might only be left with $150 per day. For ten hours of effort, that means your real wage was $15 per hour, only half of what your paycheque would have you believe.

That is your real exchange rate. If something costs you $45, that's three hours of your life. The question then moves from, "*Do I want this?*" to "*Is this worth the hours of my life it will cost me?*" How many hours, weeks, or even years of your life are you willing to pay? More becomes far less appealing when you see the real cost.

Let's say you want to upgrade your car to a newer model. If it costs $30,000, the real price of that upgrade is 2,000 hours of your time. Is that trade worth it to you? Only you can decide. You may consider it a fair deal, or you may find that it's robbing you of the very freedom you're trying to obtain.

The goal isn't to *avoid* the trade but to understand the *exchange rate*. The higher you climb the fulfilment curve, the steeper it becomes. While it may only take a day's work to fill your fridge, it can take years to afford a new car that barely changes your happiness. As the curve flattens, each additional dollar spent costs more of your life but delivers less in return. Eventually you'll reach the point where your time spent earning the money could have been exchanged for greater fulfilment elsewhere. This is the trap that many people fall into. They miss the turning point where the exchange is no longer worth it.

I learned this the hard way. For years, I believed more money meant more freedom. So, I chased the next milestone, be it a bigger pay rise, another property, or a higher net worth. Each one felt like progress, yet every time I arrived, the goalposts moved. The *enough* I thought I was chasing was just *more* in disguise, a mirage that faded the closer I got. I was using financial prudence as an excuse for postponing life. "*More money, more freedom*" was just two versions of *more* hiding in plain sight.

Eventually I realised that in chasing my freedom, I had traded it along the way. I was working myself to the bone, juggling investments and a full-time job, only to accumulate wealth beyond my needs. I'd already mastered my spending habits and kept lifestyle creep in check. The only thing keeping me shackled was my desire for more, creating stress and headaches without any real gain to show for it. My version of more may have been grounded in security rather than luxury, but that didn't make it any less of a trap. I had forgotten the very reason I started this journey in the first place.

That's the real danger. You get so used to running that you forget that stopping was ever an option. The pursuit of more keeps you on the treadmill long after you've already reached enough, trading your time and energy for things you didn't need in the first place.

Choose your terms of trade

Ultimately, we each get maybe 70-odd years if we're lucky. That's your real bank balance. How you choose to spend it is up to you; just make sure you check the price tag first. This isn't about settling. It's about living. And the best way to do that is to make sure you're getting value for the time that you spend.

Pause for a moment and look at the exchanges you're making right now. Are they moving you closer to the life you want, or simply towards the next temporary high? How do they *feel*? Do they energise you and provide meaning? Or do they drain you, twisting the deal by demanding more time after the trade just to decompress? If you feel alive in the process, perhaps the trade is fair. If your days feel like transactions, however, maybe it's time to reconsider the terms.

Get clear on your vision of enough, not in dollars, but in life. What would fulfilment feel like if you stripped away every external measure of success? What would your days look like if money were no longer the reason behind your decisions? Would you still work the same job and live the same routine, or would you make space for something different?

If the answer is the latter, then why wait? Freedom is rarely found in the distant "someday". It's found in small daily choices that align what you do with who you are. You might not yet have the financial freedom to quit your job, but you can start living by the same principles by investing your energy where it truly counts.

Get crystal clear on your *why*, the deeper reason that gives your time meaning, and then be honest about the cost of pursuing it. Maybe you'll find that some of what you've been chasing isn't worth the price. Better still, you may discover that the cost of living aligned with your values is far lower than you first imagined.

In the end, the real measure of wealth isn't the size of your portfolio, but the peace you feel in how you spend your finite time. Would you rather die with more money and more regrets, or with fewer possessions but having lived a life that was deeply your own?

That's the *Freedom Exchange*. You can't escape the trade, but you can choose which terms you're willing to accept. To do this, you first need to understand how you value both sides of the equation.

◇

EXERCISE 16

Defining enough

Before you can move towards financial freedom, you need to understand what you're actually aiming for. This exercise is about clarity, not precision. The aim is simply to understand what you're chasing and why.

Step 1 – What does enough mean to you?

Describe, in practical terms, what financial freedom looks like to you. Be as specific as you can. Consider the following:

- What would you spend more time doing?
- What would you spend less time doing?
- Are there things you would cut completely?

Focus on how you want your days to feel and function, rather than the financial figure required to get there. For example, you might say, "*I want sufficient funds to ensure that I can cover any bills or emergencies, while also travelling twice per year.*" Ground your definition in what it *provides* rather than what it costs. This ensures you're chasing something meaningful instead of an arbitrary figure. The price can come later.

Step 2 – How close are you right now?

Now reflect on your current situation.

- Which parts of your life already feel sufficient or satisfying?
- Where are you still pursuing more, and why?
- If your financial position stayed exactly the same, what would need to be true for you to feel content?

This step separates what genuinely improves your life from what is driven by habit, comparison, or expectation. If you already have what you need yet your target continues to expand, it may be a sign that you're valuing the number itself more than what it enables.

Step 3 – What are you really chasing?

Think about something you're currently working towards, such as a large purchase, a financial milestone, or even a promotion.

- What do you believe it will give you?
- Why does that matter? Use the *Five Whys* to go deeper than the first answer.
- Is there another way to access that same outcome or feeling?

Step 4 – Understand the price

Now consider what this pursuit requires of you:

- What is it costing in time, energy, or attention?
- How does it affect your stress, focus, or relationships?
- Does the pursuit itself feel meaningful, or only the outcome?

You don't need to quantify anything here. The task is to honestly reflect on the trade.

Step 5 – Alignment check

Return to your definition of enough. Does this pursuit move you closer to that life, or further away? If you already had enough, would you still choose it?

If the answer is no, it's worth asking why it's on your path at all. Once you see the trade more clearly, it becomes much harder to ignore.

CHAPTER 18

THE THREE FINANCIAL LEVERS

One of the most persistent beliefs about money is that financial freedom simply isn't possible for the average person. It's often framed as something reserved for a select group armed with complex strategies, technical jargon, and expensive degrees. In reality, the underlying mechanics are neither complicated nor sophisticated. They're basic arithmetic.

What makes money feel complex is the volume of noise surrounding it. Headlines, hot tips, and opinions on how to get rich are everywhere, often sold by people with ulterior motives. Contrary to what they'd have you believe, you don't need to become an expert at stock picking, tax structures, or predicting the market to achieve financial success. You simply need to understand the small set of variables that drive the outcome.

It's a similar story to what we saw with fitness and nutrition. There's endless debate over methods, yet most results are driven by a handful of fundamentals. It's easy to get pulled into the detail, while overlooking what actually moves the needle.

Strip everything back, and your financial trajectory is determined by three moving parts. Understand how they interact, and everything else becomes optional refinement.

The financial triad

No matter who you are, how much you earn, or how much you own, your financial trajectory is governed by three simple levers: how much money comes in, how much goes out, and what you do with the difference.

Think of it as a simple system. Money flows in through income, while some flows out through spending. Whatever remains can either sit idle or be put to work where it compounds over time, generating additional inflows into the system.

We'll explore each part of this triad in more detail over the coming chapters, but for now, let's introduce them at a high level.

Money in

This is the most straightforward and visible component. It is every dollar that flows towards you. Salary, business income, freelance work, side hustles, bonuses, investment income, and interest all count.

At the beginning of your financial journey, most of your income comes from your time. You work hours and get paid accordingly. Later, if you play the game well, a greater portion comes from your assets. Your money begins to generate income on its own.

Money out

This is everything you spend to live your life. Housing, food, transport, insurance, holidays, subscriptions, and everyday purchases are all included here.

Whether it's essential or an impulse purchase you barely remember the next day, it all flows out the same. Every dollar spent here is a dollar that can't be put to work elsewhere.

Investing

If money in and money out were the only factors, building wealth would be nothing more than a savings contest. Investing is what allows your surplus to grow and compound over time.

Some investments produce income of their own, while others grow in value. Many do both. Early on, investing often looks unimpressive. Over time, however, it becomes the dominant force in achieving financial freedom.

Surplus comes first

Before anything else can happen, money in must exceed money out. This is non-negotiable. Without a surplus, there is nothing to invest. Without investment, there is no growth. No growth means you're forever dependent on trading your time for money.

This is not philosophical; it's mathematical. You cannot build financial freedom by consistently spending more than you earn. It's the financial equivalent of trying to lose weight while eating more calories than you burn. You must first create a gap, even if it's a small one. As soon as your money out is less than your money in, a surplus begins to form.

This is the first step towards achieving financial freedom, but it's also where many people stop. As their surplus grows, they begin to accumulate cash but never put it to work. Keeping some money aside as a buffer is sensible, but money that never leaves the sidelines cannot move you forward. To change your trajectory, that surplus needs a role.

When you begin investing, the system starts to build momentum. Your money begins working alongside you. At first, progress is largely driven by your own contributions. Over time, as your investments generate returns, the balance shifts. With enough time, they begin to contribute more than you do. Eventually, you reach the point where your assets produce more than you need to live on. At that point, work is no longer required to fund your life. It becomes a choice. This is what it means to be financially free.

Where that point sits for you depends entirely on the lifestyle you choose to maintain. Higher spending requires a larger asset base to sustain it. A more frugal lifestyle lowers the threshold significantly. Neither approach is inherently better. Just remember the real cost of more and make sure you're comfortable paying the price.

If it were so easy...

Once you strip everything back, the process is remarkably simple. Spend less than you earn, invest the difference, and give the system the time it needs to generate results. That is the entire system. There are no hidden steps, no special qualifications, and no need to rely on luck over the long term. At this point, many people's natural reaction is to dismiss the concept entirely. Surely if it were this simple, more people would have already done it?

While the system is simple, it is far from easy. The process demands sustained discipline, delayed gratification, and an ability to act rationally throughout. As we saw earlier, money is tied closely to emotion. Being able to keep a level head is a necessary ingredient for long-term success. Understanding the system is straightforward. Following it consistently and over long enough periods of time, however, is where most plans fall apart.

The underlying mechanics don't change. If you create a surplus and put it to work, the trend follows from the mathematics over time. Your starting point influences the timeframe, not the basic principle. Applied consistently and diligently, the system compounds in your favour. That consistency is the key. The objective is not to optimise perfectly, but to build an approach that is sustainable over years and decades, through good times and bad.

You will need to use all three levers. Each one amplifies the others, while weakness in one will limit the entire system. Without sufficient income, a meaningful surplus never forms. Without control over spending, increases in income are absorbed just as quickly. Without investing, the surplus remains static and never compounds.

When they are aligned, however, the system begins to build momentum. The surplus grows, investments start contributing, and your progress begins to feel tangible. What begins as a slow, deliberate process becomes increasingly self-sustaining over time.

Set a course

In the following chapters, we'll explore each of these levers in more detail. How do you manage spending without feeling deprived? How can you increase income without burning out? How can you invest sensibly and manage the risks? Before refining any of those, however, one step remains. To plan any journey, you must understand your current position as well as your destination. That means quantifying where you are today and what enough looks like for you.

In the next chapter, we will establish both. You'll calculate your current net wealth, and define your *Freedom Figure*, the level at which the value generated by your assets is sufficient to support your lifestyle.

◇

CHAPTER 19

KNOW YOUR WEALTH

Financial freedom requires a plan. It means understanding where you are, where you want to go, and mapping a path to get there.

For most people, that plan never materialises. They may talk about retiring early or being financially free, but few understand what that actually means in practice. Many people don't know their net wealth, their annual spend, or how much they truly need to sustain the lifestyle they want. Without that knowledge, financial freedom remains an abstract concept rather than a goal.

It's no wonder it feels complicated and out of reach when so many people don't know exactly what it is they're chasing. Without a clear target, there's no path. Drift sets in and hope replaces a plan. But hope isn't a strategy.

Gaining control over your financial future starts with clarity. What does it take to become financially free? What do you need to do to get there? Before you can answer these, you first need to take stock of where you are right now.

Your two key financial indicators

To plot a course to any destination, you need to know where you're starting from. We'll calculate an initial estimate of your position at the end of the chapter, but first you need to understand the basic concepts.

Start with what you own. These are your assets. This includes anything that has value, such as your home, savings, superannuation, shares, businesses, or your car. Then look at what you owe. These are your liabilities. Common examples are mortgages, loans, credit cards, and anything else that needs to be repaid. Subtract the value of your liabilities from your assets and you're left with your *net wealth*.

Next, you'll need to see where your money is going. Take your total money in and subtract your total money out. This gives you your *net cashflow*. If it's positive, you're building savings. If it's negative, you're eating into them.

These are your two most important financial indicators. Net wealth shows the capital available to you. Net cashflow reveals whether your lifestyle is adding to that capital or draining it. Understanding these two measures is key to realising your financial freedom.

Diagnose your financial health

Once you have your net wealth and net cashflow, the next step is to understand what it tells you. Like any data, the numbers by themselves are meaningless without context. You need to understand what they say about your financial health.

Think of financial health like a ladder. The path to financial freedom tends to follow a fairly predictable sequence, even if people begin on different rungs. Moving up the ladder isn't complicated, but it isn't guaranteed either. It takes discipline and consistency applied over a long enough period of time. In broad terms, there are seven stages. The ladder on the following page shows how each stage typically feels in practice.

The Financial Health Ladder

Rung	Financial reality
Dependency	• *Assets and cashflow are zero or negative* • *Reliance on others to stay afloat* • *Money is about survival, not choice*
Paycheque to paycheque	• *Income covers costs, but only barely* • *Nothing meaningful accumulates* • *Little margin for error between paycheques*
Treading water	• *You are no longer sinking, but still fragile* • *Savings are starting to build* • *One large expense can wipe out months of effort*
Stable	• *A savings buffer is in place* • *Unexpected bills are manageable* • *Day-to-day money stress starts to ease*
Accumulating	• *Investing has become regular* • *Assets are growing and starting to generate income* • *Your financial future starts to feel lighter*
Financial freedom	• *Your assets can fund your lifestyle* • *Paid work becomes optional* • *Your time starts to feel like your own again*
Financial abundance	• *Wealth grows faster than you reasonably spend* • *Money becomes a tool for choice, not security* • *Contribution and legacy become realistic options*

At the lower rungs, your biggest wins come from cashflow. When you are dependent, living paycheque to paycheque, or only just treading water, your income is still made almost entirely by trading your finite time and energy. Increasing your hourly rate, or making your money go further by cutting your expenses, has an outsized impact. Until you can generate a surplus, there is nothing to invest, making growth largely irrelevant at this stage.

Once you're stable and accumulating a surplus, the focus turns to directing that surplus into productive assets. Increasing your income and controlling your expenses are still useful, but growth starts to pull more of the weight. From here, progress increasingly becomes a function of time. Your job is to stay the course, keep investing consistently, and let compounding do what it does best.

Later, when your capital base is large enough, investment returns do most of the heavy lifting. They move the needle far more than another pay rise or minor spending cut ever could. You still need to ensure your expenses don't get out of hand, or you may find yourself stuck on the hedonic treadmill, but your margin for error is much greater. At this point, the balance of power has shifted. Your money is now doing most of the work instead of you.

You may already have an idea of where you sit on this ladder. If not, the exercise at the end of this chapter will give you a rough idea. With that understanding, the next step is to choose a clear destination. First, let's be clear on exactly what you're chasing.

Net wealth, not worth

If you've looked into finance before, you may notice that what I'm describing here as net *wealth* is often referred to as net *worth*. Technically, it's the same calculation, but the choice of wording here is intentional. As we saw with NLP, the language we choose to use matters.

What happens if you calculate your net worth and it comes out negative? Does that mean you're worthless and that you have no value? Of course not. Money measures resources, not character. Your value as a person cannot be defined by the number of arbitrary pieces of paper sitting in your bank account.

Calculating net worth subtly turns the number into a judgement. It invites comparison, tempting you to chase a bigger figure simply to feel more successful or more important. Attention turns from what you need to how you compare.

Wealth keeps it practical. It treats money for what it is: a resource. Calculating your net wealth becomes an audit, not a scorecard. It becomes an honest assessment of the facts, rather than an emotional judgement on your perceived success. You're simply taking inventory of your available resources.

This is just as important when setting your financial goals. When you detach money from identity, you become clear about what it is you actually need. You stop chasing a number to prove something and start choosing a number that supports the life you want to live. Your mindset moves from *more* to *enough*.

Choose a SMART destination

So how do you choose a financial destination? "*I want to be financially free*" sounds good in conversation, but it's a vision, not firm coordinates. You can't move towards something you haven't clearly defined. Imagine setting off on a road trip without knowing where you're going. You pack the car and head off. Initially you might feel like you're making progress as the kilometres tick away. But eventually you realise you're just burning fuel with no idea where you'll end up. Vague goals lead to burnout and drift, but clear ones create purposeful and aligned action.

One of the simplest and most reliable ways to set a destination is the SMART framework. Goals should be specific, measurable, achievable, relevant, and time-bound. Each part plays a role. Specific gives you a clear target so you don't drift towards the wrong destination. Measurable lets you see progress, keeping you motivated. Achievable protects confidence so you don't quit halfway through. Relevant ensures the goal is aligned with your core values and beliefs, not your ego. Time-bound adds a sense of urgency, preventing "someday" from stretching into years.

Together, they work as a system. They turn a vague intention into a commitment you can act on. Without that structure, it's easy to collect dozens of goals while achieving none of them. This approach isn't just unique to money. It works for training, health, business, or any other area of life. The clearer the target, the easier it is to make decisions that move you towards it.

To turn financial freedom into an achievable goal, we need to do the same. The first step is to define what it looks like for you in practice. What does your lifestyle cost to maintain on an ongoing basis? Once that's clear, all that remains is to calculate the assets required to sustain it.

Find your Freedom Figure

The mechanics of financial freedom are simple in principle. Wealth generates returns, returns generate income, and income covers expenses. Generate enough income from assets, and you no longer need to sell your time to make up the difference.

If your spending is less than the income generated by your capital, you don't need to touch the capital itself. Keep it invested, and it can continue to generate returns year after year. If those returns are sufficient to cover your expenses, you can fund your lifestyle entirely from the income generated by your wealth. In principle, the same pool of capital can continue supporting you indefinitely. That's financial freedom.

At a high level, we can use some basic maths to estimate what that might require. Using a simple five per cent return assumption, $1,000,000 of invested wealth would generate roughly $50,000 per year. If your annual spending remained at or below that level, the returns could cover it.

This is a direct relationship: the higher your annual spending, the more capital you'll require to fund it. Under the same five per cent return assumption, you'd need $2,000,000 of invested capital to cover an annual spend of $100,000.

It won't be exact in practice. Markets move up and down, affecting your annual returns. Taxes reduce how much of those returns you keep. Inflation increases your future expenses. Think of this as a planning tool, not a guarantee. It's a compass, rather than a precise GPS, but for setting a course financially it's more than good enough.

Once you understand this relationship, you can work backwards. You no longer need to fantasise about an arbitrary amount of money. Instead, you can define the level of wealth you need for your investments to cover your lifestyle. That number is your *Freedom Figure*, and you only need two inputs to estimate it.

First up is your annual cost of living. How much do you actually need each year to support the lifestyle you want? This is where you begin to see the true cost of *more*. Every lifestyle upgrade will cost a portion of your remaining time to fund it. Double your spending and you roughly double the wealth required to maintain it. In practice, progressive tax systems often make the deal much worse. Higher incomes mean a larger share of your returns is taxed away, so the assets required can be significantly more than double.

Once you have your annual spend, you'll need to estimate your expected rate of return. For many people, something around four to six per cent from diversified, lower-risk investments is a reasonable long-term assumption. Higher returns are certainly possible, but they usually come with higher volatility, which may not suit your needs. The key here is consistency and a strategy you can stick with through both good years and bad.

Once you have those two numbers, the maths is straightforward.

Want $75,000 per year from a five per cent investment return?
$75,000 ÷ 0.05 = $1,500,000 of income-generating assets.[52]

How about $100,000 with eight per cent?
$100,000 ÷ 0.08 = $1,250,000.

The actual numbers will vary and that's to be expected. These aren't hard predictions, but simply targets for you to aim at. They turn a vague notion of financial freedom into something clear and measurable.

As your understanding deepens and your circumstances evolve, this figure may change. Your lifestyle, priorities, and approach to investing won't remain fixed, and neither should the number that reflects them. What's important is that you're no longer chasing an idea, but a clear destination. From there, the focus turns to how you intend to reach it.

A different philosophy

Before moving on, it's worth noting one key assumption in this strategy. Everything here assumes you leave your capital largely untouched and live off the returns indefinitely. It's a conservative strategy, but is it optimal?

There's another school of thought, popularised by Bill Perkins in *Die With Zero*. Instead of preserving capital forever, you deliberately spend it down across your lifetime, aiming to finish with little or nothing left – to "*die with zero*".[53] In theory, this lowers the amount you need upfront. A smaller *Freedom Figure* means you reach financial freedom sooner.

---

[52] Percentages are converted into decimals for calculations by dividing by 100, so five per cent is written as 0.05.
[53] Bill Perkins, *Die with Zero: Getting All You Can from Your Money and Your Life*, Houghton Mifflin Harcourt, 2020.

There's real logic to that approach. Money only has value while you're alive to use it. Experiences delayed too long are experiences lost. But it does introduce a different type of risk. Live longer than expected, face poor market returns, or encounter major expenses late in life, and you may run short when you have the least ability to recover. In trying to die with zero you may end up living with zero instead.

Neither philosophy is right or wrong. They simply optimise for different things. One prioritises maximising consumption and experiences earlier. The other prioritises security, resilience, and optionality.

Personally, I prefer the more conservative approach. Watching my wealth steadily decline in later years would create the very stress I'm trying to avoid. I'd rather risk dying with money left over than risk outliving my savings.

You may choose differently. Decide which risks you're more comfortable carrying and plan your journey accordingly.

◇

EXERCISE 17

Establish your baseline

Now it's time to establish where you stand today.

Focus on completeness over precision. This is a baseline estimate only, not a detailed analysis.

Step 1 – Calculate your net wealth

Start by listing everything you own:

- Cash and savings;
- Superannuation or retirement accounts;
- Shares or exchange-traded funds (ETFs);
- Property;
- Vehicles;
- Business interests; and
- Any other saleable assets (art, watches, high-value furniture).

If you're unsure of exact values, use conservative estimates.

Next, list everything you owe:

- Mortgages;
- Personal loans;
- Credit cards;
- HECS/HELP or other education debts; and
- Any other liabilities.

Subtract your total liabilities from your total assets to calculate your net wealth. Remember this is not a scorecard. It's a snapshot of your current position so you can work from reality rather than assumption, and focus your efforts accordingly.

Step 2 – Estimate the cost of your ideal lifestyle

Before choosing a number, reflect on what is important to you.

Think back to your values. What does a typical week aligned with those values look like in practice? What would that cost to support?

Now extend that to an annual figure. Use the following as a guide:

- Start with a rough idea of what you're currently spending;
- Remove spending that no longer aligns with your values; and
- Add in spending you would willingly increase if you had the funds to do so.

Keep this high-level. A rough estimate is sufficient. In the next chapter, you'll track actual spending and compare it to this assumption. For now, you're simply estimating what you believe your ideal life should cost.

Step 3 – Estimate your *Freedom Figure*

Now convert your estimated lifestyle cost into a capital requirement.

For simplicity, assume a conservative long-term return of five per cent. You can adjust this later, once we've covered investing in more detail. Use the following formula:

Annual spend ÷ Return = Freedom Figure

For example, $80,000 in annual spending, using a five per cent return gives:

$80,000 ÷ 0.05 = $1,600,000

To sanity-check your estimate, you can also run the calculation at four or six per cent to see how much the number changes.

Keep in mind that this is a planning estimate only, not a precise forecast. Tax will reduce how much of that income you keep, inflation will increase costs over time, and investment returns will vary.

You don't need to account for these yet. This is simply your starting point. You'll refine these numbers as your understanding improves.

CHAPTER 20

CUT THE LEAKS

Before you can put a surplus to work, you first need to have one.

Financial freedom relies on compounding investments. That can only happen when there's money left over to invest. For many people, this is the first stumbling block. No surplus, no engine. No engine, no growth. Without growth, you're left forever treading water.

The first step, therefore, is to create that surplus. You only have two levers available: earn more or spend less. Both are important, but they aren't equal. Spending has a lower ceiling, as there's only so much you can realistically cut. Income, on the other hand, has almost unlimited upside, making it the more powerful lever over the long term.

At first glance, it might seem logical to focus on income first. In practice, this approach rarely produces lasting results. True financial freedom begins with mastering your spending.

Fix your spending first

Spending is largely behavioural. We must start here for the simple reason that no level of income can save you from bad spending habits. Just as you can't out-train a bad diet, you can't out-earn bad spending. It's not uncommon for someone to double their salary and feel no better off six months later. If your expenses increase in line with your income, you'll never create a surplus. It's like pouring fuel into a tank riddled with leaks; the more you add, the faster it seems to disappear. That's not an income problem. It's a spending problem.

Beyond behaviour, there are also some basic mathematical reasons to start here. You've probably heard the phrase, "*A penny saved is a penny earned.*" Thanks to taxation, that's rarely the case in practice. Every dollar you spend comes from income that has already been taxed. Depending on your marginal tax rate, an extra dollar of spending money may require between $1.50 and $2 of pre-tax income. For example, at a marginal tax rate of 40%, cutting spending by $10,000 has the same effect on your surplus as increasing your pre-tax income by $16,667. In other words, a dollar saved is often worth significantly *more* than a dollar earned.

The leverage doesn't stop there. Lowering your spending also reduces the amount of capital required to sustain your lifestyle in the first place. The less your life costs, the smaller your *Freedom Figure* becomes. Every dollar you don't need to spend lowers the amount of capital required. Reducing spending also increases your investable surplus, accelerating the timeline in the process. In other words, it increases the fuel going into your financial engine while simultaneously shortening the distance you need to travel.

The best part is that it's a lever you can pull immediately. Spending decisions happen constantly, with each day presenting dozens of small opportunities to adjust your behaviour. By becoming mindful of your patterns, you can start to move the needle right now. Income, on the other hand, often depends on promotions, new skills, opportunities, or broader market conditions. It can take months or even years to meaningfully change.

This is why spending is such a powerful lever. Understand it, and you define how much money you need. Master it, and you make reaching that number far easier.

The consumption parallel

Mastering your spending follows a similar pattern to mastering your diet. When you compare money to calories, you'll soon realise that both operate under closely related behavioural and mechanical rules.

Calories are your body's energy budget, while money is your financial budget. Building muscle and exercising increase the number of calories you can consume each day, in the same way that earning more income increases your available spending. Both are finite, and both follow the simple equation of resources in, resources out. The balance of this equation dictates your outcomes. But as we saw with diet, the maths isn't the hard part.

Just as eating is rarely only about hunger, spending is rarely about survival. Most purchases are made from convenience, impulse, ego, or simply habit. Our spending is often just as mindless as our eating. The two are mechanically and behaviourally linked. This means that the same awareness and discipline you applied to cleaning up your diet can also be used here. Before you can do that, however, you need to reframe how you think about spending altogether.

Maximise your fuel efficiency

For many people, the idea of cutting spending is met with immediate resistance. It feels like sacrifice, or even deprivation. What we're really talking about here is optimisation. We live in a world of finite resources, which means we must allocate them carefully. Our time, calories, and money are all limited. It's why we spent so long working through your map. Once you know what you truly value, you can start directing your resources accordingly.

People with a frugal mindset understand this instinctively. It's often misunderstood and lumped in the same basket as stinginess. In truth, they're almost opposites. Stinginess is driven by fear. It stems from a belief that money is scarce, so cost becomes the only consideration. The cheapest option is chosen even if it makes your life objectively worse. Experiences that would enrich your life are dismissed entirely because of their price tag. It feels restrictive because it is.

Frugality, on the other hand, recognises that money is finite. Whether you see money as scarce or abundant, the truth is that it is limited. That distinction grounds frugality in reality. Even the ultra-wealthy still live in a world of finite resources. There are always trade-offs; you still need to choose. Frugality simply means extracting the most value from those choices. Since your money was earned with your time, it's really about getting the most value from your life.

It also allows you to reduce your cost of living, lowering your *Freedom Figure* in the process. You buy back your remaining life at a cheaper rate, without diminishing the quality. Frugal people recognise money as the valuable tool that it is. It is something to be optimised for our benefit, not hoarded indiscriminately.

The key to this mindset is recognising that price and value are not the same. In Chapter 12, we saw how some foods are calorie-dense with little nutrition, while others are nutritional powerhouses for relatively few calories. Similarly, some purchases and experiences are hollow regardless of their price tag. They empty our bank account without ever filling our cup.

Others pay us lasting dividends, dramatically improving the quality of our lives.

A $200 purchase affects your bank balance the same way, whether it's a purchase you barely remember or the experience of a lifetime. The price may have been the same, but the return is not. In contrast to stinginess, the goal of frugality isn't to spend less money. It's to buy more value. It's the financial equivalent of saving your calories for meals that you'll actually enjoy. Frugality is optimisation. Stinginess is starvation. Frugality is maximising your fuel efficiency, while stinginess is refusing to drive at all.

Applying a frugal mindset is as simple as using the following three principles:

- Cut spending on the things that don't matter to you;
- Spend intentionally on the things that do; and
- Wherever possible, get the same value for less.

Cut the leaks, choose roads worth travelling, then improve your fuel efficiency so you can go further with the same amount of fuel. That's the essence of frugality.

Early on, this may require tightening a few areas to create the surplus needed to start your financial engine. As your finances grow stronger over time, more of that surplus can be directed towards the things that genuinely matter to you. The goal is simply to use your money mindfully, extracting the greatest value from your finite resources. That process begins with understanding what you're spending, and more importantly, why.

The drivers of spending

Before we can evaluate our spending, we must first recognise what is driving it. Most purchases aren't the result of calm, rational decision-making, but rather a range of influences operating beneath the surface.

The first is your individual relationship with money. Earlier, we explored how your upbringing, experiences, and beliefs work together to create your money mindset. Some people grow up viewing money as scarce and fragile, while others see it as abundant and easily replaced. Some are naturally cautious, while others are more comfortable spending. These underlying beliefs influence how you feel about parting with money in the first place.

We've seen how beliefs can trigger an emotional response. The same pattern plays out here, with much of our spending being driven by an underlying emotion. Whether it's stress, frustration, or simply boredom, buying something can temporarily improve our mood. The danger of this retail therapy is that while the boost itself is short-lived, the behaviour can easily become ingrained.

These behaviours are often reinforced by psychological biases. We've already seen how a present bias can trigger a YOLO mindset. Spending is one of the most common ways it manifests. When the present moment is given disproportionate weight, spending becomes an easy way to chase instant gratification while pushing the consequences further into the future. Once a budget or spending goal is broken, it's easy to abandon the plan entirely. Anyone who has ever blown their diet and decided to "start again tomorrow" will recognise the pattern.

Another common bias is *mental accounting*.[54] It's our tendency to value money differently depending on where it came from. A dollar earned through hard work often feels more valuable than a dollar received through a tax refund or unexpected windfall,

---

[54] Richard H. Thaler, 'Mental Accounting Matters', *Journal of Behavioral Decision Making* 12, no. 3 (1999): 183–206.

despite having the same purchasing power. Money that arrives easily is often treated as disposable and spent far more freely simply because it didn't feel hard to obtain. It's another reason why lottery winners often manage to blow through life-changing sums. A frugal mindset avoids this trap entirely. By recognising that a dollar is a dollar regardless of its source, the cost is fixed. What varies is the value you can extract from it.

It's not only our individual psychology that reinforces our behaviours, but social forces too. Whether it's FOMO, a perceived need to keep up with peers, or simply ego, marketing and advertising amplify these pressures. Meanwhile, modern payment systems have removed much of the friction from spending. With contactless payments, saved cards and one-click purchases, it has never been easier to part with our money.

When you combine your money mindset, emotional triggers, cognitive biases, and social forces, clear spending patterns begin to form. Just as eating patterns develop over time, financial behaviours gradually become routines that no longer feel like decisions at all. Many purchases begin to happen automatically. Discretionary spending becomes embedded in rituals, while recurring expenses no longer attract scrutiny. Money starts coming out of your account without you ever questioning whether it was worth the cost.

Over time, these behaviours slowly erode your path to financial freedom. The first step in addressing them is recognising that it's happening. That awareness begins with tracking.

Create visibility

In the same way that tracking calories helps you understand your diet, tracking spending reveals the structure of your financial habits. Many people tend to dramatically underestimate both.

Tracking helps correct the error. By shining a light on where your money is actually going, tracking exposes behaviours and hidden expenses you may not even realise are there.

Without that visibility, it's easy for spending to slowly creep higher over time. Your income increases, but not your surplus. You remain stuck on the hedonic treadmill, working harder, earning more, yet no closer to becoming free. Without awareness, the treadmill simply keeps accelerating. We've already seen how you can step off the treadmill by choosing enough instead of more. Tracking helps you realise that you're on it in the first place.

So how do you start tracking your finances? For a period of time, you'll track every dollar you spend. As with calorie tracking, the purpose is to understand your habits, not to punish yourself for them. Think of it as gathering data. The goal here is simply to gain visibility.

There are many ways to do this. You can use a spreadsheet, a budgeting app, or even a simple notebook. The method doesn't matter, provided that you record everything. This may feel tedious at first, but the habit forms quickly. After a week or two it becomes routine. You don't need to do it forever, just long enough to develop a clear picture of your spending patterns.

One bonus of tracking is that it can start to change behaviour almost immediately. The Hawthorne effect we saw with tracking calories applies here too. When every purchase is written down, you begin to pause and consider whether it was worth it. Frivolous expenses get harder to justify now that you have a record of them.

Most people are surprised by what this exercise reveals. Just as many people underestimate how much they eat until they track calories, most people underestimate their spending. Tracking shows you the actual numbers. Hidden costs become visible.

Some you may be unaware of, others you may have forgotten about entirely. You may discover that some items are costing much more than you realised due to processing fees or other charges. Many people discover that a single category of expense consumes far more of their income than they ever realised.

None of this is a cause for judgement. It's simply what happens when spending occurs largely on autopilot. Bringing awareness to your patterns and behaviours is the first step in turning automatic decisions into mindful ones.

For many people, this exercise is what turns opportunity cost from a theory to a practical mindset. By revealing the true cost of your expenses, you can start to weigh them up against each other. You might not have realised that a twice-daily coffee habit was costing you $60 per week, or roughly $3,000 per year. Perhaps that is worth it for you and perhaps it's not. At least now, you understand the real price.

With your spending laid out in front of you, you can finally ask the most important question. Was it worth it?

Become a mindful spender

Your tracking has identified the cost. Now you must determine the value.

The aim is simply to align your spending with what's important to you. That means removing the spending that contributes little, protecting the spending that does, and getting the same value as efficiently as possible. When you do this consistently, your spending begins to reflect your priorities rather than your habits.

The following exercise will walk you through this process. Once you've completed it, you'll have a clearer picture of where your money is going and what it's delivering in return. Only then does it make sense to formalise things further through a budget. Budgeting simply allocates your money according to the priorities you've identified. To do this effectively, you must first understand where it is currently going. For now, your objectives are simply to make your spending visible, determine its value, and begin aligning it with the life you actually want to build.

This is how a surplus is created in practice. By allocating your resources with intention, you speed up your journey to financial freedom while also making it more enjoyable and purposeful along the way.

◇

EXERCISE 18

Review your spending

For the next four weeks, track every expense. A spreadsheet is ideal, as it allows for sorting and simple analysis, although a budgeting app or notebook are also fine.

Record everything as accurately as possible. If you don't have an exact figure, estimate and round to the nearest dollar. At the end of each week, complete the following steps.

Step 1 – Categorise your spending

Group your expenses into categories. Examples might include:

- Housing (rent or mortgage);
- Bills;
- Groceries;
- Eating out;
- Entertainment;
- Subscriptions; and
- Transport.

Use categories that reflect your own life. The aim is to understand where your money is actually going. Which categories consume the largest share?

Step 2 – Separate out the essentials

Identify your essential expenses. Focus on what is required to live and function, not simply what you've become accustomed to. Food is essential, eating out is not.

Set these aside for now.

Step 3 – Assign value

For all remaining expenses, rate the value they provide on a scale from zero to ten.

The purpose is not precision, but comparison. You are building a hierarchy of value across your spending, separating those that genuinely improve your life from those that add very little.

Step 4 – Cull low-value spending

Look for expenses that are high cost but low value. These are your easiest opportunities to create a surplus. This might include unused subscriptions, convenience purchases made out of habit, or small recurring leaks that accumulate over time.

Keep opportunity cost in mind. Every dollar wasted on low-value items could be redirected to something more meaningful, or invested towards your *Freedom Figure*.

Step 5 – Optimise what remains

For the expenses that stay, ask one final question: "*Can the same value be achieved for less?*"

For essentials, this might involve switching providers or improving efficiency. For non-essentials, it may involve finding lower-cost alternatives that deliver similar satisfaction. It's the financial equivalent of finding a low-calorie version of your favourite junk food. Sometimes you can have your cake and eat it too.

Just remember that your time has value as well. Only invest effort where the potential savings justify it. Prioritise the largest expenses first.

Final reflection

This exercise turns abstract ideas into concrete decisions. You can now see where your money is going, how much each area consumes, and what you're getting in return. More importantly, you can weigh those choices against each other.

Consider eating out, for example. Many people value the convenience and experience. When tracked honestly, however, this category can easily exceed $10,000 per year for some people. That isn't inherently a problem. It's simply a trade-off against every other category where you could have spent those funds instead.

You may decide it's worth every dollar. Or you may realise that even a small adjustment could free up thousands of dollars a year without reducing your enjoyment of life. Either way, the difference is that the decision becomes conscious, rather than automatic.

That's the real value of this exercise: to move from unconscious spending to deliberate allocation, so your spending reflects what you truly value.

CHAPTER 21

FILL THE TANK

Now that you've cut the leaks and improved your fuel efficiency, it's time to learn how to fill the tank.

In this chapter, we'll explore the different types of income and how to increase them. Later chapters will examine how to build systems where your money begins to generate more money on its own. To harness that investment engine, however, you first need fuel in the tank.

The many forms of income

Whether it's the food that fuels your body or the money that fuels your journey, both come in many different forms, and not all forms are equal. Each dollar may carry the same purchasing power, but the effort required to earn it, the reliability of that income, and its ability to scale can vary dramatically.

Some forms of income are directly tied to your time and effort. Other forms can grow independently once established. Some are stable and predictable. Others are more volatile but offer greater upside in return. Some of the most common ways of earning income include:

Salary and wages: The familiar and predictable paycheque earned by exchanging time and effort for compensation.

Bonuses and commissions: Performance-based income tied directly to results or productivity.

Freelancing and consulting: Selling specialised skills or expertise independently, often with greater flexibility but still tied closely to personal effort.

Side hustles and gigs: Flexible, often low-barrier ways to generate additional income outside of traditional employment.

Business ownership: Profits generated from a business you own. Leverage begins to emerge as systems, employees, or technology create value beyond your own labour.

Rental or property income: Ongoing cashflow from assets that generate revenue without daily effort.

Dividends, interest, and investment returns: Income produced by capital itself, rather than direct labour.

Royalties and intellectual property: Payments from creations, ideas, or inventions. Once created, these assets can continue paying over time.

Most people spend their entire lives standing at a single fuel pump, unaware that many others exist.

You don't need to use all of these to achieve financial freedom. The goal here is simply awareness. Once you recognise that income can take many forms, the number of viable paths to your *Freedom Figure* expands. That said, for most people, the first and most accessible lever is still their salary.

Expand your fuel line

It's likely that the first income you ever received was through paid employment. You're not alone. It's the default model many of us grew up with. You study, get a job, and an employer pays you in exchange for your time and effort.

It's not the most glamorous of income streams, but it does have several advantages:

- Provides predictable income;
- Requires no upfront capital;
- Fits naturally into your routine; and
- Can often be increased faster than people expect.

That last point is frequently overlooked. When people think about increasing their income, they sometimes jump straight to starting a business or investing in complex ventures. Those may come later, but the simplest and fastest gains usually come from improving the income stream you already have. Salary is the primary fuel line feeding your tank. Expand it, and the tank fills much faster.

Even modest pay rises can have an outsized impact on your surplus. Say you're earning $100,000 per year and are able to save $10,000 after tax and expenses. What effect would a $15,000 pay rise have on your surplus? After income tax, you might keep $10,000 of the pay rise. If you manage to avoid lifestyle creep and save the entire amount, you'll now have an annual surplus of $20,000. A relatively modest 15 per cent pay rise has doubled the amount of fuel available. This effect compounds even further once that fuel enters the investment engine.

As income rises, however, this effect begins to diminish. Progressive tax rates begin to take a larger share of any additional income, meaning less money is added to your surplus. It's also likely that with a higher income, you're already generating a decent surplus, meaning each additional dollar has a smaller relative impact.

Suppose instead you had an annual income of $150,000 and were already saving $60,000 per year. A $50,000 pay rise might yield about $30,000 after tax. Even if you save all of it, your surplus only increases by half, despite a 33 per cent pay rise. This is still meaningful, but less transformative, especially relative to the effort required. It's far easier to secure small pay rises on a lower salary base than a 33 per cent increase on a much higher one.

Once you appreciate the value of those first few pay rises, the next step is understanding what you need to do to earn them.

Know your value...

Before you can increase your income, you need to understand what you actually bring to the table.

Most people define themselves by their job title, but this usually undersells what they have to offer. Your true value is determined by the sum of the parts. Your skills, experience, problem-solving ability, reliability, perspective, network, and even your personality all combine to form your unique value proposition.

There has never been anyone exactly like you before, and there never will be again. It sounds like a self-help cliché, but it's a simple statistical reality. Your particular combination of experiences, strengths, interests, and capabilities is what makes you unique. Most people assume they have to be the best at something to be valuable. In practice, your true value often lies in the rare combination of skills and experiences that makes you who you are.

This is where awareness becomes critical. The more clearly you understand your own value, the easier it becomes to position yourself in the market. Many people believe the market cares how hard they work. It doesn't. You're not rewarded for *effort* – you're rewarded for *results.* Organisations pay people who create value for them, whether that's generating revenue, improving efficiency, or solving difficult problems that others can't.

Your income is determined by how effectively your capabilities solve problems that organisations care about. The more useful your skills become in this context, the more valuable you become in the marketplace.

...then increase it

If you want to earn more, you need to increase your value. That might involve developing new skills, gaining experience, improving your ability to communicate ideas, or deepening your understanding of the challenges your organisation faces. If you don't yet possess the capabilities required to command higher compensation, invest in yourself until you do. Improving your value increases your earning potential for the rest of your career. It's one of the highest return investments you can make.

Most people try to deepen the skills they already have, aiming to become experts in their field. It can work, but it's a high-risk, high-reward strategy. Unless you become exceptional, it can be difficult to stand out. Experts are everywhere.

An alternative approach is to seek breadth over depth by developing competence across several complementary areas. An engineer who communicates clearly will often outperform someone who is more technically capable, but unable to explain their ideas. Creative thinking paired with operational discipline is far more valuable than either skill alone. Financial knowledge combined with leadership ability creates opportunities that a single discipline may not. Individually these skills are valuable, but together they become far more powerful. When multiple capabilities overlap, your usefulness expands dramatically.

The challenge here is accountability. No one else is responsible for building or positioning your value in the market. That responsibility sits with you. In many workplaces, career development is largely self-directed. Organisations may provide opportunities, but they rarely manage your growth for you. If you want to increase your value, you need to actively invest in your own skills, experience, and capabilities.

The same applies when it comes to communicating that value. You may have advocates that support you, but ultimately it's your responsibility to ensure your contribution is recognised. You need to become a sales expert, and the product you're selling is you. Some people take this a step too far, exaggerating or even outright lying about their abilities. Selling snake oil might get you in the door, but it won't keep you there. Your claims must be backed by real capability and results.

Just like any good salesperson, it helps if you genuinely believe in your own product.

You get what you accept

As you were reading this, did you notice any internal resistance? Did you observe any stories about your capabilities and what you can and can't achieve? If so, you've encountered another common barrier. Income is not determined solely by ability. It is also influenced by what you believe you deserve.

Many people accept the first offer placed in front of them. They assume that the company knows their value better than they do. In reality, compensation is often determined through negotiation, perception, and positioning. Employers typically operate within ranges, and where you land inside that range often depends less on your skills and more on your boundaries.

As with other areas of life, you tend to get what you accept. Of course, this doesn't mean walking into your boss's office and demanding an arbitrary salary. It must be justified based on the value you offer. But you still need to believe that you're worth it. Assume you're worth less and that's exactly what you will unconsciously communicate. Believe that your contribution has real value and you'll approach those same conversations very differently.

It's why recognising your value is the first necessary step in increasing your income. Most people have far more to offer than they realise. They go into salary negotiations without confidence because they underestimate their bargaining position.

The next step is to make sure that you actually deliver. Potential only gets you so far. Like a first draft pick that fails to perform, you'll soon find yourself stagnant on the bench if not discarded entirely. Once you start achieving results, ensure that they are recognised through compensation, promotion, or opportunity. If it's not recognised where you are, you need to look elsewhere.

This mindset is not about entitlement. It is about knowing your value and taking responsibility for ensuring that it's priced accordingly.

Choose the right pond

Once you get clear on your value, you may realise one of two things. Sometimes you discover you're in the wrong industry. Other times you realise you're playing the wrong game entirely.

Not every industry is the same. Different sectors generate very different levels of revenue and profit. Some industries, such as mining and technology, operate on higher margins or larger scales, allowing for higher compensation ceilings. Others, such as government entities, place structural limits on what employers can pay. More importantly, different skills are valued more highly in some sectors compared to others.

If you're highly capable but working in an industry where your skills aren't particularly valued, you'll never be paid what you're worth. Aligning your skills with an industry that's willing to pay for them can dramatically increase income, often without any effort required other than the move itself. You're not required to upskill or demonstrate higher value. You're simply selling your product to the right buyer.

Many people don't realise this, instead choosing to pursue a career in fields that simply pay more. If your work isn't aligned with your natural interests or abilities, however, you'll likely find yourself competing against people for whom those skills come far more easily. You're usually better off financially working in an industry where your natural skills already command a premium. You'll be rewarded for the strengths you already possess, rather than fighting to become something you're not.

Sometimes, however, the issue isn't the industry at all. It's the game itself.

As your skills and experience grow, you may reach the point where a salary is no longer the most effective way to capture the value you create. Knowing your value also means recognising when you have outgrown the pond entirely. In those situations, your capabilities may be better applied building assets or creating systems rather than continuing to sell your time.

A salary is undoubtedly useful, but it's not without its limitations. The fact it's dependent on your time means it's ultimately capped by your hourly rate. Even highly paid professionals can only work so many hours. It's also dependent on an employer, diminishing the level of control you have over your financial freedom. Organisational budgets, market conditions, restructures, and leadership decisions can all influence what you can earn, and whether you even have a job at all.

Relying on salary alone places natural constraints on how much you can be paid for the value you deliver. Once your value outgrows your salary, it's time to zoom out and look at other forms of income.

Change the game

A useful way to understand income is through a model known as the ESBI framework. [55] It divides income sources into four categories: *Employee*, *Self-Employed*, *Business Owner*, and *Investor*.

Most people earn their income as employees, trading time and effort for wages or salary. Self-employed individuals still trade time for money, but they now work for themselves instead. In doing so, they gain more control over their financial future but also take on additional risk. Consultants, freelancers, and contractors all fall into this category. Income potential may increase, but it still depends heavily on personal effort and is still capped by your time.

Business owners are playing a different game entirely. They create systems that generate income beyond their own labour. Employees, technology, and processes allow the business to produce value even when the owner is not directly involved. With this constraint removed, your earning potential is no longer limited by your time.

---

[55] Robert T. Kiyosaki, *Rich Dad's Cashflow Quadrant: Rich Dad's Guide to Financial Freedom* (1998).

Finally, we have investors. Investors allocate capital into assets that produce returns. Here, money itself becomes the working force. Similar to business owners, there is no ceiling to your earning potential. The primary difference here is effort. Businesses often demand a large amount of time, especially early on, for a pay-off that may or may not arrive. Investments, on the other hand, can be largely passive, requiring little ongoing effort once the capital has been deployed.

Each step along this spectrum increases leverage. Employees rely primarily on their *time*. Self-employed people rely on their *skill*. Business owners rely on *systems*. Investors rely on *capital*.

Financial freedom rarely emerges solely from the employee quadrant, simply due to the constraints it places on our income. Eventually, some portion of income must come from assets that continue generating returns without requiring our effort.

This is where investing becomes essential.

Growing the gap

Now that we've explored both sides of the financial equation – money in and money out – there's one final piece to bring them together.

Managing expenses is immediate but ultimately limited. Income growth takes longer but has far greater upside. Both are important, but neither is sufficient on its own. Spending all your time climbing the corporate ladder will be worthless if you spend every extra dollar you earn. Cutting expenses to the bone will only go so far if your income never increases. What ultimately drives financial progress is not the absolute level of either, but the gap between them.

It's why a higher income doesn't automatically translate to better outcomes. Someone earning $100,000 per year and consistently generating a $30,000 surplus is in a stronger position than someone earning $150,000 but only saving $20,000. The gap is the number you need to care about. Without a surplus, there is nothing left to invest. Your income is forever capped by the number of hours you're able to work.

Building that surplus is your first and most important objective. In practice, that means working on both sides of the equation. You increase income where the return on effort is worthwhile and reduce spending where it adds little value. How you balance the two, however, depends on your situation.

We've seen how at lower income levels, it makes sense to focus more on your earnings. Pay rises are proportionally more valuable while marginal income tax is modest and your existing surplus is small. At higher income levels, the opposite is often true. With higher tax rates and a surplus that is already substantial, the easier win is preventing lifestyle inflation from eroding the gap.

Regardless of where you focus your effort, the measure of progress remains the same: how much of a gap are you able to create and maintain? Some money will be reserved as a buffer against the uncertainty of life. The rest becomes your investable surplus, the fuel that will power your financial engine.

Once you're able to consistently generate an investable surplus, the next step is to put it to work. In the next chapters, we'll explore what this looks like in practice and how to build your investment engine.

◇

EXERCISE 19

Monetise your capabilities

This exercise is about translating your capabilities into income. Reflection here is a direct investment in your future earnings. Take your time and be honest with yourself.

Step 1 – Know your capabilities

List your skills across three categories:

- Technical or domain skills (e.g. accounting, coding, engineering, analysis);
- Transferable or soft skills (e.g. communication, problem solving, leadership); and
- Experience and context (e.g. industries, projects, systems, scale of work).

Aim for at least 10 to 15 items in total. Which capabilities stand out as your strongest?

Step 2 – Identify where you create value

Think about how you currently earn your income. What are you actually being paid for? Ask yourself the following questions:

- What challenges am I solving?
- Who benefits from the value I deliver?
- How do I impact outcomes such as revenue, cost, risk, or quality?

Step 3 – Assess current utilisation

Which skills are currently doing the heavy lifting and generating most of the value? Which are underutilised, or not used at all?

If a skill isn't contributing, either it's not valuable in your current environment, or it's not being leveraged effectively. Be honest about which is more likely.

Underutilised but valuable skills often represent immediate upside. Skills with little market value, however, may be better used for hobbies, unless you can apply them in a way that creates value.

Step 4 – Define what you bring to the table

Now put it all together.

Based on your answers above, write a short, clear description of what you bring. Ask yourself the following:

- What am I consistently good at?
- What do people rely on me for?
- What kinds of situations or challenges do I handle better than most?
- Where do my skills overlap in a way that makes me particularly useful?

The goal here is to clearly define your strengths and how they create value in the real world.

Step 5 – Expand and strengthen your value

Consider how your current skills could be applied more effectively, and where they could be improved:

- Are you in a role that fully uses what you're capable of?
- Are there environments or industries where your skills would be valued more highly?
- Could you combine your skills in a way that creates more value than you currently deliver?

- Is there a way to use these skills outside your main job, through freelancing, consulting, or some other side income?
- Are there any skills you could invest in to meaningfully increase what you have to offer?

This will help identify where your best opportunities lie.

Step 6 – Take action

Choose two or three actions you will take in the next 30 days. Be specific, for example:

- Start a small side-income stream using an existing skill;
- Begin developing a complementary capability; or
- Prepare evidence of results delivered at work and schedule a salary review.

Outcome

By the end of this exercise, you should have:

- A clear understanding of what you have to offer;
- A view of where it is most valuable; and
- A defined plan to convert that value into higher income.

Once you secure a higher income, the next step is to put those funds to work.

CHAPTER 22

THE POWER OF INVESTING

Now that you've learned how to build a surplus, the next step is to deploy it.

You can't save your way to financial freedom. No matter how high your income, or how much you cut your expenses, your progress will remain linear. Each additional dollar you save only moves you forward by one dollar. Investing changes that equation.

At its simplest, investing means using your money to buy assets that can produce income or grow in value over time. That might mean owning a share of a business, lending money in exchange for interest, or holding an asset such as property that generates income or increases in value over time. Instead of sitting idle in a bank account, your money is put to work.

Once invested, that money has the potential to generate returns of its own. Those returns can then be reinvested, producing further returns in the future. Instead of simply adding to your wealth, you multiply it. Over the long term, the two produce completely different outcomes. One steadily adds to your bank account, while the other one eventually removes your dependence on it entirely.

Part of the reason we fail to appreciate exponential growth is that it's easier to see than it is to explain. Add in the fact that results only appear in the long term, and it becomes clear why it's so often underestimated. To help you see just how powerful it is, consider the legend about the invention of chess.

The rice and the chessboard

As the story goes, a wise scholar presented his new game to a powerful king. The king was so impressed that he offered the inventor any reward he wished. The scholar made an unusual request. His reward was to be paid over 64 days – one for each square on the chessboard. On the first day, he would receive a single grain of rice. On the second day, the reward would double to two grains. On the third day, it would double again to four, and so on.

The king laughed at what appeared to be a trivial request and ordered the reward to be granted. Only later did he realise the problem.

The next day, the scholar received his first payment: a solitary grain of rice resting on a small ornate plate. The king's royal attendants were puzzled, wondering why anyone would accept such a small reward. The scholar simply smiled and thanked them. The next day, the plate contained two grains. The following day four, then eight, then sixteen. After two weeks, the scholar had barely enough rice for a single meal.

But as the doubling continued, the scale escalated rapidly. By the end of the third week, the payment was being delivered in large bags. Soon, entire carts were arriving at the scholar's door. By the time half the payments had been made, the scholar had already amassed more than 100 tonnes of rice. The kingdom's rice stores were stripped clean long before the 64 days could be completed.

What the king had assumed was humble was anything but. To fulfil the scholar's request would have required

18,446,744,073,709,551,615 grains of rice, a number so large that most people struggle to comprehend it at all. To put it in perspective, that's about 461 billion metric tonnes, or roughly the weight of three Mount Everests.

This is the incredible power of exponential growth. At the beginning, the increases are barely noticeable. Like ripples before a tidal wave, they offer little indication of the extraordinary scale that is building beneath them. Our intuition struggles with processes like this. We are used to thinking in straight lines, where progress arrives in steady, predictable steps. Exponential growth is a different beast entirely. Just like the scholar's rice payments, the early stages of compounding feel insignificant. The true power only becomes visible once time has already done most of the work.

As a mathematician, I understand exponential growth better than most, yet the sheer scale of it still amazes me. You might think that, of all people, I would be the first to start investing. Instead, I began my investing journey much later than I would have liked. As it turns out, the barriers to investing are rarely technical.

What's the catch?

If investing is so powerful, why don't more people do it?

The first barrier is practical. Many people never manage to create a surplus, making investing impossible. It's why we spent the last few chapters addressing that specific challenge first. Yet even among those who build a surplus, many still choose not to invest it. Sometimes that's simply due to a lack of awareness; they don't realise investing is even an option. More often, however, the barrier is psychological.

People tend to hold very different views about what investing represents. For some, investing is simply participation in the economy. When you buy shares in a company, you are purchasing a small ownership stake in a business that produces goods, employs people, and generates profits over time. In that sense, investing is a way to share in the growth of productive activity and, ultimately, a path towards greater financial freedom.

Others see it very differently. Some view financial markets as little more than a glorified casino, associating investing with speculation, greed, or the excesses of modern capitalism. In that frame, investing looks less like prudent wealth building and more like degenerate gambling.

These beliefs influence how accessible investing appears to be. If you see it as participation in the economy, it becomes something almost anyone can do. See it as a casino, however, and it'll appear complicated and full of risk, reserved only for the wealthy, or those with the specialised knowledge to navigate it.

These reactions are understandable. Our views about money are often among the most deeply rooted beliefs we hold. It would be unusual not to carry some assumptions or reservations about investing. The key is not to ignore those beliefs, but to become aware of them. Once you recognise the stories you carry about money and investing, you can begin to question them. Which ones are grounded in reality? What parts might be incomplete? Which ones are simply inherited assumptions that have never been examined closely? In some cases, those beliefs will turn out to be accurate. Other times they may be exactly what is holding you back.

If your beliefs go unexamined, they often give way to the greatest barrier of all: fear. We've already seen how money carries emotional weight. It doesn't just represent dollars, but the years of work, discipline, and sacrifice it took to earn them. The idea of placing those hard-earned savings into something that might fall in value can feel deeply uncomfortable.

For me, this was the greatest blocker. I justified my hesitation with a compelling thought: *"If it's so easy, why isn't everyone doing it?"* It simply sounded too good to be true. I wasn't expecting the impossible returns of the scholar, either. Doubling your money every day is obviously unrealistic, as demonstrated by his unfathomable payment. Yet the maths shows that even modest rates of growth produce extraordinary returns over time.

At ten per cent per year, money only grows by about 33 per cent in the first three years. That feels perfectly reasonable; a little more than ten per cent each year as the gains begin to compound. It takes over seven years for your money to double for the first time. Leave it alone for 30 years, however, and the result becomes far less intuitive. That same money now grows to more than 17 times its initial value. While the early years make sense, the end result seems to almost defy reason.

Surely it couldn't be that easy? Between the fear of losing my savings and the suspicion that something this powerful must come with a hidden catch, I convinced myself that investing wasn't for me. So, for years, I let those beliefs stop me from investing. Instead, I saved. I hoarded my surplus and left it sitting in the bank while inflation slowly eroded its value.

Looking back, I wish I had started sooner, but that doesn't mean those years were wasted. Saving taught me to live below my means and gave me a capital base to work from. This is worth remembering if you feel you have started too late. Earlier is better, but later is better than not starting at all. If you have built discipline, reduced expenses, increased your income, or accumulated any capital at all, you are not starting from zero. You have already built the base. Investing is how you begin to put that base to work.

The lesson is not to ignore scepticism altogether. In a world filled with scams, spruikers, and speculative fads, it's wise to be cautious. If something sounds too good to be true, it usually is. The trap is allowing that caution to lead to avoidance. Investing is not a get-rich-quick scheme; it's a get-rich-slow strategy. The growth is very real, but it requires patience, consistency, and a willingness to allow time to do its work.

There isn't a catch, but there is a price.

The price of admission

The principles of investing are not particularly complicated. Successful investing can be surprisingly simple, but simple does not always mean easy.

Unlike the story of the scholar, meaningful results do not appear in a matter of weeks. Real investment returns unfold over decades. Over that time, returns are rarely consistent. Markets don't move in straight lines. Some years deliver strong gains while others deliver losses. Occasionally those losses can be large and arrive without warning. When that happens, the value of your investments may fall sharply in the short term, even if the long-term trend remains intact.

This is where the real challenge begins. Markets do not test your intelligence nearly as much as they test your temperament.

When prices rise quickly, investors often feel tempted to chase whatever appears to be performing well. When markets fall, the instinct is often to retreat to safety and wait for things to stabilise. Both of these instincts can tempt investors into making trades, rather than holding for the long term. Yet even professional investors struggle to consistently outperform the market.

Warren Buffett once captured this dynamic with a simple observation: investors should aim to be "*fearful when others are greedy, and greedy when others are fearful.*" The quote is not meant as a trading instruction, so much as a reminder that the crowd's emotional response to markets is often backwards. When optimism reaches its peak, prices are often already elevated. When fear dominates headlines, prices have often already fallen heavily in response. Acting on emotion in either direction tends to produce poor results.

The trap here lies in how compound growth works in a volatile environment over time. If returns were perfectly consistent, moving in and out of the market would have predictable results. Missed time in the market would simply reduce your returns proportionally. This is not the case for rapidly moving markets like shares.

A surprising portion of long-term market returns tends to occur during a relatively small number of trading days. One famous example analysed the performance of the US share market over the 20 years from 2003 to 2022.[56] An investor who remained fully invested in the S&P 500 during that entire period earned an average return of roughly 9.8 per cent per year. Over those two decades, an initial $10,000 investment would have grown to about $64,000, producing a profit of $54,000.

Now consider what happened if that same investor missed just the best ten trading days during those twenty years. That same $10,000 investment now only grows to roughly $29,000. Instead of earning $54,000 in profit, they'd have made only $19,000.

[56] J.P. Morgan Asset Management, *Guide to the Markets*, "The Impact of Missing the Best Days in the Market," data covering 2003–2022.

Missing just ten days in 20 years would have erased roughly two thirds of the total return. The same analysis showed that if an investor had missed the best 30 days, their return would have disappeared entirely.

This is the danger of trying to time the market. Missing just a handful of the market's strongest days can erase the majority of long-term returns. Of course, the opposite is also true. Avoid the worst days and your returns improve dramatically. That's exactly the trap that many investors fall into. Large market falls are often followed by sharp rebounds. Over that 20-year period, seven of the best ten days occurred during market downturns. By trying to avoid the worst days, many investors inadvertently miss some of the best ones as well.

Although this example focuses on the share market, the same logic applies in any volatile market. It leads to one of the most commonly repeated principles of investing: "*Time in the market beats timing the market.*"

Consistently predicting short-term movements in any market is extraordinarily difficult. There are always factors outside of your control and information you're not aware of. What investors can control, however, is whether they remain invested long enough for compounding to do its work. Invest for the long term and you're far less likely to miss the days that drive most long-term returns. The bad days are simply the price you must pay for the good ones.

Volatility is not a flaw in financial markets. It's a feature. Prices move up and down in response to economic events, investor sentiment, and countless other factors. Those fluctuations can feel uncomfortable, particularly when the numbers on your screen suddenly turn red, but volatility itself is not a sign that something has gone wrong. It is part of the mechanism that produces long-term returns. If markets were perfectly stable, there would be little reward for investing in them. The uncertainty that causes prices to fluctuate is the same uncertainty that creates opportunities for growth.

It's one thing to understand this principle, but another to live by it in practice. One of my first investing experiences was a sensible, long-term investment product. I knew that higher expected returns usually meant accepting some volatility along the way, yet that knowledge didn't help much once my own investment started falling in value. In just a few months, my investment fell by more than ten per cent and I did exactly what I wasn't supposed to: I panicked and pulled my money out. The issue wasn't the investment itself, but my mindset. I had enough knowledge to begin investing, but I wasn't yet mentally prepared to pay the price.

Today, my response would be very different. Some parts of my portfolio now carry far more risk than I'd ever thought I'd take on in the past. I still don't enjoy losses, nor have I become reckless in my approach. The difference is that I now have the experience, capital base, and temperament to sit through larger swings without panicking. Of course, this doesn't mean every investor should accept higher levels of volatility. Other investors may be far better served by a steadier approach. The principle is not to seek volatility for its own sake, but to choose investments whose ups and downs you can live with over the long term.

That experience taught me something most investors eventually come to realise. Progress does not arrive in a smooth, uninterrupted line. There will be periods of optimism, but also periods of fear. Stretches of rapid growth are often preceded or followed by stretches of stagnation. The question is not whether there will be volatility, but whether you can stomach it when it arrives. Avoiding volatility usually means accepting lower returns, but too much volatility may test your resolve, leading you to abandon your strategy entirely.

This leads to one of the most important, yet often overlooked, parts of investing: understanding yourself.

Find what works for you

Knowing *who* is investing is just as important as knowing *what* to invest in.

Before investing a single dollar, you need to reflect on what is right for you. Investing is often presented as a purely analytical exercise, where you weigh up different opportunities based solely on the numbers and allocate your capital accordingly. In reality, successful investing is just as much about behaviour as it is about mathematics. A strategy that looks solid on paper is not always the one an investor can stick with in practice. Investing works best when the strategy aligns your financial goals with your temperament, meaning you need to be aware of both.

The obvious example here is risk tolerance. Different investors can have very different appetites for risk and uncertainty. Some investors are comfortable watching the value of their portfolio fluctuate significantly if it offers the potential for higher long-term growth. Others find large swings deeply stressful and prefer a more stable approach, even if it means accepting lower expected returns.

Neither preference is inherently right or wrong. It simply tells you something about the kind of strategy you are likely to sustain. Investing is not a one-off decision. It is a process that unfolds over decades. For that process to work, you need to remain committed through both good times and bad.

If an investment strategy keeps you awake at night or leaves you constantly checking market prices, it's unlikely to be sustainable. Peace of mind can be just as important as potential returns. Discomfort creates friction, and that friction makes it harder to stay disciplined, especially when markets become volatile.

A strategy that aligns with your temperament removes much of that friction. When you feel comfortable with the approach you have chosen, it becomes far easier to follow it consistently. The best investment strategy, therefore, is usually the one that gives you the confidence and peace of mind to stick with it. While others may look more impressive on paper, they often fall short if they cause investors to abandon them, missing out on some of the best days in the process.

Your own financial circumstances also play an important role in determining your approach to investing. How much cash do you need readily available? How soon might you need the funds that you're planning to invest? Maintaining an adequate cash buffer can prevent the need to sell investments during periods of market stress – one of the most common ways investors undermine their own results. These funds act as your own private insurance policy, protecting you when unexpected expenses arise. Like any insurance policy, you pay a premium: in this case, the growth foregone in exchange for having those funds available. Understanding your unique circumstances helps you decide how much money to keep in reserve before committing the remainder to longer-term investments.

Effort and involvement are other factors worth considering. Some investors favour a more passive approach, happy to let time and compounding do most of the work. Others prefer actively managing their portfolios, researching businesses and analysing potential investment opportunities. Just as we saw with income, however, the market doesn't necessarily reward effort. Spending more time on your investing does not automatically lead to better results.

That's not to say you should only passively invest. Some level of involvement can still be valuable. Many investors enjoy feeling engaged in the process. Taking an active interest in your investments can create a sense of ownership and agency over your financial future. Even if time and compounding are doing most of the heavy lifting, being involved can make the journey feel more intentional. That sense of ownership can make it easier to remain committed over the long term.

While increasing your effort may not improve your results, focusing it can. Many investors find they achieve better outcomes by aligning their investment choices with their personal interests and strengths. Some enjoy analysing numbers and financial statements, while others prefer tangible assets they can see and understand more directly. Some people are naturally drawn to property, while others prefer shares or businesses.

As we'll see in the next chapter, there are many ways to invest. You don't need to master them all to be successful. In many cases it is better to focus on a small number of areas that you understand well rather than trying everything at once. Not only is it simpler, but it also helps develop your skills and expertise, increasing your confidence and peace of mind. Lean into areas you enjoy, and the process becomes easier to sustain.

After considering all these factors, you may decide that investing simply isn't for you. That's perfectly fine. Just be aware that choosing not to invest is still a financial decision, and like any other, it carries risks of its own.

The risk of doing nothing

Every investment comes with risks. Many people avoid it entirely as a result, believing it to be the safest possible choice. What they often don't realise is that they're simply replacing one risk with another.

Risk is commonly viewed in a negative light, yet it is a fundamental part of life. Every decision we ever make carries some degree of uncertainty. We are constantly taking on risk, whether we're aware of it or not.

Stepping outside exposes us to countless potential diseases, injuries, and accidents, yet we leave the house most days without hesitation. Travelling introduces additional risks we wouldn't face at home, yet we eagerly plan our annual getaways. Relationships, careers, and family all carry uncertainty, yet most of us would never choose to live without them. Just as volatility is the price of admission for investing, risk is simply the price of living. Trying to eliminate risk completely only results in a life not truly lived. Instead, life is about understanding the trade-offs and choosing which risks you are willing to accept.

The same holds true for investing. For many people, the greatest risk of avoiding investing is that it makes financial freedom far more difficult, if not impossible, to achieve. Without investment growth, wealth can only increase through income and saving. That process is inherently linear. As we saw earlier in the chapter, exponential growth is a different beast entirely. Over long periods of time, it produces results that are impossible to replicate through saving alone. Choosing not to invest means deliberately choosing not to leverage the power of compound growth.

This becomes an even riskier prospect once you factor in the effects of inflation. Over time, the purchasing power of money slowly erodes. The same amount of cash buys fewer goods and services as prices rise. The number on your bank balance might look the same, but the value behind it gradually declines. Meanwhile, productive assets such as businesses, property, and other investments have historically increased in value over the long term. Investing is one way of protecting against inflation, ensuring that your money remains just as effective tomorrow as it is today.

When these forces are combined, the limitations of relying solely on income become clear. Achieving financial freedom without investment income typically requires earning significantly more money, maintaining a higher savings rate for longer, and accumulating a far greater *Freedom Figure* to offset the effects of inflation. Even then, another risk remains. If your plan relies primarily on accumulated savings rather than investment growth, those savings must last for the rest of your life. Inflation continues to erode their purchasing power year after year, gradually increasing the risk that your money runs out before you do.

This creates an interesting paradox. In the short term, investing often feels like the riskier option because markets fluctuate and values can fall. Over longer time horizons, however, the picture begins to change. Short periods are dominated by randomness. A handful of good or bad years can dramatically alter the outcome. Over longer periods, however, the underlying forces of economic growth and compounding begin to assert themselves. As the number of years increases, the random noise that was once deafening begins to be drowned out by the long-term trends.

For this reason, many people eventually come to view investing as the safer path over extended time horizons. As with life, there will always be risks, but here they are balanced by the powerful forces of compounding and time.

Before we continue

Before we dive deeper into the mechanics of investing in the next chapter, it's worth clarifying the purpose of the discussion that follows.

The intent of these chapters is to explain how investing works and provide a framework for thinking about money and long-term wealth. It should not be interpreted as financial advice. Each individual's circumstances are different. Income, expenses, tax considerations, time horizons, and risk tolerance vary from person to person. Most importantly, your money mindset is unique to you. Your views and beliefs about investing, and about money more broadly, will strongly influence how you invest, including whether you choose to invest at all.

The ideas explored here are meant to help you understand the principles behind investing and the beliefs that drive common behaviours. How those ideas apply to your own situation is something only you can ultimately decide.

With that said, now that we've explored the power of investing, it's time to look at the basics.

In the next chapter, we'll dive into the fundamentals. We'll look at the different types of assets available, how they generate returns, and the principles investors use to combine them into long-term portfolios.

◇

EXERCISE 20

Your investing mindset

Before investing a single dollar, you need to understand how you think and feel about it.

The decisions that most affect outcomes tend to occur during periods of uncertainty, when emotions are heightened and logic is harder to apply. This exercise is designed to surface the beliefs, assumptions, and reactions that will influence your behaviour when it counts the most.

Step 1 – Your current beliefs

Write down your immediate thoughts about investing:

- What do you believe investing represents?
- Do you see it as ownership, opportunity, risk, speculation, or something else?
- Where do these beliefs come from?
- If you've invested before, briefly describe that experience and how it felt.

Step 2 – Identify your concerns

List your top three concerns about investing. For each one, classify it as:

- A real and unavoidable risk;
- A risk that can be managed or reduced; or
- An assumption you have not yet examined closely.

Notice whether any concerns are based more on perception and stories rather than experience or evidence.

Step 3 – How do you handle uncertainty?

Imagine that you've invested an amount of money that is meaningful to you. Within a year, the value falls by 20 per cent. Consider the following:

- What is your first instinct or reaction?
- Would you hold, invest more, or sell?
- How confident would you feel staying invested?

Now consider the opposite. Imagine your investment rises quickly over a short period:

- Would you feel comfortable leaving it alone?
- Would you be tempted to take profits or invest more?

Step 4 – Compare the trade-offs

For this step, you will rate statements according to how true they feel to you. Use the following scale:

- Always true;
- Often true;
- Sometimes true;
- Rarely true; or
- Never true.

There are no right or wrong answers. Focus on your instinctive reaction rather than what you think should be true.

- I am comfortable accepting short-term losses if there is a reasonable expectation of higher long-term growth.
- I would prefer my money to remain stable, even if it means slower long-term progress.
- I am willing to tolerate uncertainty in how my investments perform year to year.

- I would find it difficult to stay invested if the value of my portfolio declined for an extended period.
- I am comfortable relying primarily on my income and savings to build wealth, even if that means it'll take longer before I can reduce or stop working.
- I am willing to accept a less predictable path if it increases the chance of having greater flexibility later in life.

After answering each, review your responses as a whole:

- Which statements felt easiest to agree with?
- Which created the most discomfort or hesitation?
- Do your answers lean more towards stability, or towards growth despite uncertainty?

Step 5 – Define your boundaries

If you choose to invest, define the conditions required for you to remain consistent:

- What level of fluctuation would you find difficult to tolerate?
- What would cause you to change course?
- What would need to be true for you to remain invested over the long term?

Final reflection

Investing is not just about understanding how markets work. It is about understanding how you respond to them. Before investing, you must be willing to accept the trade-offs involved. The next chapter will explore different investment types, but you must first decide if it's something that's right for you.

CHAPTER 23

PUT YOUR MONEY TO WORK

Now that we've covered the critical role of investing in achieving financial freedom, the next step is to understand how it works in practice. What can you actually invest in? How do different investments behave? What factors do you need to consider when deciding where to put your money?

This chapter provides a brief introduction to the core principles of investing. Once you have this foundation in place, you can begin to build your own personal investment strategy. Investing is not a one-size-fits-all approach. Building a portfolio requires choosing the products that are right for your goals and your circumstances.

This is not purely an analytical exercise. The numbers are important, of course, but practical considerations will heavily influence how investors build their portfolios. Before we dive into that detail, let's first explore the different investment options available.

How to put your money to work

Just as there are many ways to earn income, there are many ways to invest. While the financial world offers thousands of investment products, most tend to fall into a small number of broad categories.

At their core, investments usually work in one of three ways. Your money is either being lent to someone else, used to purchase ownership of an asset or business, or pooled with the money of other investors to buy a collection of investments. Most investment products are simply different ways of applying these principles. Some of the most common types of investments include:

Cash and fixed-income investments: These involve lending your money to a bank, government, business, or other borrower in exchange for regular interest payments. Examples include savings accounts, term deposits, and government or corporate bonds.

Shares and equities: These involve purchasing a small ownership stake in a business. As an owner, you may benefit if the company grows in value and may also receive a share of its profits through dividend payments.

Property and real estate: These involve owning physical land or buildings, such as residential homes, apartments, or commercial properties. Returns typically come from rental income and any increase in the property's value over time.

Managed funds and exchange-traded funds (ETFs): Rather than selecting individual investments yourself, these pool money from many investors to purchase a diversified portfolio of assets. Depending on the fund, this may include shares, bonds, property, commodities, or a combination of different investment types.

Alternative investments: This broad category includes investments outside the traditional asset classes, such as private equity, venture capital, commodities, infrastructure, and cryptocurrencies. These investments often have different risk and return characteristics from more conventional investments.

Each category represents a different way of putting your capital to work, along with its own set of potential rewards, risks, and trade-offs. Understanding these differences is an important first step in building an investment portfolio that aligns with your goals and circumstances.

Before we can compare these investment types in more detail, we first need to understand how investments generate returns.

How money creates money

Investments typically generate returns in two ways: *income* and *capital growth*.

Income refers to cash paid out to you while you own the investment. This might include interest from bonds, rent from property, or dividends from shares. Growth, on the other hand, occurs when the value of an investment increases over time. If you buy an asset for $10,000 and later sell it for $15,000, that $5,000 increase represents capital growth.

The balance of income and growth varies depending on the type of investment. Some assets provide only income, while others offer only potential growth. Most investments provide some combination of both. For example, many shares pay dividends while also increasing in value, while property investments often generate rental income alongside potential capital growth. Regardless of the balance between the two, the overall return on an asset is simply the sum of the income received and the capital growth. If a $10,000 investment pays you $300 income and is worth $10,700 by the end of the year, the total return is $300 plus $700, or ten per cent.

In any given year, $1,000 of income and $1,000 of capital growth increase your wealth by the same amount. The long-term wealth gain can vary significantly, however, depending on when those gains are taxed. In many tax systems, income is taxed in the year it is received, while capital gains are taxed only when the investment is sold. Over time, this can lead to vastly different outcomes thanks to the effects of compounding.

Imagine investing $50,000 into one of two different assets, both generating a hypothetical ten per cent annual return for 20 years. The first asset pays that return entirely as an annual income, while the second pays no income but appreciates by ten per cent per year instead. For the first asset, assuming you're taxed at 30 per cent, the after-tax return drops to seven per cent per year. Reinvesting that income each year would grow your investment to roughly $193,000 after two decades.

For the second asset, the gain is usually taxed only when your investment is sold. Without an annual tax bill reducing the amount left invested each year, the same investment grows to roughly $336,000 over the same period. Even if the gain were eventually taxed at the same rate, you'd still keep more than $250,000. Delaying the tax bill simply allows the full balance of your investment to compound for longer.

Some tax systems widen this gap even further by incentivising long-term investing. Under a system where only half of a long-term capital gain is taxed, that initial $50,000 would result in roughly $293,000 in your pocket after tax. That's an extra $100,000 compared with the income investment, despite the same underlying return. This example illustrates that while return is clearly a key consideration for any investor, it's not the only one. Factors such as timing and tax can significantly affect what you ultimately keep.

The characteristics of an investment also influence how returns are achieved over time. Investments vary in how stable their values are, how long they typically take to deliver results, how easily they can be converted into cash, and how much effort they require to manage. Some fluctuate dramatically in the short term but reward patience over many years. Others are relatively stable but grow slowly. Some can be sold instantly while others may take months to exit.

These characteristics affect not only the financial outcome, but also the psychological experience of investing. Understanding them is essential to building a portfolio that will work for you and your unique circumstances.

The key characteristics of investments

Although investments vary widely, most can be evaluated using a small number of core characteristics. By understanding them, you can better determine what role an investment might play in your portfolio and whether it suits your particular needs.

Return

The primary reason people invest is to grow their wealth, so it's no surprise that return is usually the first consideration for any investment. Both the expected return and how it will be paid are important. Naturally, every investor wants the highest possible return. The balance between growth and income, however, will depend largely on the investor's circumstances. Investors seeking regular cashflow may prioritise income-producing assets, while those focused on long-term wealth accumulation may prefer investments that emphasise growth.

Inflation also affects how meaningful your returns are in practice. A five per cent return sounds positive, but if prices rose by the same amount, your purchasing power remains unchanged. Over long periods, it is your inflation-adjusted real return that determines whether your wealth is genuinely growing or merely keeping pace with rising prices.

It's another reason why returns should be treated as estimates rather than guarantees. Investments may perform better or worse than expected, while rising prices can erode more of your gains than you anticipated. You can't control inflation, but you can decide how much risk you are willing to accept in pursuit of higher returns. Investments offering higher potential returns usually involve greater uncertainty along the way, while safer investments usually offer less financial reward. This relationship between risk and return is one of the most fundamental principles of investing, making risk the next major consideration for any investment.

Risk

All investments carry risks. For the most part, the impact of these risks is usually financial. You may lose some of your capital, or returns may be far lower than expected. The converse is also true, and your returns could exceed your expectations. Some risks are specific to an individual investment, such as poor performance in a company. Others are more broad-based, like overall market uncertainty or geopolitical tension.

Taking risks is a necessary part of investing, but by choosing what to invest in, you can still manage which risks you choose to accept. Some investments are inherently riskier than others. While they typically offer higher potential returns, you can also lose your investment entirely. Others are far safer but offer less potential upside. Ultimately, how much risk you take on is a matter of personal preference.

The important thing is that you understand the risks attached to each investment. This allows you to build a portfolio that reflects your temperament, goals and circumstances. The responsibility of an investor is therefore not to avoid risk altogether, but to decide which risks are worth accepting, and which ones are not.

Time horizon

Your risk appetite will often be correlated with the time horizon of your investments. Some investments have clearly defined and relatively short timeframes. A term deposit, for example, might lock in a fixed return over a period of months or years. Other assets often require longer periods of time for their value to materialise.

Volatile investments can fluctuate significantly in the short term, making short investment windows a far riskier prospect. The longer an investor can remain invested, however, the greater the opportunity for short-term fluctuations to even out and for long-term trends to emerge. Assets such as shares and property have historically produced stronger returns over longer periods.

In some cases, the investment itself may also impose time constraints. Certain assets cannot easily be exited until a particular period has passed. Some alternative investments like venture capital may not be able to be exited until certain milestones are reached.

Matching investments to your particular time horizons is critical in managing your finances. If you're looking to buy a house in the next year, for example, it would be unwise to place your deposit funds in high-risk investments in the meantime. If you don't need to touch the funds for ten to 20 years, however, you have far more options as to where you may choose to invest.

Liquidity

A related concept to the time horizon of an investment is its liquidity, or how readily it can be converted into cash. Some assets are highly liquid. Shares in large publicly listed companies can usually be bought or sold within seconds during market hours. Other investments can be far harder to dispose of. Property, private businesses, or specialised investments may take weeks or months to sell.

How liquid an asset is often depends on how easily it can be divided and traded. Larger assets are usually less liquid because they require a large one-time commitment to buy or sell. Shares in a large company, however, are highly liquid because they are so divisible. A single share can be bought for a few dollars, with some exchanges even allowing the purchase of fractional shares, making them one of the most liquid investments available.

Liquidity is an important consideration for investors as financial plans rarely unfold exactly as expected. Having some investments that can be accessed quickly provides flexibility if circumstances change. If the majority of your investments are illiquid, you'll usually need to keep more cash in reserve as insurance.

Transaction costs

Buying and selling investments usually involves costs, reducing your overall return. Depending on the asset, these might include brokerage fees, legal expenses, stamp duty, or other transaction costs. These vary drastically between asset classes and, like liquidity, influence how readily you can move between investments. Assets with low transaction costs such as shares are easier to buy and sell, while buying or selling a house can cost a small fortune.

Transaction costs become particularly relevant when investments are held for shorter periods. When assets are bought and sold frequently, these costs can consume a meaningful portion of the return. For long-term investments held over many years, the impact of transaction costs is usually much smaller.

Access and capital requirements

Not all investments are equally accessible. Some require substantial capital before participation is even possible.

Purchasing an investment property, for example, usually involves a significant deposit, borrowing capacity, and transaction costs. Other investments allow participation with relatively small amounts of money. Many share market investments or managed funds can be accessed with minimal starting capital. These constraints often influence how investors construct their portfolios, particularly in the early stages of wealth building.

Effort required

A final consideration for investors is how much effort an investment requires to maintain. Some are largely passive, requiring little ongoing effort. Once established, they operate mostly in the background. Others are active, requiring regular decision-making, management, or oversight. Importantly, greater effort does not necessarily lead to greater returns. In many cases, simple and low-maintenance approaches perform just as well as more complex strategies.

Peace of mind plays a role here as well. Truly passive investments operate silently in the background, without you ever lifting a finger. If, however, you find yourself constantly checking prices, monitoring news, or moving in and out of investments, that is still time and energy being spent.

There is nothing wrong with putting effort into your investments, but you should be aware of how much time they demand. If you eventually reach financial independence but spend all your days managing your portfolio, you may simply have replaced one form of work with another.

Ultimately, your investment approach should align not only with your financial goals, but also with the level of involvement you are willing to sustain over the long term.

Comparing investment types

Now that we've explored the key characteristics of investments, it's useful to see how they apply in practice. The following table compares some of the most common investment types across several important characteristics. While individual investments will vary, it highlights the typical trade-offs investors consider when building a portfolio.

The key message to keep in mind is that no investment is universally "better" than another. Each asset class has its own strengths and limitations. Cash provides stability but generally offers the lowest long-term returns. Shares have historically generated some of the strongest long-term returns, but they can also experience substantial fluctuations in value over shorter periods. Property can generate both rental income and capital growth, but it generally requires a larger initial investment and is far less liquid than shares or managed funds. Understanding these trade-offs, rather than searching for a perfect investment, is one of the most important skills an investor can develop.

Investment types at a glance

Investment type	Return source	Expected return	Volatility	Liquidity	Capital required	Effort
Cash and fixed income	Interest	Low	Very low	Very high	Very low	Very low
Shares	Dividends + capital growth	High	High	Very high	Very low	Low
Property	Rent + capital growth	Moderate to high	Moderate	Low	High	Moderate to high
Diversified managed funds / ETFs	Distributions + capital growth	Moderate to high	Moderate	Very high	Very low	Very low
Alternative investments	Varies by asset	Varies widely	Often high	Varies widely	Varies widely	Moderate to high

Note: *This is an indicative guide only. Characteristics vary by product, structure, provider, and market conditions. Alternative investments are broad by definition, so their characteristics can vary materially.*

Investing is personal

Once you understand the characteristics of different investments, it becomes clear why investing is such a uniquely personal experience. Every investor wants strong returns, but the path taken to achieve those returns can vary widely. Some people are comfortable with large fluctuations in value, while others prefer stability. Some have decades before they need their money, while others may require access much sooner.

It's not just your goals that will influence your strategy, but also where you are right now. Factors such as available capital, income needs, cash reserves, and tax considerations all play a part in determining which investments make sense for you. Investors must also consider how much time they are willing and able to spend managing their portfolio.

Retirement accounts add another layer to this. In Australia, this includes superannuation. In other countries, it may involve pensions, retirement accounts, or other tax-advantaged structures. These are not usually separate investments in themselves, but vehicles through which investments are held. Because they are often highly regulated, tax treatment, access restrictions, contribution rules, fees, insurance, and investment options can all vary significantly. A sound investment plan needs to account for both the money you can access freely today and the money held inside retirement structures, so it is important to understand how the system works where you live.

For these reasons, there isn't a single correct investment approach that applies to everyone. The most appropriate strategy depends on the individual circumstances of the investor. That said, there are still broad strategies and principles that appear repeatedly in investing discussions. While they are not rules, understanding them can help clarify some of the trade-offs investors face when building a portfolio.

Diversification versus concentration

One of the most widely discussed concepts in investing is diversification. Diversification involves spreading investments across multiple assets rather than relying heavily on a single opportunity. By doing so, the impact of any one investment performing poorly is reduced. It's the financial equivalent of "*don't put all your eggs in one basket.*"

Concentration takes the opposite approach. Instead of spreading capital broadly, an investor allocates a larger portion of their wealth to a smaller number of investments, magnifying both gains and losses.

Warren Buffett has referenced this trade-off explicitly with his well-known observation that, "*Diversification may preserve wealth, but concentration builds wealth.*" The statement is not intended as advice, but rather a reflection of how the market tends to reward risk over long periods.

Concentrated portfolios can produce exceptional outcomes when the underlying investments perform well. However, they also expose investors to the possibility of significant losses if those investments fail. As a result, they're often better suited to investors who have strong conviction in a particular asset or investment thesis.

Diversification, on the other hand, rarely produces extreme outcomes in either direction. Instead, it reduces the likelihood that a single investment will dramatically alter the trajectory of a portfolio. For many investors, this trade-off provides greater stability and peace of mind.

As wealth grows, many investors gradually tend to move towards greater diversification as a way to protect the assets they have already accumulated. It often makes little sense to risk a small fortune in pursuit of an even greater one, particularly when your accumulated wealth can already generate substantial income on its own.

Understanding which approach suits you depends on your knowledge, unique skills, goals, risk tolerance, and overall financial position.

Dollar-cost averaging versus lump sum investing

Another common discussion revolves around the timing of investing.

When an investor has capital available to invest, they must decide how and when to deploy those funds. One option is to invest the entire amount at once, often referred to as lump sum investing. An alternative approach is dollar-cost averaging, where the investment is split across multiple smaller purchases over time. For example, you might choose to invest $10,000 per month for 12 months, rather than $120,000 all at once.

From a purely mathematical perspective, lump sum investing tends to produce better results on average.[57] This is largely because markets have historically risen over long periods, meaning that the earlier money is invested, the longer it has to compound. While dollar-cost averaging reduces the risk of investing all capital immediately before a market decline, it also increases the chance of missing gains if markets rise during the waiting period.

---

[57] See Anatoly Shtekhman, Christos Tasopoulos, and Brian Wimmer, *Dollar-Cost Averaging Just Means Taking Risk Later*, Vanguard Research, July 2012.

This trade-off parallels the conventional wisdom we saw earlier: *time in the market* versus *timing the market*. Lump sum investing maximises time in the market, allowing your capital to begin compounding immediately. Dollar-cost averaging, on the other hand, spreads the timing risk by investing gradually rather than committing everything at once.

Despite the mathematical argument for lump sum investing, many investors prefer dollar-cost averaging for psychological reasons. Spreading purchases over time removes the pressure of deciding when to deploy a large amount of capital. For some people, investing a significant sum of hard-earned money only to see markets fall shortly afterwards can be discouraging enough to avoid investing altogether. In that sense, the choice between dollar-cost averaging and lump sum investing is often as much psychological as it is mathematical.

In practice, this decision most often arises when investors are first starting out or when they receive a large windfall. Once a portfolio is established, ongoing contributions from income naturally create a form of dollar-cost averaging, as new money is invested regularly over time. Conversely, certain investments inherently require lump sum investing simply because of their size. Purchasing a property or acquiring a business, for example, usually involves committing a large amount of capital at once rather than spreading the investment across many smaller purchases.

There is no right or wrong approach here. The best option will be the one that allows you to invest consistently for the long term without second-guessing every decision you make.

Maintain a cash buffer

Alongside diversification and investment timing, another important consideration when building a portfolio is maintaining a financial buffer. While investing is essential for long-term wealth creation, most investors benefit from keeping some capital in reserve rather than committing every available dollar to the market.

Holding a cash buffer provides several practical advantages. First, it creates peace of mind. Knowing that you have funds available for unexpected events can make the natural ups and downs of investing far easier to tolerate. Cash provides a straightforward safety net for life's unexpected expenses, from medical bills to job loss or major repairs. If markets fall sharply, having accessible cash reduces the likelihood that you'll be forced to sell investments at the worst possible time.

A cash reserve can also create opportunity. Market uncertainty can offer attractive entry points, allowing investors with available funds to buy at more favourable prices. But holding cash is not without trade-offs.

Money sitting in a bank account typically earns far lower returns than long-term investments. Cash can feel like the safest option, but if it earns less than the rate at which prices are rising, its purchasing power slowly declines. Even when cash does keep pace with inflation, it still creates an opportunity cost over time, as funds that could have been compounding in productive assets remain idle. Some investors reduce this effect by keeping their reserves in high-interest savings accounts or mortgage offset accounts. These allow cash to remain accessible while still providing some financial benefit.

Choosing the size of your cash buffer is ultimately a personal decision. Too little cash leaves you exposed to financial shocks, while too much can significantly delay financial freedom. Some investors are comfortable keeping only a small reserve so that most of their money remains invested, while others prefer larger buffers that provide greater stability and peace of mind. The right balance depends on many factors, including your risk tolerance, job stability, existing financial obligations, and how aggressively you wish to invest.

Putting together a plan

Diversification, investment timing, and cash reserves all serve a similar role, allowing investors to decide how they wish to manage their risk. None of them eliminate risk entirely, but they can influence how those risks appear over your financial journey. How that risk is structured will largely determine whether you can stick with your strategy over time.

The most effective investment strategy is not necessarily the one that targets the highest return. It is the one that allows you to remain invested through the inevitable ups and downs of markets without abandoning your plan. Just like diet and exercise, consistency beats optimisation. Build a portfolio you understand, choose an approach you can stick to, then give it time to work.

In the next chapter, we will bring these elements together and examine how spending, income, and investing interact over time. By looking at the numbers in practice, you'll see how small financial decisions compound into meaningful long-term outcomes.

◇

EXERCISE 21

Define your investor profile

This exercise helps clarify how you approach investing. The aim is not to select specific investments, but to define the requirements of your portfolio.

Focus on what you would actually do in practice, not what you think you should do.

Step 1 – Determine your risk and return preference

Which of the following best reflects your preference?

- Lower volatility, more stable returns;
- A balance between stability and growth; or
- Higher growth, accepting larger fluctuations.

If you're unsure, refer back to the previous exercise. How comfortable are you seeing your portfolio in the red, even if it's only temporary? What level of decline can you tolerate without affecting your peace of mind?

Step 2 – Assess your time horizon and liquidity needs

When are you likely to need access to a meaningful portion of your investments? Allocate your expected needs across the following:

- Short term (zero to three years);
- Medium term (three to ten years); or
- Long term (more than ten years).

Also consider how much cash you want to keep in reserve for emergencies. How much financial flexibility do you need before committing the rest to longer-term investments?

Step 3 – Choose your level of effort and involvement

How much time are you willing to spend managing your investments?

- Minimal (set and review occasionally);
- Moderate (periodic review and adjustments); or
- High (active involvement and decision-making).

Some investments require more ongoing attention than others, whether through monitoring, decision-making, administration, or dealing with third parties. Remember that higher effort does not guarantee higher returns. This is about matching your investment approach to the time and involvement you are realistically able to sustain.

Step 4 – Consider any other personal constraints

List any other factors that may influence your investment decisions. For example:

- Income needs or reliance on investment returns;
- Tax considerations;
- Access to capital;
- Existing assets or financial commitments; and
- Any other constraints or preferences.

Final reflection

When you combine all your answers, you should have a clearer picture of your investment profile and the constraints it needs to operate within. This is the foundation for selecting an investment approach that you can maintain in practice.

CHAPTER 24

BUILD YOUR FREEDOM PLAN

The goal of these chapters has been to equip you with the tools necessary to reach financial freedom. The challenge now is turning those ideas into a plan that works in practice.

You've seen how income is generated, how your spending determines what remains, and how you can invest the difference. It's not your income or spending in isolation that count, but the surplus you're able to consistently generate, and what you do with it. All that remains is to see how these elements combine to determine your financial trajectory in practice. From there, you can revisit your *Freedom Figure* and develop an approach that suits your needs.

For the purposes of the examples in this chapter, we only need to focus on two variables:

- **Investable surplus:** The amount of money you can set aside to invest each year; and
- **Rate of return:** How effectively that capital grows once it has been invested.

Each year, your portfolio grows through a combination of the two. Together, they determine both the pace of your portfolio growth and how that growth evolves over time. Contributions add steadily, while returns build on themselves and accelerate. Let's start by looking at how these two variables translate into real outcomes.

How investments grow over time

To demonstrate the principles in this chapter, we'll follow Ally, a hypothetical investor working towards financial freedom. After reviewing her current position, she decides to model her investment outcomes using the following assumptions:

- She can invest $10,000 at the start of each year, beginning immediately; and
- She expects to be able to earn 7.5 per cent on her investments.

For simplicity, she ignores factors such as inflation, salary increases, tax on investments, and changes to expenses. After 30 years, Ally will have accumulated over $1.1 million. But where does that figure actually come from? Her annual contributions account for $300,000, while the remaining balance of more than $800,000 comes entirely from investment returns. The chart below shows how these two components evolve over time.

How investment returns dominate your portfolio over time

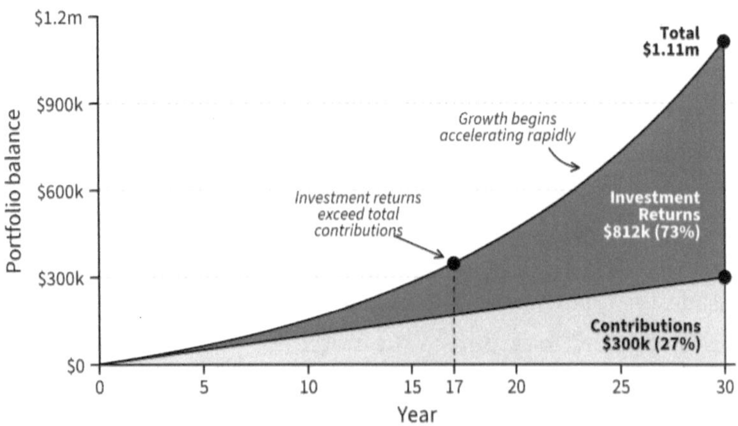

Contributions increase steadily as $10,000 is invested each year.
Investment returns start slowly, but gradually dominate the overall portfolio value.

As expected, contributions increase steadily as she invests $10,000 per year. The growth component, however, accelerates as returns build on prior returns. Early on, it adds little to her portfolio, but over time, its influence becomes overwhelming. After ten years, only about a third of the portfolio value comes from growth. It takes 17 years for investment returns to overtake contributions. By the end of the investment period, investment returns dominate, accounting for nearly three quarters of the final result. In the final year alone, the growth component contributes nearly $80,000.

This highlights the first key dynamic of investing. As your investment balance grows, your contributions become far less impactful than your investment returns. In Ally's case, once her portfolio exceeds $133,333, her annual investment returns will be worth more than her yearly contributions.[58] The relationship scales quickly from there. By the time her portfolio reaches $400,000, her returns are roughly three times her annual contribution, with the gap continuing to grow each year.

While contributions drive progress early on, their relative impact declines as your portfolio grows. Over time, investment returns become the dominant driver of outcomes. This has a practical implication. Early in the journey, increasing the amount you can invest has the greatest effect. It doesn't matter whether that comes from a higher income or lower spending. The more you can invest, the faster the base is built. Later, once that base is established, the focus turns towards the return generated on your existing capital. Contributions are still important, but their influence is overshadowed by the return generated by your existing capital.

[58] With a balance of $133,333.33, a 7.5% investment return will yield $10,000 – equal to her annual contribution.

The irony of long-term investing

The delayed nature of this shift is part of what makes investing so difficult in practice. While long-term outcomes are driven largely by investment returns, those returns often feel insignificant in the early years. In Ally's case, even after seven years, growth accounts for barely a quarter of the total value of her portfolio.[59] For a long time, the progress she sees is driven almost entirely by what she puts in.

This creates a disconnect. Successful investing depends on consistently contributing and staying invested long enough for those contributions to compound, yet the payoff isn't visible until much later. By the time the results are obvious, the behaviour must already be well established for the portfolio to have reached a meaningful size in the first place.

Most habits are reinforced quickly. You go to the gym and begin to see results. You improve your diet and feel better within weeks. The feedback loop is short, making the behaviours easier to sustain. Investing works very differently. For years, it can feel as though your effort is producing very little return. Push too hard early on, by cutting too aggressively or overextending yourself, and it can start to feel like punishment.

This is where delayed gratification becomes non-negotiable. Consistency must be built without any immediate reinforcement. It requires discipline that won't be validated by short-term results. Over time, however, this dynamic reverses. As your portfolio grows, the impact of returns becomes more visible. Progress accelerates, and the results begin to reinforce the behaviour. Eventually, your habits become easier to maintain,

---

[59] After seven years, Ally has contributed a total of $70,000, while her balance has grown to $94,464. That difference of $24,464 accounts for about 25 per cent of her total balance. The remainder has come entirely from her own contributions.

but by this point, your contributions play a much smaller role in driving the overall outcome.

This becomes clearer when you break down the impact of each individual contribution over time. While each of Ally's investments is identical, the value each one produces after 30 years depends entirely on when it was made. This shouldn't come as a surprise. Earlier contributions will clearly be worth more as they have the most time to compound. What's less obvious, however, is the magnitude of this difference.

The chart below shows the value that each $10,000 investment will have generated by the end of the 30-year period.

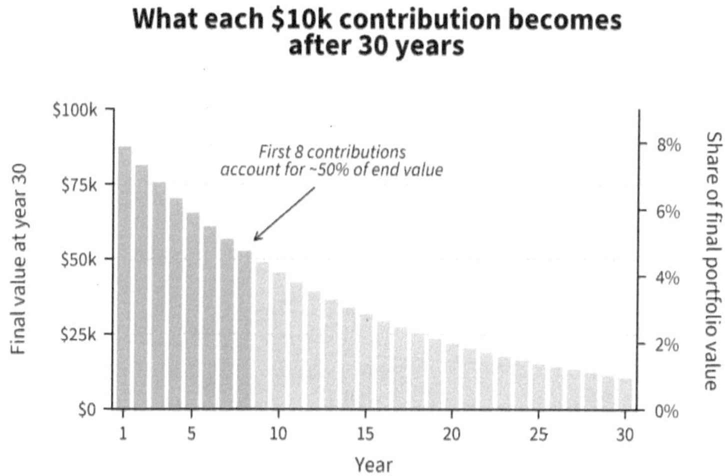

As earlier investments compound for longer, they contribute far more to the final portfolio balance.

When you look at the percentage that each investment contributes to the total value, the importance of the early years becomes hard to ignore. The first eight years account for roughly half of the total value, with the first year alone contributing about eight per cent. Missing that single contribution would leave Ally nearly $90,000 worse off, a comparable result to missing the final seven years *combined*. Yet despite the lower value of these later-year investments, they're the ones she's most likely to consistently make.

That's the irony of long-term investing. The behaviour that matters the most is hardest to sustain when it has the greatest impact. Early contributions carry the most weight, but offer the least feedback, requiring conviction and discipline to maintain. Later, as results become visible, motivation is easier to maintain, but each additional contribution now has a much smaller influence on the outcome. The positive feedback arrives too late to influence your earlier decisions. You don't get to go back and alter your investment decisions with the gift of hindsight.

This is why discipline and consistency are so important early on. You need to make those contributions early, before the results provide any motivation of their own. One way to bridge this gap is to create your own kind of positive reinforcement. Automating contributions, tracking progress, or attaching small, immediate rewards to the act of investing can help build consistency during the early years when it's needed the most.

The compounding effects of returns

So far, we've focused on the importance of regular contributions, particularly in the early stages of the journey. As we saw in the previous example, however, it is the investment returns themselves that become the dominant driver of outcomes in the long term.

To see how powerful the rate of return can be, let's return to Ally's base case of investing $10,000 per year. Assume she now has three investment options to choose from: a low, medium, and high-risk option, returning four, seven, and ten per cent per annum respectively. A few percentage points can seem insignificant, and over shorter timeframes that's largely true.

Over decades, however, the outcomes diverge significantly. The chart below shows the trajectory of all three options over a 30-year period.

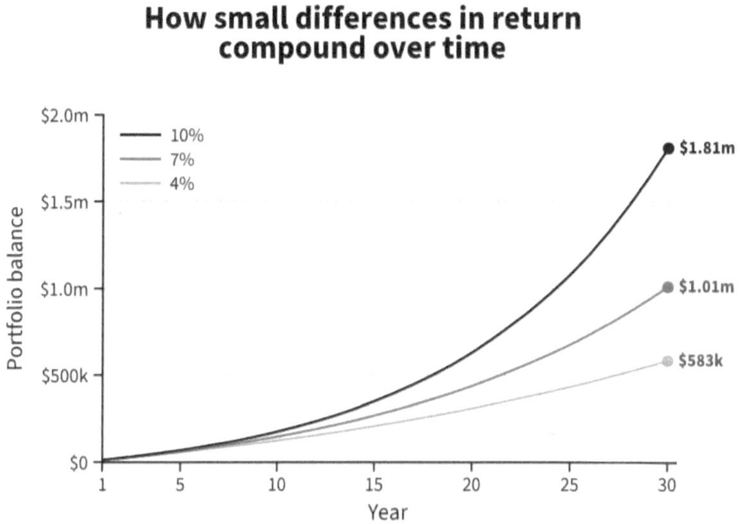

When returns vary, the same contributions can lead to vastly different outcomes.

Ally contributes the same total of $300,000 under each scenario. In the early years, the difference in value between each investment option is barely noticeable. As time passes, however, the gap begins to widen. By the end of the 30-year period, the ten per cent option is worth more than three times the four per cent option. Yet even this still understates the true result.

To truly appreciate the impact of the rate of return, you need to remove Ally's contributions from the final result. When you factor out her contributions, the four per cent investment option yields a profit of about $283,000. At ten per cent, that figure exceeds $1.5 million, almost six times the profit. This is the power of compounding. As returns build on prior returns, small differences in rate are magnified over time.

Note that this also works in reverse. Costs such as management fees, transaction costs, and tax inefficiencies all reduce your effective return. These often appear insignificant, typically under one per cent per year. Over time, however, this starts to add up. This cost drag compounds in exactly the same way as returns, meaning that even a small difference can have a substantial impact. Over a 30-year period, a seemingly small fee can translate into hundreds of thousands of dollars erased from your final outcome.[60]

It's why minimising fees is often one of the lowest-risk levers for improving your overall outcome. You don't need to find better investments or take on more risk. Simply reducing unnecessary costs and inefficiencies can materially improve your long-term results.

Improving returns, on the other hand, is not as straightforward. Higher return investments usually come with the price of greater uncertainty and volatility along the way. As returns can vary significantly from year to year, periods of underperformance are inevitable. As we saw earlier, this is a necessary trade-off with investing. Higher long-term returns are earned by accepting a less predictable journey along the way.

When you put these examples together, it becomes clear that what you focus on depends on which stage of the journey you're at.

Focus your effort

Early on in your financial journey, your results are largely driven by your own investments, with growth barely even registering. Your most important goal here is to build the foundation for your

[60] See William F. Sharpe, 'The Arithmetic of Investment Expenses', *Financial Analysts Journal* 69, no. 2 (2013): 34–41.

investment engine. Despite the apparent absence of growth right now, the value of the investments made now will far outweigh those made later. This means focusing on increasing income and managing your expenditure as much as possible. While your asset base is still small, increasing your surplus is the most immediate and effective lever at your disposal. The more you can invest early, the faster you build your asset base, and the sooner it can begin to grow on its own.

As your investment base grows larger, returns become increasingly important. The engine starts to contribute more towards the outcome, while ongoing investments accelerate the process. Attention turns towards optimising your approach, whether it's refining your risk profile or reducing unnecessary investment costs. At this stage, periodic review becomes important to ensure your strategy remains aligned with your goals.

Eventually, time becomes your most powerful ally. Your primary job now is simply to stay invested and allow compounding to work. When your investment base is large enough, most of the heavy lifting has already been done. Additional contributions have a diminishing impact, with small increases to your surplus barely moving the dial. So long as your expenses remain under control, your investment engine can do the rest.

When people don't recognise this, they tend to misplace their effort. Some focus on fine-tuning returns too early, before they've accumulated enough of an asset base for it to make a difference. Others who are further along the journey sometimes focus on pay rises or cutting expenses, even though small optimisations to their investment strategy would prove far more meaningful.

Understanding where you are is what allows you to plan effectively. Know where you stand, set a destination, then focus your effort accordingly.

Life is never a straight road

The examples in this chapter are heavily simplified to make the mechanics easy to understand. If investment returns played out as neatly as they're portrayed here, the decision to invest would be straightforward. In reality, the path is far less predictable.

Markets don't rise smoothly year after year. Returns can vary dramatically. If you inadvertently invest just prior to a downturn, it can take many years for your portfolio to recover. For many people, this fear of investing at the "wrong" time often results in the decision to delay or avoid investing altogether.

It's not just the markets that are volatile, but life itself. Your income may change dramatically, whether it's through promotions or setbacks. Expenses evolve as your lifestyle and priorities change. Unexpected costs arise, but also opportunities. While these factors are unpredictable in the short term, the long-term outcome is determined far more by your financial habits than by any individual event.

Next steps

You now have the complete system. There are no additional levers hiding elsewhere, and no complexity required beyond what you've already seen. At the core is your relationship with money. You've seen how it influences every financial decision you make, despite being built from surprisingly few experiences. By examining the stories and beliefs behind it, you begin to see how those patterns translate into behaviour, which in turn drives outcomes.

You've learned what "more" truly costs. Recognising those trade-offs allows you to step off the hedonic treadmill and choose "enough" instead. This is where your direction is set. Knowing what you're working towards, and why, gives the system purpose.

With that foundation in place, progress is built through the financial triad. Spending is brought under control through awareness and intention, while income is expanded by understanding and positioning your value more effectively. As a surplus begins to form, you now understand how to put it to work and what to consider. Your net wealth and net cashflow provide a clear view of where you stand and where to focus, while your *Freedom Figure* gives the process a measurable endpoint.

The framework may be clear, but finance is a broad field. You will need to decide how to implement your approach in practice. The specifics will vary based on your circumstances, but the principles do not: earn more where you can, spend with intention, and invest the difference in a way that aligns with your needs. Most importantly, stay invested long enough for compounding to take effect. These are the behaviours that define your financial path.

From here, progress depends on what you do next. You have the awareness to understand your position, the tools to define a meaningful destination, and the framework to build a strategy around it. Apply what you know, refine your approach as you go, and stay consistent long enough to give the process time to work.

◇

EXERCISE 22

The path forward

The exercises in this part of the book have focused on building awareness of your financial situation and the behaviours underpinning it. Now it's time to turn your attention to the path ahead. This exercise is about understanding where you stand, and what that means for how you move forward.

Step 1 – Identify what stage of the journey you are at

Which stage best describes your current position?

- You are building consistency, with little or no regular surplus to invest;
- You have a consistent surplus and are actively building your investment base;
- You have a meaningful investment base, with returns beginning to contribute noticeably; or
- Your investment base is doing most of the work, with contributions playing a smaller role.

There are no hard boundaries here; it is simply a subjective assessment of where you are compared to where you want to be.

Step 2 – Identify your primary constraint

At this point in your journey, what is the main factor limiting your progress? Is it:

- Your ability to generate a surplus;
- Inconsistency in applying your plan;
- Uncertainty or hesitation around investing;
- The structure or efficiency of your current approach; or
- Something else entirely.

Step 3 – Define your focus

Based on your answers, where do you need to focus your attention? Resist the urge to do everything at once. Progress tends to come from addressing the single most important constraint first.

You are not locking in a permanent plan. As your situation evolves, your focus will change with it.

EPILOGUE

THE ROAD AHEAD

We began with a journey. Yours.

Whether you realised it or not, you were already on a path long before you picked up this book. You already had a map, even if you had never stopped to examine it. You already had a vehicle, even if you had sometimes taken it for granted. You already had fuel, even if you had not always understood what it was really for. And somewhere beneath the noise, the habits, the inherited beliefs, and the demands of everyday life, there was a driver.

The trouble is that the driver isn't always the one holding the wheel.

Instead, the journey is often steered by old stories, automatic reactions, fear, comparison, pressure, expectation, or even convenience. The ego starts calling out directions from the back seat, leaving you on a route chosen by default rather than design. That is not a failure. It is simply part of being human.

Most of us do not begin with perfect clarity. We inherit maps before we learn to question them. We form habits before we understand their cost. We absorb beliefs before we realise we have a choice. We chase goals before asking whether they are truly ours. We spend years moving, reacting, and ultimately drifting before we pause long enough to ask a simple question: "*Where is all of this actually taking me?*" That question sits at the heart of this book.

The purpose of your map isn't to choose the path for you. It may help you understand the terrain and plot a course, but it cannot remove every obstacle or decide your direction. Its role is to show you where you are, where you have been, what you value, what you believe, and where you may want to go next. But for a map to be useful, it still needs to be read, questioned, and refined.

Your vehicle isn't just a means to get you from A to B. It is your irreplaceable vessel through which all of life's experiences are filtered. How you care for it influences how clearly you think, how freely you move, how well you work and recover, and how fully you are able to engage with life. Looking after it is not vanity – it's stewardship.

Fuel doesn't exist simply to be accumulated for its own sake. The true value of money lies not in the number itself, but in the paths it makes available to you. It can create safety, options, time, generosity, and room to breathe. Used unconsciously it can keep you trapped. Used deliberately, it allows you to build a life of choice rather than constraint.

The map, the vehicle, and the fuel are not separate aspects of your life. They are connected parts of the same journey. A clear map without a functioning vehicle will never be fully explored. A strong vehicle without enough fuel can only go so far. Plenty of fuel without clear direction can simply mean you move faster towards a life you never consciously chose.

But none of these things matter much without the driver.

So who or what, exactly, is the driver? The driver is your *awareness*. It is your capacity to notice and observe, to pause before reacting, to question a story before believing it, and to recognise when your ego has taken hold. It is the part of you that can look honestly at a habit, a relationship, a belief, or a goal, and ask whether it is still serving the life you want to build.

The driver is not the loudest voice in your head. It is not the part of you that needs to be right, look impressive, avoid discomfort, or defend old decisions. It is far quieter than that, but also far more powerful. It is the awareness beneath the noise, the agency beneath the excuses, and the capacity to choose your next response, even when you cannot control the road itself.

Freedom is not found in controlling everything, nor does it come from an absence of responsibility. In many ways, it is the opposite. Freedom is owning your role in the journey. It is not found in having endless money, perfect health, total certainty, or a life without difficulty. Freedom begins when the driver takes the wheel. It is the practice of choosing a destination that is genuinely yours, then consciously steering towards it.

That doesn't mean you'll never veer off course. There will be days when the old map feels easier to follow, when the vehicle is neglected, or when accumulating fuel begins to take priority over the life it was meant to enable. There will be moments when your backseat driver takes over, steering you in a different direction. Drifting is normal. Your job isn't to prevent it, but to recognise when it happens.

This is the role of awareness. It gives you the chance to check in, notice when your autopilot has taken over, and correct your course before the gap grows too wide. Each time you do, you see more clearly where your choices are taking you. You begin to distinguish between comfort and alignment, between motion and progress, between success as others define it and freedom as you experience it. And perhaps most importantly, you begin to remember that this journey is temporary.

Your vehicle will not last forever, no matter how well you care for it. Your fuel cannot come with you, no matter how much you manage to accumulate. Even your map, no matter how carefully it has been studied, marked, or refined, belongs to this lifetime. One day, this particular journey will end. Perhaps the driver moves on to another journey, or perhaps the mystery is larger than we can ever understand. But you don't need certainty to recognise that the point was never to possess the vehicle forever, stockpile endless fuel, or cling to your map. The point is simply to travel well while you are here.

To wake up. To choose. To learn. To love. To contribute. To take responsibility where you can. To experience this brief, uncertain, and extraordinary journey with as much awareness as you can. You don't need to have it all figured out, nor do you need a flawless plan before you begin. You only need to notice where you are, decide where you are willing to go, and take the next step in that direction. Then another. And another.

The road ahead will not always be smooth. There will be detours, wrong turns, and moments when the way forward is hard to see. But you are not powerless. You are not merely a passenger on this journey, condemned to watch your life pass by. You can adjust your map, care for your vehicle, and manage your fuel wisely. And, when you drift, you can return to the wheel.

So, as this book ends and your journey continues, it's time to ask yourself: Will you travel it asleep, or awake? Will you hand the wheel back to old patterns, or take it for yourself? Will you keep waiting for life to change, or begin participating in it more consciously now?

You don't need to control the whole road, nor map the entire journey. You only need to wake up, take the wheel, and choose the next turn.

◇

A PERSONAL NOTE FROM THE AUTHOR

Thank you for reading *The Freedom Framework.*

Wherever this book has found you, I hope it has offered something useful for the road ahead. If something in these pages inspired you, challenged you, helped you see your life differently, or encouraged you to take even one meaningful step forward, I would genuinely love to hear about it. You can reach out through www.thefreedomframework.com.au.

If you know someone who may benefit from this book, sharing it with them or leaving a review is one of the most meaningful ways to support its message. Reviews and recommendations help the book reach people who may need it at the right time.

I wish you every success on your journey.

ACKNOWLEDGEMENTS

This book is the culmination of a lifetime of experiences, relationships, and lessons. I am deeply grateful to everyone who has influenced, challenged, supported, and encouraged me along the way. Every experience has contributed to the person I am today and, ultimately, the ideas within these pages.

I am especially grateful to my family and friends for their unwavering support, and to the many authors, teachers, mentors, and thinkers whose work challenged my thinking, broadened my perspective, and inspired me to keep learning and growing. This book would not exist without the countless lessons you have shared.

Finally, I want to thank you for reading this book. In a world full of distractions and competing demands for attention, I am honoured that you chose to spend some of your time with these pages. I am truly grateful, and I hope the ideas explored in this book can help you create the freedom to live life on your own terms.

ABOUT THE AUTHOR

Peter Chemello believes that we are all capable of far more than we realise.

He has long been fascinated by how we can be the best version of ourselves and make the most of the one life we are given. This pursuit led him to a lifelong commitment to personal growth, with health and financial independence becoming important complements to that broader journey. Throughout the years, he became increasingly interested in the recurring patterns that appear across different areas of life and the underlying principles that remain true regardless of the domain in which they are applied.

Drawing on an actuarial education and years of personal study, Peter gradually adopted and applied the principles explored throughout this book. In his thirties, he achieved a lifelong goal of financial freedom, retiring from full-time work. As he approaches forty, he continues to enjoy the highest levels of health, fitness, and vitality of his life. He views each achievement not as a destination, but as the beginning of the next challenge. Upon retiring, he decided to dedicate himself to sharing the ideas that had most influenced his own life, ultimately inspiring the writing of this book.

The Freedom Framework reflects much of what Peter wishes he had understood earlier. It distils the knowledge and insights he gathered across multiple disciplines, tested and refined through years of personal application. While many books provide valuable pieces of the puzzle, he saw a need for a practical framework that connected those pieces into a coherent whole.

At a time when many people feel overwhelmed, uncertain, or powerless to change their future, Peter hopes this book helps readers develop greater awareness, take ownership of their choices, and recognise their true potential. He believes that awareness is the foundation of freedom, and that lasting change begins when we stop operating on autopilot and instead consciously choose the direction of our lives. To learn more or get in touch, visit www.thefreedomframework.com.au.

www.ingramcontent.com/pod-product-compliance
Lightning Source LLC
LaVergne TN
LVHW100255210926
848480LV00003B/931
* 9 7 8 1 7 6 4 8 1 5 8 0 2 *